OREGON

OFF THE BEATEN PATH®

OFF THE BEATEN PATH® SERIES

TWELFTH EDITION

OREGON

OFF THE BEATEN PATH®

DISCOVER YOUR FUN

MYRNA OAKLEY

REVISED AND UPDATED BY
KIM COOPER FINDLING

Globe
Pequot

Guilford, Connecticut

All the information in this guidebook is subject to change. We recommend that you call ahead to obtain current information before traveling.

Globe
Pequot

An imprint of The Rowman & Littlefield Publishing Group, Inc.
4501 Forbes Blvd., Ste. 200
Lanham, MD 20706
www.rowman.com

Distributed by NATIONAL BOOK NETWORK

Maps by Melissa Baker

British Library Cataloguing in Publication Information available

Library of Congress Cataloging-in-Publication Data available

ISBN 978-1-4930-5361-2 (paper: alk. paper)
ISBN 978-1-4930-5362-9 (electronic)

♾️™ The paper used in this publication meets the minimum requirements of American National Standard for Information Sciences—Permanence of Paper for Printed Library Materials, ANSI/NISO Z39.48-1992.

To all those wonderful dining and lodging hosts and the dozens of volunteers and staff at regional and local visitor information centers who stand ready to offer local information and helpful advice to travelers; to all those travelers who enjoy finding out what's just around the bend; to family members and friends who return to their favorite places year after year; and to everyone who enjoys exploring Oregon's byways and finding those enticing and scenic places off the beaten path.

OREGON

PORTLAND
& ENVIRONS

Astoria

Pendleton

The Dalles

Portland

COLUMBIA RIVER GORGE
&
HIGH
CASCADES

La Grande

Salem

NORTHEASTERN
OREGON

Newport

THE
OREGON
COAST

CENTRAL
OREGON

THE
WILLAMETTE
VALLEY

Bend

Ontario

Coos
Bay

Burns

SOUTHEASTERN
OREGON

Jordan
Valley

SOUTHERN
OREGON

Lakeview

Brookings

Medford

Contents

About the Author

Myrna Oakley has traveled the byways of the Northwest and western British Columbia since 1970, always with a camera in hand and an inquisitive eye for natural and scenic areas, as well as for wonderful inns, gardens, and places with historical character and significance. In this process, she has developed an affinity for goose-down comforters, friendly conversations by the fire, and intriguing people who generally prefer to live somewhat off the beaten path.

In addition to *Oregon Off the Beaten Path,* she has written *Washington Off the Beaten Path; Recommended Bed & Breakfasts: Pacific Northwest; Public and Private Gardens of the Northwest;* and *Bed and Breakfast Northwest.* She also teaches about the business of freelance writing, novel writing, and travel writing.

About the Reviser

Fifth-generation Oregonian **Kim Cooper Findling** writes about the people and places of her home state. She is the editor of *Bend Magazine,* the publisher of Dancing Moon Press and the author of *The Sixth Storm,* with Libby Findling; *Day Trips to the Oregon Coast: Getaway Ideas for the Local Traveler; Bend, Oregon Daycations: Day Trips for Curious Families; Day Trips from Portland: Getaway Ideas for the Local Traveler;* and *Chance of Sun: An Oregon Memoir.* She lives in Bend, Oregon, with her husband, three teenagers, and two cats.

Acknowledgments

I have worked two decades as a travel writer and author, and I am blessed beyond words for the journeys to fantastic destinations both physical and metaphysical that have ensued. My books would not come to fruition without the support and assistance of many others. First to thank in a cosmic shout-out is the Pacific Northwest, for existing as such a diverse, fascinating, and richly beautiful place. I am unbelievably fortunate to reside and write here. I owe thank yous to dozens of tourism and travel professionals and longtime colleagues who contribute to my work—too many to name here, but you are all unparalleled. Personal thanks to friends and acquaintances who regularly contribute travel destination ideas. Finally, I extend endless gratitude to my family, my steady traveling companions. You are the best road trip sidekicks on the planet, and I am so very lucky.

Introduction

Growing up on the Oregon Coast in the 1970s and 1980s, I was aware that I lived in a beautiful and remarkable place. I was born to a family of wanderers, and as we traveled from the blustery coast to the lush Willamette Valley, from the austere high desert to the alpine forests of the Cascade Range, from the bustling city to the wide-open rural stretches, I reveled in the diversity, grandeur, and hidden delights of my home state. Later, when I became a writer, it was no surprise that Oregon itself would be my subject and my muse. Sharing with readers stories of this state's people, hidden pockets and many pleasures has been my privilege for twenty years.

Exploring 101: Favorite Oregon Highways and Byways

Historic Columbia River US Highway 30: Starting at Troutdale, east of Portland, and continuing in several sections roughly paralleling I-84, to The Dalles. **Note**: Several sections of US Historic Columbia River Highway 30 (US 30), including a number of tunnels, have been reopened for walking, hiking, and bicycling (hcrh.com).

US Highway 101 (US 101): The more than 300 mile-length of the scenic Oregon coast starting at Astoria in the north or starting at Brookings on the south coast

Highway 126: From Florence, on the central coast, to Eugene, then east and onto Highway 242 at the small community of McKenzie Bridge and winding up and over McKenzie Pass to Sisters and the central Oregon high desert region (or, if Highway 242 is still snowbound, go instead to Highway 22 over Santiam Pass to the high desert)

Highway 138: From Roseburg winding east along the scenic Umpqua River to Diamond Lake and Crater Lake

John Fremont Highway 31: Heading southeast from Bend and La Pine (on US 97) and continuing on US Highway 395 to Lakeview

Highway 205: Scenic route from Burns south through the Malheur National Wildlife Refuge to Frenchglen and on to the Alvord Basin desert region and returning back to Burns

Highway 82: From La Grande to Elgin, Enterprise, Joseph, and into the scenic Wallowa Mountains area and the end of the road at Imnaha, all in northeastern Oregon

Highway 86: From Baker City to Halfway and on to Hells Canyon Dam, then the paved back road around to Joseph

Highway 395: Traversing the center of the state north at Pendleton to south at Lakeview, through the John Day Country and the high desert

TOP HITS IN THE BEAVER STATE

Columbia River Gorge
from Troutdale east to Umatilla

Covered bridges
Willamette Valley and southern Oregon
covered-bridges.org

Crater Lake National Park
southern Oregon

Hells Canyon National Recreation Area
northeastern Oregon

Historic Columbia River
US 30
from Troutdale to The Dalles

Klamath Basin National Wildlife Refuge
Klamath Falls

Lava Lands and Newberry National Volcanic Monument
central Oregon

Lewis and Clark Corps of Discovery sites
Columbia River Gorge, Long Beach Peninsula, and Astoria
nps.gov/focl

Malheur National Wildlife Refuge
south of Burns in southeastern Oregon

Oregon coast lighthouses
from Astoria on the north coast to Brookings on the south coast

Oregon farmers' and Saturday markets
small towns and cities statewide, Mar through Oct
oregonfarmersmarkets.org

Oregon Trail sites
northeastern Oregon to the Willamette Valley

Public, historic, botanic, and display gardens
Portland and environs, the Willamette Valley, and the Oregon coast

Whale-watch weeks in March
Oregon coast
whalespoken.org

In that time, too, Oregon's delights have been discovered by many. Traveling off the beaten path has become a well-worn habit, one shared by fellow Oregonians as well as visitors. Our wide ocean beaches and spectacular coastline remain a favorite destination—fully preserved for everyone to enjoy. A sense of the mid-1840s pioneer past still permeates much of the state, and sections of the Oregon Trail, including the actual wagon ruts, have been identified and preserved in eastern and central Oregon.

History and heritage are reflected in sites you can visit throughout the Columbia River Gorge and at the mouth of this mighty river at the Pacific Ocean. Along this route, some thirty-three members of the Lewis and Clark Corps of Discovery, including Clark's Newfoundland dog, Seaman, met and traded with local Native Indian tribes, collected plant and animal specimens, and camped during the rainy winter of 1805 to 1806.

While modern explorers will enjoy more amenities and pleasant accommodation choices in Oregon than Lewis and Clark did, it is worthwhile to be mindful of the weather when planning a trip. The Pacific Northwest has four distinct seasons and two distinct weather patterns.

The eastern half of the state, the high desert, at elevations of 3,000 to 5,000 feet and higher, offers crisp, cold winters and hot, dry summers. Destinations east of Bend and east of US 97 offer quieter byways and many undiscovered and less crowded destinations. This is real cowboy and cowgirl country, and you'll find longer distances between towns and cities. (***Note:*** Always fill the gas tank before heading into the rural stretches.) In these outback areas, however, there are ample visitor information centers as well as friendly locals glad to help travelers with directions. If you enjoy snow and winter sports, plan treks to the Cascade Mountain regions from mid- to late November through March. (See these chapters: Southeastern Oregon, Central Oregon, Northeastern Oregon, and Columbia River Gorge and High Cascades.)

The western half of the state, situated between the Cascade Mountain Range and the Pacific Ocean, offers low elevation, green, and lush regions with mild temperatures year-round. Hundreds of public gardens and nurseries, vineyards and wineries, and major metropolitan and coastal areas are discovered here. If you want less traffic and less crowded places, especially along the coast, visit midweek. Or, travel early spring, April through June, and early fall, September (after Labor Day) and October. Autumn in the entire Northwest is generally sunny and warm. (See these chapters: The Oregon Coast, Southern Oregon, Portland and Environs, Columbia River Gorge and High Cascades, and The Willamette Valley.)

At the end of each chapter, places to eat and places to stay are listed, including resorts, inns, historic hotels, RV parks, and luxury lodgings, along with coffeehouses, bakeries, cafes, breweries, and restaurants. Casual, informal, and friendly are the bywords here; however, open hours can change and may be highly seasonal, so it's always best to call ahead to determine hours and to ask about the current weather (which might still change five minutes later).

Hundreds of day-use parks and overnight campgrounds located in scenic areas throughout the state are managed by Oregon State Parks, city and county parks, the USDA Forest Service campgrounds, and the Bureau of Land Management (BLM) campgrounds. You can call the Oregon State Parks reservation line (800-452-5687) or register online (oregonstateparks.org) up to six months ahead to reserve full-service RV sites and tent sites. For general information about state park accommodations, call (800) 551-6949. A number of state parks are open year-round, and many of them offer cozy cabins, camping yurts, and even deluxe yurts with kitchens. For more information obtain a copy of *Oregon Parks and Heritage Guide* from any local visitor information center.

I hope you enjoy this field trip through the Beaver State—walking in the footsteps of yesterday and today. Happy travels!

Take Care Out There

As Oregon has been discovered, visitor numbers have increased and along with them, the impact on the state's amazing destinations. Keep yourself and the landscape safe with these tips from the folks of Travel Oregon.

Prepare—Plan Ahead
Prepare before you head out, consider what you want to see and experience, your group's physical abilities and what's realistic to do in the time you have. Can you visit off peak to avoid crowds?

Be Ready
Check conditions. Pack your Ten Essentials. Got the right shoes for the terrain? Water? Cell phone? You may not always have coverage, so take a picture of the trail map or bring one with you. Consider hiring a guide.

Don't Forget
Let someone know where you're headed and when you plan to be back. Tuck some cash in your pocket for park fees (which help maintain Oregon's natural spaces).

Care—Make Smart Choices
Know your limits and when to stop for the day. Follow the signs; they're there to tell you important stuff like how to avoid injuries and not get lost.

Be Respectful
If you're lucky enough to spot wildlife, use your zoom lens and observe from afar. Share trails with others. Know who manages the land you access and what the rules and regulations are.

Keep It Natural
Stay on designated trails and areas to protect the landscape. Don't take anything home but your trash—and please, please take your trash with you. Make wildfire prevention a top priority.

Connect—Enjoy Yourself
Experiencing the quiet, awe-inspiring beauty of nature can not only uplift your spirits, it can improve your health. Think of Oregon's vast outdoors as your place to relax and recharge.

Say Hello
Greet fellow adventurers and spark a conversation. Check in at a visitor center, ranger station, and/or local business to learn from the locals, grab a map and gather local insight.

Spread Goodwill
Share your knowledge with others if it's helpful. Support the community—eat, drink, shop, and stay local. Stop by cultural centers to learn our history and relationship to place.

Oregon Fast Facts

- **Area:** 97,073 square miles
- **Capital:** Salem, located in the central Willamette Valley about one hour south of Portland
- **County names (36 in all):** Baker, Benton, Clackamas, Clatsop, Columbia, Coos, Crook, Curry, Deschutes, Douglas, Gilliam, Grant, Harney, Hood River, Jackson, Jefferson, Josephine, Klamath, Lake, Lane, Lincoln, Linn, Malheur, Marion, Morrow, Multnomah, Polk, Sherman, Tillamook, Umatilla, Union, Wallowa, Wasco, Washington, Wheeler, and Yamhill
- **Highest point:** Mount Hood (11,237 feet), located approximately 50 miles east of Portland
- **Major rivers:** Columbia River, which flows south then west from its source in the Canadian Rockies and empties into the Pacific Ocean at Astoria on the north coast; the Willamette River, which flows north from its source in the Umpqua National Forest in the southern Cascade Mountains and empties into the Columbia River just north of downtown Portland
- **Mascot and colors, Oregon State University:** Beavers, orange and black (located in Corvallis, central Willamette Valley)
- **Mascot and colors, Portland State University:** Vikings, green and white (located in Portland)
- **Mascot and colors, University of Oregon:** Ducks, green and yellow (located in Eugene, southern Willamette Valley)
- **Nickname:** the Beaver State
- **Population:** 4.2 million
- **State animal:** beaver
- **State bird:** western meadowlark
- **State birthday:** February 14, 1859
- **State fish:** Chinook salmon
- **State flower:** Oregon grape
- **State gem:** sunstone
- **State rock:** thunder egg
- **State tree:** Douglas fir

Bites, Sips, Pours, and Plates

Whether rambling along the Oregon coast for a day or a long weekend, travelers often look for great coffee stops and perhaps a bite to eat and delicious pastries at a local cafe or pub. Check out these coffeehouses, cafes, bakeries, and pubs as you work your way along the Oregon coast!

- **Astoria Coffeehouse & Bistro,** Astoria
- **Bandon Coffee Cafe** on 2nd Street in Bandon

- **Barnacle Bistro** in Gold Beach
- **Bread and Ocean Bakery**, on Laneda Avenue in Manzanita
- **Blue Scorcher Bakery & Café**, Astoria
- **Buoy Beer Company**, Astoria
- **5 Rivers Coffee Roasters & Coffeehouse**, US 101 north, Tillamook
- **42nd Street Café**, in Seaview, Long Beach Peninsula
- **Green Salmon Coffee Company** on 2nd Street, Yachats
- **The Cafe on Hawk Creek**, Neskowin
- **Kaffe 101** on South Broadway in Coos Bay-North Bend
- **Lost Roo**, Long Beach Peninsula
- **MacGregor's Whiskey Bar & Restaurant**, Cannon Beach
- **Manzanita News & Espresso**, Laneda Avenue in Manzanita
- **McMenamins Lighthouse Brewpub**, Lincoln City
- **Mo's West** at Otter Rock north of Newport
- **Nana's Irish Pub**, Newport
- **Pacific Grind Cafe**, on US 101 north, Lincoln City
- **Pelican Pub & Brewery**, Pacific City
- **River Roasters**, Old Town Florence
- **Rogue Brewer's on the Bay** at Yaquina Bay Marina in Newport
- **Sleepy Monk Coffeehouse**, N. Hemlock Street, Cannon Beach
- **Stimulus Espresso Café**, Pacific City
- The restaurant at the **Tillamook Creamery**, Tillamook

The Oregon Coast

The Oregon Coast ranges 363 miles along the Pacific Ocean from Brookings, at the southern end of the coast, to Astoria, a many hour's drive to the north where the Columbia River separates the Beaver State from Washington State. The Astoria-Megler bridge arches high above the Columbia River offering drivers wide views and safe access to Washington's Long Beach Peninsula and destinations from there into the Evergreen State.

Although some portions of this trek move inland and away from the ocean a few miles, travelers will find many established waysides on the ocean side to pull off US 101, particularly along the central coast section from Florence north to Newport and Lincoln City. These are safe places to enjoy wide views of sea stacks, lighthouses, the ocean, and myriad sea birds flying about. You'll also find a number of state campgrounds and day picnicking waysides along the way and many of these are close to the sandy beaches. The best news is that nearly every inch of the Oregon coast and its sandy beaches are open to the public.

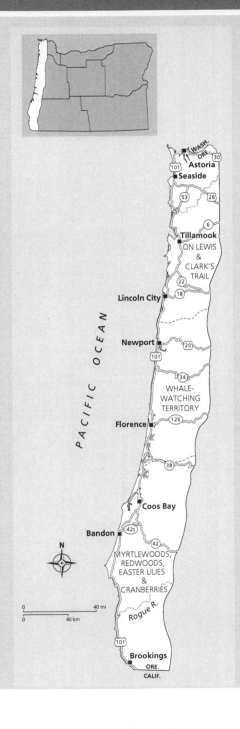

Myrtlewoods, Redwoods, Easter Lilies, and Cranberries

With its mild, relatively dry winters, the southern Oregon coast offers many appealing options—clamming, crabbing, hiking, fishing, beachcombing, museum hopping, and just plain solitude beckon visitors to linger awhile.

Brookings and Gold Beach

From late June to early September, fields of lilies, both Easter lilies and Oriental hybrids, nod in colorful profusion along US 101 just south of **Brookings**. At **Flora Pacifica**, 15447 Oceanview Drive, Harbor (541-469-9741; florapacifica. com), you can enjoy the colorful viewing garden and several acres of flowers for cutting, such as calla lilies, astilbe, delphinium, larkspur, and fragrant lavender. You can see where the flowers are dried and made into gorgeous swags and wreaths as well as browse the well-stocked gift shop seven days a week from 8:30 a.m. to 5:00 p.m. Before continuing north, stop to pick up current maps and information at the **Oregon Welcome Center** located at 1650 Hwy. 101 and near Harris Beach State Park, open daily May through October.

You can then head out the Chetco River Road from Brookings and spend an hour or so hiking the 1-mile **Redwood Grove Nature Trail**, located 8.5 miles inland from US 101 and 0.5 mile north of Alfred A. Loeb State Park, on the north bank of the Chetco River. Aided by the helpful interpretive brochure, you and the kids will pass some fourteen numbered stations and identify trees, shrubs, ferns, and flowers that are characteristic of this coastal region. The centuries-old giant redwoods range between 300 and 800 years in age and may reach heights of 350 feet and girths of 25 feet. To travel into the heart of the awesome redwoods and **Redwood National Park**, continue south from Brookings to Crescent City, California.

For other wilderness hiking information, including wilderness cabins, contact the Gold Beach Ranger District at 29279 Ellensburg Avenue (541-247-3600; fs.usda.gov/rogue-siskiyou). You can also obtain helpful information from the nationwide reservation service website for USDA Forest Service campgrounds, recreation.gov (888-448-1474, information; 877-444-6777, reservations).

Guided rafting and drift-boat fishing trips are also available on the Chetco River; information about local guides can be obtained from the ranger station or from the Brookings-Harbor Visitor Information Center, 16330 Lower Harbor Road (541-469-3181; brookingsor.com).

Enjoy evenings of live local theater while you're in the Brookings-Harbor area. Both the *Chetco Pelican Players* (541-469-1877; chetcopelicanplayers.org) and *Brookings-Harbor Community Theater* (541-373-3680; brookings harborcommunitytheater.com) perform throughout the year and offer contemporary, light comedy and melodrama as well as popular Broadway musicals.

History buffs may want to plan a visit to the *Chetco Valley Historical Society Museum* (541-469-6651) located in the *Blake House*, the oldest standing house in the Brookings-Harbor area. The vintage red-and-white structure served as a stagecoach station and trading post on the south coast during the early 1800s. The museum is located at 15461 Museum Road in Brookings and is open mid-March through November, Saturday and Sunday, noon to 4:00 p.m. For good eats in Brookings, pop into *Black Trumpet Bistro* (625 Chetco Avenue, Ste. 200; 541-887-0860), which is open Monday through Friday for lunch and dinner; Saturday and Sunday for dinner only. Head down to the harbor area for delicious coffee and espresso at *The Bell & Whistle Coffee Shop* at 16350 Lower Harbor Road, Brookings (541-469-2218), open daily. Or, pop into *The Hungry Clam* also on Lower Harbor Road for tasty fish and chips, great burgers, dogs, and chowders (541-469-2526). Enjoy views of the water from both eateries. For tasty Italian fare, try *Zola's Pizzaria*, 16362 Lower Harbor Road (541-412-7100), which boasts over 100 craft beers, and for fresh-baked goods try *Bakery by the Sea* at 1105 Chetco Avenue, Brookings (541-251-3665); go inside the building and down the hall to find the bakery entry. If time permits, detour at *Cape Sebastian*, located just north of Brookings and Pistol River, and some 5 miles south of Gold Beach. Rising 500 feet from the Pacific Ocean, the cape offers spectacular views of the coastline north and south, as well as hiking trails and picnic areas. Don't be deterred by the weather; this sight is not to be missed, even on a blustery day.

For one of the best side trips on the south Curry County coast, take one of the *Rogue River mail boat trips* (800-451-3645; mailboat.com) from Gold Beach up the lower Rogue River. Here passengers and daily mail are transported in open and safe hydrojet-powered launches across ripples and easy rapids about 32 miles upriver, to Agness. Good-natured pilots (Coast Guard certified) point out wildlife, birdlife, and geological features along the way, often recounting lively tales of early river life. A hearty lunch at rustic *Singing Springs Resort* and the 32-mile return trip to Gold Beach complete this memorable foray into the Rogue River's pioneer past. Information about the mail boat trips and overnight options can be obtained from the Gold Beach–Wedderburn Visitor Information Center, located at the south edge of Gold Beach at 94080 Shirley Ln. (800-525-2334; goldbeach.org).

A longer, 102-mile round-trip mail boat excursion up into the federally des-ignated Wild and Scenic section of the Rogue River is also available. You could spend the night at remote **Lucas Pioneer Ranch & Fishing Lodge** (541-247-7443) upriver near Agness. Also up the river from Gold Beach is the wonderful, rustic, and peaceful yet luxurious **Tu Tu' Tun Lodge** (800-864-6357; tututun .com). Or hang out in **Gold Beach** and pop into **Biscuit Coffeehouse** (541-247-7733) located next door to **Gold Beach Books**, 29707 Ellensburg Avenue/ US 101, for great coffee drinks, fresh-baked pastries, and good reads. Find tasty clam chowder, fish and chips, burgers, and sweet potato fries at **Barnacle Bistro**, 29805 Ellensburg Avenue/US 101 (541-247-7799; barnaclebistro.com). Or, try **Porthole Café** down on the harbor in the historic Cannery Building, Gold Beach (541-247-7411; portholecafe.com).

As you head north on US 101, the coastal headlands press close to the ocean, and the highway, once a narrow Indian trail, curves along a shelf high above the waves and around Humbug Mountain to **Port Orford**. In 1828, moun-tain man Jedediah Smith trekked through the area with more than a dozen men and some 250 horses loaded with furs obtained by trapping and trading in Cali-fornia. Crossing the mouth of the Rogue River, Jedediah reported in his journal that twelve horses drowned, but the furs, ferried across in canoes, were saved.

Bed-and-Breakfasts, Historic Inns, and Lodges on the South Coast

Floras Lake House Bed and Breakfast
Langlois
(541) 348-2573
floraslake.com

Mt. Emily Ranch Bed & Breakfast
Brookings
(541) 661-2134 or (541) 469-3983
mtemilyranch.com

Requa Inn Hotel
Klamath, CA, near Redwood National Park
requainn.com

South Coast Inn Bed & Breakfast
Brookings
(541) 469-5557
southcoastinn.com

Tu Tu' Tun Lodge
Gold Beach
(800) 864-6357
tututun.com

At Port Orford visit the scenic local harbor, a natural deepwater area where fishing boats are hoisted in and out of the churning waters each day with an enormous converted log boom. You'll often see the boats resting high and dry on long trailers atop the pier.

Gather more information at Port Orford's Visitor Information Center, located at the south end of the town at *Battle Rock City Park* (541-332-4106; enjoyportorford.com). Be sure to ask about the Port Orford Lifeboat Station grounds and museum and the Bioswale Garden near the visitors center. *Wild-Springs Guest Habitat* at 92978 Cemetery Road (541-332-0977; wildspring .com) is a magical forested overnight retreat with five eco-friendly, comfortable cabins. The grounds also include views of the Pacific, a soaking pool and trails.

If time allows, drive about 5 miles west of US 101—just north of Port Orford—to *Cape Blanco State Park* to see the *Cape Blanco Lighthouse*. Constructed in the 1870s, the lighthouse is the oldest still standing on the coast, and its light still shines 21 miles out to sea. The lighthouse is open for tours April through October, Wednesday through Monday, from 10:00 a.m. to 3:30 p.m. Nearby, the restored *Historic Hughes House*, ca. 1898, sits in a small meadow above the winding Sixes River. It was built as a dairy ranch by pioneers Patrick and Jane Hughes and is now part of the Cape Blanco State Park complex. The house is open from April through October, Wednesday through Monday, from 10:00 a.m. to 3:30 p.m. Call ahead to arrange a visit (541-332-0248).

Of the nine original lighthouses on the Oregon coast, light beams from six of them continue to guide mariners, fishing parties, sailors, and pleasure boaters along coastal waters. Although newer technology in marine navigation—radio beacons and such—has retired the other three lighthouses from active service, there is growing interest in preserving these vintage maritime structures as historic sites, interpretive centers, and museums. See a list of Oregon lighthouses on page 26.

The nearby *Sixes River* offers fishing for fall chinook, spring and fall sea-run cutthroat, and winter steelhead. Cape Blanco State Park is open from April to November and offers facilities for day and overnight use, in addition to a hiker-biker camp. There are large state campgrounds in each section of the coast that remain open all year; many offer roomy yurts, small cabins, and tepees as alternatives to tent or RV camping. Browse oregonstateparks.org; call (800) 551-6947 for information and (800) 452-5687 for reservations.

TOP HITS ON THE OREGON COAST

Azalea Park Gardens Brookings	**Columbia River Maritime Museum** Astoria
Cape Kiwanda and dory fishing fleet Pacific City	**The Connie Hansen Garden Conservancy** Lincoln City

Darlingtonia Wayside	Shore Acres Gardens and Sunset Bay
Florence	State Park
	Coos Bay–Charleston
Devil's Churn and Cape Perpetua	
Yachats	Tillamook Naval Air Station Museum
	and World War II blimp hangar
Fort Clatsop	Tillamook
between Astoria and Gearhart	
	Umpqua Discovery Center
Historic Seaside Promenade	Reedsport
Seaside	
	Yaquina Head Lighthouse
Oregon Coast Aquarium	Newport
Newport	
Rogue River mail boat trips	
Gold Beach	

Bandon

Located at the mouth of the Coquille River, where the river surges into the Pacific Ocean, the community of **Bandon** is known for its cheese and its cranberries. Milk for the original Bandon Cheese and Produce Company, founded in 1927, was hauled from nearby Coquille Valley dairies by stern-wheel riverboats, and both cheddar cheese and butter were shipped to San Francisco by steamboat.

Some 900 acres of **cranberry bogs** are under cultivation near Bandon. The original vines were brought from Cape Cod, Massachusetts, in 1879 by pioneer grower Charles McFarlin. In those days, the Coos Indians helped pick the bright red berries with wooden-toothed scoops each autumn. The Bandon community celebrates a cranberry festival every September. Displays of Indian artifacts and old photos of the cranberry harvest, as well as exhibits of local history—the town burned to the ground twice, in 1914 and 1936—can be seen at the **Bandon Historical Society Museum** (541-347-2164; bandonhistoricalmuseum.org), located at 270 Fillmore Avenue and US 101 and near the harbor and Old Town shops and eateries. The museum is open Monday through Saturday from 10:00 a.m. to 4:00 p.m. (closed Sunday, October through May, and entirely in January). If time allows, from here drive several blocks west out to the bluff overlooking the ocean and turn onto **Beach Loop Drive**. Wind along the ocean drive to see enormous **sea stacks**—giant rock formations left over from eons-old underwater volcanoes—and large rocks hosting colonies of seabirds. There are several places to park and walk down to the beach, one being **Face Rock State Scenic Viewpoint**. This is one of the best beach walks on the south coast. For ocean-view sleeps call the **Bandon Inn** at 355 US 101 (541-347-4417).

Within walking distance of the historical museum, you can enjoy a stroll through **Old Town** shops and galleries. For tasty espresso drinks, pastries, and deli sandwiches, pop into **Bandon Coffee Cafe** (541-347-1144) at 365 2nd Street, which opens every day at 6:00 a.m. For casual fare stop at **Bandon Brewing Company** at 395 2nd Street (541-347-3911), open daily at 11:00 a.m. for tasty homemade pizza, salads, and fresh craft beer made onsite. You're ready for dining with ocean views? Drive out to **Bandon Dunes Golf Resort** and dine at the Pacific Grill, upstairs in the clubhouse (57744 Round Lake Road; 855-220-6710); open daily for breakfast, lunch, and dinner. For current information, call the Bandon Visitor Center (541-347-9616; bandon.com).

Nestled alongside the Coquille River, just north of Bandon's Old Town marina, the **Coquille River Lighthouse**, now a museum, was built in the late 1890s. You can access the historic structure from **Bullards Beach State Park**, off US 101 just north of Bandon. Walk out the jetty trail to see spectacular ocean waves crash on the rocks that edge both sides of the Coquille River as it surges into the Pacific. The large state park offers RV sites, tent sites, and space for hiker-bicycle parties and for horse campers. Bullards Beach State Park is open year-round (contact state parks for reservations: 800-452-5687; oregonstateparks.org).

For a pleasant side trip from Bandon, head east on Highway 42 for about 15 miles to the small community of **Coquille.** The community's annual **Gay Nineties Celebration** on the first Saturday of June launches the summer season.

To experience some of the most magnificent scenery on the south coast, detour from US 101 about 10 miles north of Bandon to Charleston and then double back to Sunset Bay, Shore Acres, and Cape Arago. This area can also be accessed by heading west from Coos Bay–North Bend.

Sandstone cliffs curve around picturesque, half-moon **Sunset Bay**. Atop the cliffs are easy hiking trails. At low tide, you can walk out along the rocks on the south side to explore tide pools filled with sea anemones, tiny crabs, oblong chitons, and purple sea urchins. Keep close supervision of children and wear sturdy shoes for this trek so as not to take a spill on wet rocks and slippery seaweed. For RV, tent, and comfy yurt reservations at **Sunset Bay State Park**, call (800) 452-5687 (oregonstateparks.org).

Historic Shore Acres Gardens

Don't miss visiting nearby **Shore Acres State Park and Gardens** (541-888-3732; shoreacres.net), accessed by Cape Arago Highway from Coos Bay and Charleston, once the grand turn-of-the-20th-century estate of wealthy south coast lumberman Louis J. Simpson. Simpson's prospering business was built by his father, Asa Meade Simpson, in the late 1800s. The garden is just a mile beyond **Sunset Bay State Park** campground. A wooded walkway invites visitors past a small gift shop and display illustrating the history of Shore Acres and the Simpson family, researched by Oregon historian Stephen Dow Beckham. The beautifully restored gardens encompass more than 5 acres and feature enormous beds of elegant roses, lush plantings of dahlias, exotic tree species, tall firs, and a lovely sunken Japanese garden around a large pond with seasonal plantings. Find the small rose garden hidden beyond the pond. Paved walkways lined with low boxwood hedges in the upper garden area are wheelchair accessible. Along the nearby sea cliff is an enclosed gazebo where the mansion once perched—an excellent place to read more displays about history, watch for whales and to safely view the crashing waves of winter storms. You'll notice, too, many up-tilted ledges and massive outcroppings—ancient geology at its best on the south coast! Easy hiking trails and picnic areas are also available on the grounds. Shore Acres State Park is open year-round from dawn to dusk (no pets are allowed outside vehicles except guide dogs). The gardens are decorated with thousands of sparkling holiday lights from Thanksgiving to New Year's Eve.

Coos Bay, Charleston, and North Bend

Drive on to **Cape Arago,** at the end of the road, for another panorama of wave-sculpted bluffs, for ocean breezes, and, often, for the cacophony of barking Steller's sea lions, harbor seals, and elephant seals on **Simpson's Reef.** You'll find secluded picnic tables and hiking trails here as well. Year-round camping is also available at nearby **Bastendorff Beach County Park,** along with a wide sandy beach and good views of the ocean. This less-crowded spot is excellent for flying kites and for walking along the beach.

Driving past the county park back toward Coos Bay–North Bend, notice the colorful boat harbor at **Charleston**; here visitors can go crabbing from the dock area. Charter fishing excursions are also available at the **Charleston Marina**; for current information call the friendly folks at **Betty Kay Charters** (541-888-9021). Stop at one of the many cafes and restaurants in the boat basin, such as **High Tide Cafe** (541-888-3664; hightidecafeoregon .com) for specialty coffees, sandwiches, soups, fresh fish dishes, juicy steaks, and awesome chowder; opens at 11:00 a.m. Closed Monday and Tuesday. Don't miss a visit to the **Charleston Marine Life Center** on the campus of University of Oregon's Oregon Institute of Marine Biology at 63466 Boat Basin Road (541-888-2581; charlestonmarinelifecenter.com), which interprets coastal ecosystems. Admission is $5 for adults; children are free and donations are welcome.

From Charleston follow the signs to the towns of **Coos Bay** and **North Bend**. On US 101 South pop into **Kaffe 101** at 171 South Broadway (541-267-4894) for steaming lattes and great pastries. You can learn the best ways to brew coffee, store beans, and also order their fresh roasted coffees such as Bean Forge Blend, Lighthouse Blend, and Whiskey Run Blend at thebeanforge .com. If your taste buds cater to natural foods, try the **Blue Heron Bistro** (541-267-3933; blueheronbistro.com), which is well known for home-baked breads, tasty soups, delicious entrees, freshly made desserts, and gourmet coffee. The bistro, located at the corner of Commercial Street and US 101 in Coos Bay, is open daily at 11:00 a.m. For other casual and tasty fare, try **Shark Bites Café**, 240 S. Broadway (541-269-7475; sharkbites.com) across from the Egyptian Theatre; and **Chocolates of Oregon** at 240 S. Broadway (541-217-7415), a chocolates shop with plenty of options from around the state. **7 Devils Brewing Company**, 247 S. 2nd Street (541-808-3738; 7devilsbrewery.com) is a wonderful craft brewpub in downtown, with locally sourced ingredients on the menu and in the brews, too. Step outside and take in the expansive mural painted on the wall, depicting the greater bay area.

TOP ANNUAL EVENTS ON THE OREGON COAST

FEBRUARY
Newport Seafood and Wine Festival
Newport
newportchamber.com

MARCH
Savor Cannon Beach
Cannon Beach
Savorcannonbeach.com

APRIL
Astoria Warrenton Crab, Seafood and Wine Festival
Astoria
oldoregon.com

MAY
Azalea Festival
Brookings-Harbor
brookingsor.com

Depoe Bay Fleet of Flowers
Depoe Bay
depoebaychamber.org

Rhododendron Festival
Florence
florencechamber.com

Whale of a Wine Festival
Gold Beach
goldbeachwinefestival.com

JUNE
Pistol River Wave Bash
Gold Beach
internationalwindsurfingtour.com

JULY
Circles in the Sand
Bandon
sandypathbandon.com

Oregon Coast Music Festival
Coos Bay
oregonsadventurecoast.com

Southern Oregon Kite Festival
Brookings
southernoregonkitefestival.com

AUGUST

Astoria Regatta Festival
Astoria
astoriaregatta.org

SEPTEMBER

Bay Area Fun Fest
Coos Bay
oregonsadventurecoast.com

Cranberry Festival
Bandon
bandon.com

Mill-Luck Salmon Celebration
Coos Bay
themillcasino.com

Muttzanita
Manzanita
muttzanita.com.

OCTOBER

Lincoln City Kite Festival
Lincoln City
oregoncoast.org

NOVEMBER

Nature's Coastal Holiday Festival of Lights
Brookings

Seaside Parade of Lights
Seaside
seasideor.com

Yachats Celtic Music Festival
Yachats
yachatscelticmusicfestival.org

Works Progress Administration (WPA) History on the South Coast

Heading north from Coos Bay–North Bend, travelers drive high above the bay via McCullough Bridge, one of the longest bridges constructed by the WPA along the Oregon coast. Signed into law by President Franklin D. Roosevelt, the WPA provided much-needed work for thousands of Americans during the Great Depression of the 1930s. McCullough Bridge, designed by renowned bridge designer Conde McCullough, is nearly a mile in length and was dedicated on June 5, 1936. Channel spans rise 150 feet to accommodate large ships entering and leaving Coos Bay's large, protected harbor.

Motoring on scenic US 101, with its many bridges spanning numerous rivers, ocean bays, and estuaries, it's easy to forget this was once a windswept wilderness laced with only deer and Indian trails. Indians, explorers, and pioneers traveled on foot, on horseback, by canoe, and, later, by ferry. There were no bridges. During the late 1800s and early 1900s, the stagecoach lines traveled on sections of the sandy beach!

For a visit to a historic newspaper and job-printing shop on the National Register of Historic Places, plan a summertime stop at the **Marshfield Sun Printing Museum** (541-269-1565), located at the corner of Front Street and Bayshore Drive (US 101 North) in Coos Bay. *The Marshfield Sun* newspaper was edited and published by Jesse Allen Luse from 1891 until 1944. In the museum, you'll see the shop as it was left when Luse passed away, including a Washington handpress, a Chandler and Price platen press, and nearly 200 fonts of type in their cases on the main floor of the building. On the upper level, see exhibits on the history of printing and on early Marshfield (Coos Bay's former name) as well as a collection of original *Marshfield Sun* newspapers. The museum is open from Memorial Weekend through Labor Day, Tuesday through Saturday from 1:00 p.m. to 4:00 p.m. Plan a stop at the Coos Bay Visitor's Information Center (50 Central Avenue, 541-269-0215; ore gonsadventurecoast.com) for maps, directions, and information about lodgings in the area.

History buffs can stop at the **Coos History Museum** on the waterfront of the bay (1210 N Front Street; 541-756-6320; cooshistory.org), for a look at south coast Native American and pioneer displays, exhibits, and vintage photographs. The museum is open Tuesday through Sunday from 10:00 a.m. to 5:00 p.m.; closed Monday and holidays.

In North Bend near the McCullough Bridge is the well-stocked North Bend Visitor Information Center (800-472-9176) along with a shady picnic area and public restrooms. Ask the staff at the visitor center which plays are currently running at **Little Theatre on the Bay** (2100 Sherman Avenue, 541-756-4336; thelibertytheater.org) in North Bend. Little Theatre is the second-oldest community theater in the state, having begun in 1948. Hungry by now? For tasty Italian favorites, try **Ciccarelli's Restaurant**, 2072 Sherman Avenue (541-751-1999) and for delicious vegan food, pop into **Tin Thistle** at 1972 Sherman Avenue (541-267-0267). For specialty coffee drinks try **Books by the Bay Coffee**, 1875 Sherman Avenue, 541-756-1215, and for terrific breakfasts in generous portions, visit **Pancake Mill** (2390 Tremont Avenue; 541-756-2751).

At the small town of **Lakeside**, a few miles north of North Bend, visitors learn that most of **North Tenmile Lake** as well as **South Tenmile Lake** are accessible only by boat, its many arms reaching into Coastal Range forests. Anglers return year after year to Lakeside to stalk the black bass, bluegill, trout, and catfish in the lake's waters. Good boat ramps, a marina, art boutiques, motels, and campgrounds are found in the Tenmile Lakes area. For current information about daily flat-deck pontoon rentals, boat rentals, and the spring bass-fishing contest, call **Ringo's Lakeside Marina** (541-759-3312; ringos lakesidemarina.com).

The Majestic Oregon Dunes

The **Oregon Dunes** are the largest expanse of coastal sand dunes in North America, known for huge hills of sand formed by wind, water, and time. This natural wonder stretches 40 miles from the Siuslaw River south nearly to North Bend, interspersed with islands of trees, marsh-like low points, and access to open beach. Most people access the dunes on motorized all-terrain vehicles like dune buggies, dirt bikes, or four-wheelers. Bring your own, rent one or sign up for a tour from a recreational outfitter.

If your own two legs are your preferred method of traversing nature, visit the **John Dellenbeck Dunes Trailhead**, 5 miles south of Winchester Bay on US 101 at mile marker 222. This trail is a wonderful combination of coastal rainforest, open sand dunes, and oceanfront beach. The trailhead is near the highway, beginning in a lush forest of shore pine, alder, wax myrtle, and Sitka spruce. Choose an easy 1-mile interpretive loop hike on a good trail through rhododendrons and salal, or traverse further to trek into the loose sand of the Oregon Dunes. It's 2.7 miles to walk all the way through the dunes to the ocean beach, a stunning and rewarding hike, though be advised that hiking in dunes is more tiring than hiking a trail. Also be aware of the possibility of flooding in the wet season. The good news is that there aren't any motorized vehicles allowed in this section of the dunes, so while you may hear ATVs in the distance, you won't see any, or worse, need to dodge them on your hike. John Dellenbeck was a former state representative who advocated for protection of the Oregon Dunes.

Pet-friendly; bring a leash; don't park in the adjacent Eel Creek Campground unless you have secured a campsite.

Whale-Watching Territory

This section of the Oregon Coast offers a number of scenic waysides and pull-outs where travelers can often spot whales during January and March. Browse whalespoken.org for information about places along this section of the coast where volunteers will staff viewing stations during this time and offer helpful information.

Winchester Bay and Reedsport

Travel north again on US 101 to **Winchester Bay**, the largest salmon-fishing harbor on the Oregon Coast, and discover bustling **Salmon Harbor**—where the Umpqua River meets the Pacific Ocean—by turning west toward **Windy Cove Campground**. You'll find facilities here for launching seaworthy boats and for renting crabbing and fishing equipment; you'll also find custom canning, bait, fuel, and ice, as well as information about appropriate fishing licenses. Charter deep-sea fishing trips are available throughout most of the year at Salmon Harbor. Stop at the Reedsport–Winchester Bay Visitor Center (541-271-3495; reedsportcc.org) for maps and information about fishing, campgrounds, parks, and also current information about the *Oregon Dunes National Recreation Area*.

Continue on the loop drive, following the south shore of Salmon Harbor, to discover *Umpqua River Lighthouse*. From the impressive 65-foot tower, a bright red flash is seen some 16 miles at sea, the only colored signal on the Oregon coast. Ask about tours of the lighthouse May through October (541-271-4631). Camping options include RV and tent spaces at *Umpqua Lighthouse State Park* or nearby *Windy Cove* (800-452-5687; oregonstateparks.org for reservations). Ask about the large yurts at the Umpqua Lighthouse State Park campground that come with large double bunk beds, heater, and an outdoor picnic table and fire ring. Bring your own bedding, camping lights, folding chairs, groceries, ice chests, and outdoor barbecue gear. For RV spaces with hookups and great water views, check out *Winchester Bay RV Resort* at Salmon Harbor Marina (541-271-0287; winchesterbayresort.com).

At *Reedsport* you can walk along reconstructed boardwalks reminiscent of the industrial area that housed canneries and sawmill sheds in earlier days and also learn about the small coastal town's history at the splendid *Umpqua Discovery Center*. It is located near the boardwalk at 409 Riverfront Way in Old Town, just off US 101 (541-271-4816; umpquadiscoverycenter.com). The kids will enjoy spotting the tall totem pole at the entry and peeking through the center's periscope for a 360-degree view of the Umpqua River, nearby railroad swing bridge, and jet-boat dock. The center is open 9:00 a.m. to 5:00 p.m. June through September; winter hours are 10:00 a.m. to 4:00 p.m. Tasty eats are available nearby at the *Schooner Inn Cafe* (423 River Front Way; 541-271-3945), which offers indoor and outdoor seating with views of the Umpqua River. *Sugar Shack Bakery* offers tasty bakery treats (541-271-3514); open daily to 6:30 p.m. For a huge menu offering cedar plank salmon to peanut butter pie pop into *Harbor Light Restaurant* at 930 US 101 (541-271-3848; harborlightrestaurant.com).

If you drive east toward Roseburg and I-5 via Highway 38, be sure to pull off at the *Dean Creek Elk Viewing Area* just 3 miles east of Reedsport and near the Umpqua River. Pause at Hinsdale Interpretive Center for helpful displays and to peek through the viewing scope, then gaze out over nearly 500 acres of bottomland and 600 acres of hilly woodlands, where a hundred or more mammoth elk roam free. Depending on the time of day, you may also see a parade of other wildlife, such as porcupines, coyotes, and raccoons as well as many bird species.

Just south of Florence, detour from US 101 at the **Oregon Dunes Over-look**, a scenic pullout area with wheelchair-accessible observation decks that offer good views of the ocean and dunes. In the Oregon Dunes are twelve developed trails, ranging from a 0.75-mile stroll along a small lagoon to a 6-mile hike through Douglas fir forests and rugged sand dunes. Maps and information about other accessible sand-dune areas can be obtained from the well-stocked Oregon Dunes National Recreation Area Visitors Centernin Reedsport (541-271-6000; fs.usda.gov). Check with the helpful staff about appropriate preparation and equipment needed for visiting the dunes' areas; newcomers should arrange a guided tour prior to going alone out onto the dunes.

Florence

At the junction of US 101 and Highway 126, near the mouth of the Siuslaw River, stop and explore **Florence**, a thriving community of some 9,000 coast dwellers. **Old Town Florence**, along the river near Bay Street, is a pleasant place to stroll and poke into charming shops, galleries, and eateries housed in some of the town's most historic buildings.

Along Bay Street, in Old Town, you can stop for dinner at **Bay View Bis-tro** (541-590-3000; bwpierpointinn.com), at **Waterfront Depot Restaurant** (541-902-9100; the waterfrontdepot.com), open daily at 4:00 p.m., or at **Bridge-water Fish House and Zebra Bar** at 1297 Bay Street (541-997-1133), open daily at 11:00 a.m. Enjoy great sundaes and cones at **BJ's Ice Cream** (541-997-7286), open daily at 11:00 a.m., or stop in for a steaming cup of espresso at **River Roasters** on the river, 1240 Bay Street (541-997-3443; coffeeoregon .com) or at **Old Town Coffee Roasters** (541-997-1786), doors open daily at 8:00 a.m., on Nopal Street near the port of Siuslaw. An old-fashioned gazebo in tiny **Old Town Park** offers a cozy spot to sit with a view of the Siuslaw River and its graceful drawbridge, ca. 1936, constructed by the 1930s WPA (Works Progress Administration). For a local's favorite visit **Hukilau Pacific Fusion** at 185 US 101 (541-991-1071). Find good breakfast at the **Dunes Cafe** (541-997-5799), open daily at 5:00 a.m., near the junction of US 101 and Highway 126.

If you haven't time to try catching your own crabs but would like to see how it's done, drive a couple of miles south to the **South Jetty**, walk out on the large wooden pier, and watch folks lower bait-filled crab rings into the churning waters. Here you're on the Siuslaw River estuary, where the river meets the Pacific Ocean—surging against the oncoming tides. If you visit from November through February, look for the squadron of some 200 snowy white tundra swans that winter on the Siuslaw River's marshes near South Jetty. It's a good idea to bring rain gear, waterproof boots, and binoculars.

After this invigorating trek, head back to Old Town in Florence to **Mo's Seafood & Chowder** for their classic clam chowder or tasty fish and chips; it's located at the east end of Bay Street (541-997-2185). You can also enjoy Mo's tasty eats at sites in Astoria, Seaside, Cannon Beach, Otter Rock, Newport, and Lincoln City. For comfortable overnight lodgings and great breakfasts, check with the **Blue Heron Inn Bed & Breakfast**, a comfortable 1940s country home overlooking the Siuslaw River (800-997-7780 or 541-997-4091; blueheroninnflorence.com). You could also consider the **River House Inn**, 1202 Bay Street (888-824-2454) on the banks of the Siuslaw, or hole up at the ca. 1930s **Lighthouse Inn**, 155 Highway 101 (866-997-3221; lighthouseinn-florence.com), located within walking distance of Old Town. For other lodgings stop at the Florence Area Visitor Center, 290 US 101 (541-997-3128; florencechamber.com).

If you'd like to view the ocean astride a horse, check with the friendly folks at **C and M Stables** (541-997-7540) located 8 miles north of Florence at 90241 US 101 North, to reserve a horse for yourself or the whole family for beach and sunset rides, dune trail rides, or winter rides. The stables are open daily June through October but closed on Monday and Tuesday during winter months.

Next, turn off US 101 at the **Darlingtonia Wayside** sign, pull into the visitor parking area, and follow the shaded trail to the sturdy boardwalk that takes you out onto a marshy bog. This is one of the few small nature preserves in the United States set aside for conserving a single native species. *Darlingtonia californica* is often called "cobra lily" because it captures and actually digests insects. You can see the unusual greenish-speckled tubular-shaped plants here from spring through summer and into early fall.

Your next stop is **Devil's Elbow State Park**, just beyond Cape Creek Bridge. The park's sheltered beach offers a lovely spot to picnic and to beachcomb for shells and driftwood. Offshore, the large rock "islands," part of the Oregon Islands National Wildlife Refuge, are transient nesting grounds for tufted puffins, cormorants, pigeon guillemots, and numerous kinds of seagulls. From here you can walk the forested trail over to the ca. 1894 **Heceta Head Lighthouse**. The lighthouse is open occasionally for touring and the historic keeper's house is open for bed and breakfast lodging; call for current information (541-547-3696; hecetalighthouse.com). Parking for guests is available next to the keeper's house. Be prepared for innkeepers' hearty seven-course breakfast!

By now, midway on your coastal trek, you have surely felt the magic of the ocean seeping into your bones. Even words like "magnificent," "incredible," and "awesome" seem inadequate to describe the wide-angle views along this stretch of the Oregon coast. It's a panoramic showstopper of the first order, and nearly every inch of it is open to the public. One such dramatic encounter is found by walking down the short trail at *Devil's Churn (Wayside)* to watch incoming waves as they thunder and foam into a narrow basalt fissure. Wear sturdy walking shoes and use caution here, especially with children.

For another spectacular view, drive up to *Cape Perpetua* and its visitor center, just a short distance off US 101, perched atop a jagged chunk of 40-million-year-old volcanic basalt. The Forest Service staff offers lots to see and do at Cape Perpetua, including six nature trails, campfire talks at Tillicum Beach, and naturalist-led hikes down to the tide pools, together with interpretive nature exhibits and films. The visitor center (541-547-3289; fs.usda.gov/Siuslaw) is open daily at 10:00 a.m. fall through spring, and at 9:30 a.m. in summer. Also within the *Cape Perpetua Scenic Area* are group picnic areas, a campground, and a 22-mile self-guided auto tour.

OTHER ATTRACTIONS WORTH SEEING ON THE COAST

Fort Stevens Historic Area
near Astoria in Hammond; Peter Iredale shipwreck on beach

Port Orford Lifeboat Station at Port Orford Heads State Park
archive.is/p3VO

South Slough National Estuarine Reserve and Interpretive Center
near Charleston (541-888-5558)

Tillamook Forest Center
Highway 6 (milepost 22 near Tillamook)
tillamookforestcenter.org

Yachats and Newport

For pleasant oceanside lodgings and good eateries on the central coast, there are several possibilities near *Waldport* and *Yachats*. *The Overleaf Lodge and Spa*, 280 Overleaf Lodge Lane (541-547-4880; overleaflodge.com), offers dozens of splendid guest rooms, all with large windows facing the ocean. An onsite spa on the top floor offers views of the sea from its soaking pool. Delicious breakfasts are served each morning, and an evening reception offers light refreshments. Right out front of the property is the historic 804 Trail, once a county road and probably a footpath before that, which leads north to a sandy beach and south into town.

In the small community of Yachats, try the *Green Salmon Coffee Company*, 220 US 101 North (541-547-3077; thegreensalmon.com), for tasty coffee and espresso drinks, teas, fresh-baked scones, danish, and savories as well as homemade soups and panini sandwiches. *The Drift Inn*, a historic restaurant and bar open daily for breakfast, lunch, and dinner at 124 US 101 North (541-547-4477; the-drift-inn.com), offers fresh seafood, chowder, homemade breads, and tasty desserts. Beer lovers can visit **Yachats Brewing and Farmstore** (541-547-3884), 348 US 101 North. This delightful place was once a bank and has been transformed with the use of reclaimed woods, plenty of windows, and many living plants. Try an array of fresh craft beer and a menu boasting great food made from local products and produce. **Leroy's Blue Whale Caffe**, on US 101 near 7th Street (541-547-3399), offers delicious fish and chips. For additional information about this area, contact the Yachats Area Visitor Center (800-929-0477; yachats.org).

Continue north again on US 101 for about 20 miles to **Newport**, where two more lighthouses await—the ca. 1871 **Yaquina Bay Lighthouse** in Yaquina Bay State Park, and the ca. 1872 **Yaquina Head Lighthouse** at **Yaquina Head Outstanding Natural Area** (blm.gov); these are located 3 miles north of Newport and 1 mile west of US 101. Both lighthouses are open for touring, call ahead to check current hours (541-574-3100 and 541-265-5679; yaquinalights.org). Yaquina Head's tower, rising 93 feet on a point of land at the edge of the ocean, is especially dramatic; its light has remained active since 1872. Yaquina Bay Lighthouse, nearby, offers limited tours of a fine museum with period furnishings in all the rooms in the keeper's house; its light was constructed atop the house and is no longer in service. Be sure to visit the gardens on the grounds and also notice the colonies of seabirds on the offshore islands here. There is an entrance fee per car payable at the entry booth. Ask too about joining Friends of Yaquina Lighthouses and about the annual Pacific Coast Passport, which allows travelers to visit a variety of locations up and down the Oregon coast.

Most everyone who travels through this part of the central coast will plan a stop at the **Oregon Coast Aquarium** (541-867-3474; aquarium.org) in Newport to see all kinds of sea creatures and sea mammals swimming in enormous and enclosed underwater habitats. Both the aquarium and the **Hatfield Marine Science Center** (541-867-0100; hmsc.oregonstate.edu) are located just below the Yaquina Bay Bridge at the south edge of Newport. Both open daily at 9:00 a.m. during summer months and at 10:00 a.m. the rest of the year.

On Newport's bay front, visit the **Pacific Maritime & Heritage Center** at 333 SE Bay Blvd. (541-246-7509; oregoncoasthistory.org), which offers views of Newport's working harbor. The center offers educational maritime programs and also maritime activities at the working wharf. The center is located in a historic home built in 1925 and restored after the original home was destroyed by fire in 1924.

For a meal on the bay front, have lunch at one of the city's oldest eateries, *Canyon Way Bookstore & Restaurant*, 1216 SW Canyon Way (541-265-8319; canyonway.com), which features homemade pastas, delicious breads, meat- or seafood-filled croissants, and delectable pastries. Buy a book or a stack of books while you are there as well. Open Monday through Friday at 11:30 a.m. A true local's favorite is *Local Ocean*, a popular eatery plus fish market offering fresh oysters, seafood stew, and rock cod tacos, 213 SE Bay Boulevard (541-574-7959; localocean.net). The second-floor dining offers incredible views of the Yaquina Bay Bridge and the working harbor.

Rogue Brewery on the Bay, an Oregon Classic

Jack Joyce and Bob Woodell, University of Oregon fraternity brothers, first began brewing ales, an amber and a gold, in a basement in southern Oregon in 1988. A year later, they bought an old warehouse on the central coast, in Newport, and hired John Maier, who had been with Alaska Brewing, as the new brewmaster for *Rogue Ales*. They added the pub, recycled the back bar from the old Elk Tavern and opened to the public in spring 1989. Curious Newport locals stopped by and never left. Rogue Ales is now noted for more than fifty handcrafted ales including such intriguing names as Portland State IPA, XS McRogue Scotch Ale, Shakespeare Oatmeal Stout, and Cap'n Sig's Northwestern Ale. They feature handcrafted ales, porters, stouts, lagers, and spirits.

Pop into *Rogue Brewer's on the Bay* (2320 OSU Drive, 541-867-3664), at the Yaquina Bay Marina, Newport, or the location on the other side of the bay at 748 SW Bay Blvd., 541-265-3188.

Book Lovers Alert: Newport's Sylvia Beach Hotel Is the Place

Offering guest rooms decorated for well-known novelists such as Mark Twain, Agatha Christie, J. K. Rowling, and Ernest Hemingway, the *Sylvia Beach Hotel* (541-265-5428; sylviabeachhotel.com) also offers a cozy library on the top floor crammed with books, overstuffed chairs, and the best view of the ocean. Storm watching is excellent during winters when the wind howls, the building shakes, the rain goes sideways, and ocean waves crash some 50 feet below on the rocks and beach. Breakfast is included with your room and you can also order dinner, which is served family-style with a choice of four entrees. Hot spiced wine is usually served evenings around 10:00 p.m. *Note:* No TVs, radios, or telephones in the guest rooms, just books!

In Newport's historic *Nye Beach* area, stop at the *Newport Visual Arts Center* at 777 NW Beach Drive (541-265-6540; coastarts.org) to immerse yourself in central coast art. These exhibits are free to enter from 12:00 a.m. to 4:00 p.m., Tuesday through Sunday.

Enjoy poking into shops and eateries in Nye Beach along NW Beach Street off Coast Drive. For yummy pastries, breads, sandwiches, and espresso drinks, check out *Panini Bakery* at 232 NW Coast Street (541-265-5033). *Nana's Irish Pub* (613 NW 3rd Street; 541-574-8787; nanasirishpub.com) is a fun destination offering authentic Irish fare with seating indoors and out. Other favorites include *Georgie's Beachside Grill*, noted as a romantic eatery, 744 SW Elizabeth Street (541-265-9800; georgiesbeachsidegrill.com), and *Sorella*, 526 NW Coast Street (541-265-4055; sorellanyebeach.com).

Pleasant inns in the Newport area, most offering great ocean views, include *Newport Belle Riverboat Inn*, aboard a 97-foot-long stern-wheel-style riverboat (541-867-6290; newportbelle.com) located at the Yaquina Bay marina and offering great sunset views across the calm waters to the Yaquina Bay Bridge and the ocean; *Tyee Lodge Oceanfront Bed & Breakfast* (541-265-8953; tyeelodge.com), at 4925 NW Woody Way at ocean's edge near downtown Newport; and ca. 1940s *Agate Beach Motel* (175 Gilbert Way; 541-265-8746; agatebeachmotel.com) located 1 mile north of Newport and renovated in postmodern style with comfy rooms and decks and also overlooking the beach.

The Newport Visitor Information Center (800-262-7844; discovernewport. com) offers current information about other lodgings and the variety of goings-on in the area. For live theater offerings, check out the *Newport Performing Arts Center* in Nye Beach (541-265-2787; coastarts.org) for the current playbills.

Heading north again on US 101, you can access *Otter Crest Scenic Loop Drive*, at Otter Rock. First drive out to the bluff to peer down into *Devil's Punch Bowl*, a rounded outcropping into which the ocean thunders. The tiny *Mo's West* here offers tasty clam chowder and fish and chips. The loop drive reconnects with US 101 within a couple of miles.

If you're driving through the area at low tide—you can pick up current tide tables for a nominal cost at most visitor centers, or use an online app—stop at the *Inn at Otter Crest*, parking close to the ocean, just beyond *The Lodge Restaurant*. Walk a short path down to the beach, where you can see a fascinating array of *tide pools* formed by rounded depressions in the large volcanic rocks. Bathed by tidal currents twice each day, coastal tide pools may house a variety of species, such as sea anemones, sea urchins, goose barnacles, sea stars, sea slugs, limpets, jellyfish, and tiny crabs. *Note:* Do not disturb live sea creatures.

If your picnic basket and cooler are full of goodies and cold beverages, consider a lunch stop at one of the most charming coastal day-use parks, ***Fogarty Creek Wayside***, just north of Depoe Bay and Pirate's Cove. Here you can walk a path that meanders through the park, alongside a small creek, and through a tunnel under the highway to a small sandy cove right on the edge of the ocean. Weather permitting, you can enjoy your picnic with seagulls and sandpipers for company. In the park are picnic tables and restrooms. It's a great place for families with small children.

Depoe Bay, Gleneden Beach, and Lincoln City

If, however, you're driving through this section of the central coast early in the day and the ocean is flat and shimmering in the morning sun, stop at the seawall in ***Depoe Bay***, just south of Fogarty Creek, to see whether the gray whales are swimming past. Of the seven different kinds of whales plying the Pacific Ocean, the grays maneuver closest to the shoreline. Some 15,000 of the mammoth creatures migrate south from November to January and return north from March to May. This 12,000-mile round-trip is the longest known for any mammal. You could also hole up near Depoe Bay at the cozy ***Inn at Arch Rock*** (800-767-1835; innatarchrock.com) with panoramic views of the ocean or at ***Troller's Lodge***, 355 SW US 101 (800-472-9335; trollerslodge.com).

Equipment for ***whale watching*** is minimal—helpful are good binoculars, a camera, and warm clothing. Or just shade your eyes and squint, gazing west toward the horizon. You might be rewarded for your patience by seeing one of the grays "breach"—that is, leap high out of the water and then fall back with a spectacular splash.

During one week in January and another week in March, some 200 volunteers at whale-watching sites all along the coast offer helpful information, brochures, maps, and assistance with spotting the gray whales. Look for the familiar logo "Whale Watching Spoken Here" and for the volunteers, ranging from school kids to oldsters. For more information, check the helpful website whalespoken.org and stop at the ***Whale Watching Center*** in Depoe Bay where rangers are ready to answers your questions (541-765-3304; oregon stateparks.org).

Both at Shore Acres, located west of Coos Bay–North Bend, and at Cape Perpetua, north of Florence, you can view whales from glassed-in areas and stay dry to boot.

Just south of Lincoln City, in ***Gleneden Beach***, tucked away at 6645 Gleneden Beach Loop Road, is a good lunch and dinner stop, the ***Side Door Cafe*** (541-764-3825; sidedoorcafe.com); open at 11:30 a.m., Tuesday through Saturday. This cozy, eclectic space delivers delicious food and cocktails.

Nestled in a hillside setting of coast pine and Douglas fir, casually elegant *Salishan Lodge Resort & Spa* (7760 N. Hwy. 101, Gleneden Beach; 800-452-2300; salishan.com) offers spacious and comfortable guest suites, an art gallery, a golf course, indoor tennis courts, an indoor swimming pool, and gourmet dining in the inn's three restaurants. The wine cellar is exemplary. Directly across US 101 from the lodge, you'll find the

oregontrivia

Siuslaw is an Indian word meaning "faraway waters." Most of the lakes in this area have special Indian names: *Cleawox,* meaning "paddle wood"; *Siltcoos,* meaning "plenty elk"; and *Tahkenitch,* meaning "many arms."

lively *MarketPlace* of small boutiques, breweries, bookshops, and eateries, and, at the north end, a pleasant nature trail that skirts tiny *Siletz Bay*.

Gently Explore Oregon's Tide Pools

Cruising through tide pools is a tried-and-true coastal activity, especially with kids along for the fun. But it's wise to mind safety, both for you and for the plants and animals you wish to see. Seaweed is slippery, wear good closed-toe shoes, and avoid jumping from rock to rock; keep a wary eye on the incoming tide; watch for large "sneaker" waves, which can appear out of the regular wave pattern; stay away from rolling logs, which can move quickly onto an unsuspecting tide-pooler, particularly a small child; don't remove live marine creatures from the tide pools or take any live specimens with you; avoid walking on rocks bearing animals, including barnacles and mussels, as your weight can crush them. There are beach treasures which you and the kids can collect and take home, including limpet and barnacle shells, sand dollar and sea urchin shells, dried kelp, driftwood, beach rocks, and translucent agates. It was once common to find Japanese glass floats on the beaches of Oregon, and the folks of Lincoln City celebrate that heritage with the Finders Keepers program. Find a custom-made blown glass float in the sand and it's yours to take home.

Following all this whale-spying and gourmet eating, you and the kids can stop by *Catch the Wind Kite Shop* at 266 SE US 101 (541-994-9500) in *Lincoln City* for a look at kites of all sizes, shapes, colors, and prices. It's located just across the highway from the *D River Wayside* beach, where, on a particularly windy day, you can watch kites being flown by grown-ups and kids of all ages. For tasty eats, try the friendly *Wildflower Grill* at 4250 NE US 101 (541-994-9663; thewildflowergrill.com) that offers omelets, home-style soups and chowder, seafood dishes, and homemade desserts. The covered deck overlooks a wetland where you may dine with the ducks, herons, beavers, deer, and occasionally an eagle perched in a nearby fir tree. Call to confirm current hours. Also at the north end of Lincoln City, the legendary **Barnacle Bill's** at 2174 NE US 101 (541-994-3022) is a good stop for fresh seafood and deli items. **Pacific Grind Cafe** at 4741 SW US 101 (541-994-8314; pacificgrindcafe.com) offers great coffee, espresso, sandwiches, and soups; open Monday through Saturday. Don't miss the house coffee, which features Left Coast Blend, from nearby Cape Foulweather Coffee Company. You can pop into **Kyllo's**, also at the D River (1110 NW 1st. Ct.; 541-994-3179; kyllosseafoodandgrill.com). The ocean rolls right up to the restaurant under the right conditions, and fresh seafood from halibut to lingcod, clam chowder and an amazing happy hour compliment the view.

Also located in the Taft community, you can find comfortable sleeps at **Historic Anchor Inn**, 4417 SW Highway 101 (541-996-3810; historicanchorinn.com). A nostalgic 1940s feeling emanates in the guest rooms and comfy common area, and guests find hot popcorn, warm cookies, and a complimentary breakfast in the morning. For helpful information about the entire area, stop at the Lincoln City Visitor Center at the far north end of town, at 801 SW US 101 (800-452-2151; lincolncity.org). You can snoop **Finders Keepers** on the beach for local handblown glass floats, all colors, from mid-October to Memorial Day. Ask, too, for directions to the nearby **Connie Hansen Garden Conservancy**—a true plantswoman's botanical paradise. Lush native plantings, grassy walkways, native shrub and ornamental tree species, and watery streams ramble about on two city lots, at 1931 NW 33rd Avenue. The splendid garden is cared for and staffed by a group of dedicated volunteers on Tuesday and Thursday from 10:00 a.m. to 2:00 p.m. and is also open for visitors daily (541-994-6338; conniehansengarden.com). Located on nearby Devil's Lake just outside of Lincoln City check out **Lake House Bed & Breakfast**, a cedar home and guest cottage, 2165 N.E. East Devil's Lake Road (541-996-8938 or 888-996-8938; lakehousebb.com). Another oceanfront option is **Ocean Terrace Condominiums**, 4229 SW Beach Avenue (541-996-3623; oceanterrace.com). Small condominiums accommodate families, and the kids will love the indoor heated swimming pool.

Golfing on the Oregon Coast

Since golf's beginnings on Scotland's windswept dunes, folks of all ages have enjoyed walking the fairways, swinging the clubs, and aiming those elusive putts on the greens. Stow the golf clubs and golf shoes in the trunk and take in a number of scenic links on your travels along the central coast. Call for current rates and tee times. Enjoy!

Agate Beach Golf Course
Newport
9 holes, 6,004 yards, par 72
(541) 265-7331
agatebeachgolf.net

Alderbrook Golf Course
Tillamook
18 holes, 5,692 yards, par 69
(503) 842-2767
alderbrookgolfcourse.com

Bandon Dunes Golf Resort
Bandon, four oceanside links courses
(541) 347-4380
bandondunesgolf.com

Cedar Bend Golf Course
Gold Beach, opened 1971
9 holes, RV park nearby
(541) 247-6911
cedarbendgolf.com

Crestview Golf Club
Waldport, day-use RV parking
9 holes, 3,062 yards, par 36
(541) 563-3020
crestviewgolfclub.com

The Highlands Golf Club
Gearhart
9 holes, 2,000 yards, par 31
(503) 738-5248
highlandsgolfgearhart.com

Manzanita Links
Manzanita, no carts available
9 holes, 2,192 yards, par 32
(503) 368-5744
manzanitalinks.com

On Lewis and Clark's Trail

Leaving the busy Lincoln City area, travelers notice a quieter, more pastoral ambience along US 101, which winds north from Otis toward Neskowin, Sandlake, Cape Lookout, Netarts, and Tillamook. Those who travel through this region in the early spring will see dairy cows munching lush green grass inside white-fenced fields, clumps of skunk cabbage blooming in bright yellows, and old apple trees bursting with pale pink blossoms on gnarled limbs.

Native Oregon grape—an evergreen shrub related to barberry—crowds along the roadside, with tight clusters of bright yellow blooms; low-lying *salal*, with its pink flowers, carpets forested areas; and gangly *salmonberry bushes* show pale white blossoms. This is clearly the time to slow the pace and enjoy a kaleidoscope of springtime colors.

If your sweetheart is along, you might spend a night in *Neskowin* near *Proposal Rock*, at *Proposal Rock Inn* (48988 US 101 South; 503-392-3115; proposalrockneskowin.com). Located next door to the inn, popular *Cafe on Hawk Creek*, 4505 Salem Avenue (503-392-4400; cafeonhawkcreek.com), offers breakfast fare, fresh-baked pizza, great sandwiches, juicy burgers, fresh seafood, and espresso and coffee drinks. On tap find a variety of northwest microbrews, such as Black Bear Stout, McPelicans Scottish Style Ale, Old Speckled Hen, Three Creeks Blonde, and Deschutes Mirror Pond. For groceries, local foods, and deli items, pop into *Neskowin Trading Company* near Proposal Rock Inn.

Heading north on US 101, detour onto *Three Capes Scenic Drive*, heading toward *Pacific City*, so that you can watch the launching of the *dory fleet*, one of the coast's most unusual fishing fleets. In the shadow of *Cape Kiwanda*, a towering sandstone headland, salmon fishers from the Pacific City area launch flat-bottomed dories from the sandy beach into the protected waters near the large, offshore rock islands where those ever-present seabirds congregate. You could also arrive in the late afternoon to see the dories return with the day's catch, skimming across the water and right onto the beach. The boats are then loaded onto large trailers for the night. Then, too, keep watch for those hardy souls who can often be spotted hang gliding into the wind from Maxwell Point just north of the beach. Pacific City is one of Oregon's most popular surfing spots, as well. Watch the experts catch waves off the cape, or rent some gear or take a lesson from one of the local surfshops.

If you're hungry, stop at *Pelican Pub & Brewery* (503-965-7007; pelicanbrewing.com) for eats and locally brewed ales along with views of Cape Kiwanda and the beach. Or, grab a generous breakfast at *Grateful Bread Restaurant Bakery* (34805 Brooten Road; 503-965-7337), where bread and pastries are homemade and lunch and pizza is on the menu, too. This is also a great place to buy a tie-dyed shirt bearing the café's logo. For overnight lodging with incredible views and luxury surroundings, book a night at *Headlands Coastal Lodge and Spa* (33000 Cape Kiwanda Drive; 503483-3000; headlandslodge.com). Every room has views of the ocean, and adventure coaches are on hand to help you plan outdoor activities in the area, from biking to hiking to surfing.

Just north of Sandlake, nature trails at *Cape Lookout* offer a close-up view of a typical coastal rain forest that includes such species as Sitka spruce, western hemlock, western red cedar, and red alder. The ca. 1894 *Sandlake Country Inn Bed & Breakfast*, at 8505 Galloway Road, Cloverdale (503-965-6745; sandlakecountryinn.com), offers cozy rooms and a romantic cottage, among tall Douglas fir and native rhododendron.

Then dig out the binoculars and stop a bit farther off the beaten path, at the small community of *Oceanside*, to walk on the beach and see *Three Arch Rocks Wildlife Preserve*. These offshore islands, set aside in 1907 by President Theodore Roosevelt as the first wildlife preserve on the Pacific Coast, are home to thousands of black petrels, colorful tufted puffins, and penguin-like murres, along with several varieties of gulls and cormorants. The bellow of resident Steller's sea lions and sea pups can often be heard as well. For good eats, also beachside, pop into *Roseanna's Café* for fresh seafood, pasta, hearty soups, and tasty desserts (503-842-9351; roseannascafe.org). For overnight accommodations in nearby Netarts, call on **Surf Inn** (4951 OR 131; 503-354-2644; pacificviewlodging.com), which offers simple but welcoming rooms with kitchens. Also in Netarts is the legendary **The Schooner Restaurant** (2065 Netarts Basin Boat Road, Netarts; 503-815-9900; theschooner.net). One half bar, one half restaurant, with a huge covered patio, the Schooner has a little something for everyone, and specializes in oysters caught in the bay out front. For more information about the area, see the Tillamook Coast website, gotillamook.com.

From Oceanside return to Netarts and access this section of the Scenic Loop to the thriving dairy community of Tillamook. Continue north to **Cape Meares** and **Cape Meares Lighthouse** (503-842-2244), open daily May through October. Also walk the short trail to see the unusual **Octopus Tree**, an enormous Sitka spruce with six trunks. Then, bordering the paved path down to the lighthouse, you'll see thick tangles of ruby rugosa roses with large burgundy blossoms. You may well see folks sketching or photographing the picturesque, ca. 1890s structure; the beacon was decommissioned in 1963.

Lighthouses on the Coast

Cape Arago Lighthouse
near North Bend and Coos Bay; illuminated in 1934. It's not open to the public, but good views are available from the trail at Sunset Bay State Park.

Cape Blanco Lighthouse
near Port Orford; commissioned in 1870 to aid shipping generated by gold mining and the lumber industry. Visitor programs; (541) 332-6774.

Cape Meares Lighthouse
west of Tillamook; illuminated in 1890. Trails lead to the lighthouse and viewpoints overlooking offshore islets home to Steller's sea lions and seabirds. Gift shop, visitor programs, and Friends of Cape Meares; (503) 842-3182; capemeareslighthouse.org. The beacon was decommissioned in 2014.

Coquille River Lighthouse
near Bandon; commissioned in 1896 to guide mariners across the dangerous river bar. Decommissioned in 1939 and restored in 1979 as an interpretive center; open year-round. Access from the state park across the river from Bandon.

Heceta Head Lighthouse
north of Florence; illuminated in 1894. Its automated beacon is rated as the strongest light on the Oregon coast. Tours May through September and bed-and-breakfast lodging in the historic keeper's house; (541) 547-3416.

Tillamook Rock Lighthouse
between Cannon Beach and Seaside. Commissioned in 1881 to help guide ships
entering the Columbia River near Astoria, it was replaced by a whistle buoy in 1957.
No public access.

Umpqua Lighthouse
near Reedsport; illuminated in 1894. The structure, museum, and first-order Fresnel
lens with both red-and-white beacons are maintained by the Douglas County Parks
and Recreation Department; (541) 271-4631.

Yaquina Bay Lighthouse and Museum
north of Newport; in service from 1871 to 1874. Keeper's house and fine museum
open daily for self-guided tours May through September; group tours and special
events; 541-270-0131; yaquinalights.org.

Yaquina Head Lighthouse (and Yaquina Head Outstanding Natural Area)
north of Newport; illuminated in 1873. The beacon aids navigation along the
seacoast and at the entrance to Yaquina Bay. Open to the public; 541-574-3100;
yaquinalights.org.

Tillamook, Wheeler, and Nehalem

Stop in Tillamook at the Tillamook Visitor Center, 208 Main Avenue (503-842-7525), to get oriented to the area. You can learn about Tillamook County's history at the well-stocked *Tillamook County Pioneer Museum* (503-842-4553; tcpm.org), located in the old courthouse building at 2106 2nd Street in *Tillamook*. You'll see the stagecoach that carried mail in the county's early days, vintage horseless carriages, logging memorabilia, the replica of a fire lookout, and a kitchen of yesteryear. Hours are generally Tuesday through Sunday from 10:00 a.m. to 4:00 p.m. (closed Monday and major holidays). Also stop to see costumes, textiles, and historic and contemporary quilt exhibits at *Latimer Quilt & Textile Center*, 2105 Wilson River Loop Road (503-842-8622; latimerquiltandtextile.com). Hours are 10:00 a.m. to 5:00 p.m., Monday through Friday; noon to 4:00 p.m., Saturday and Sunday. Also consider the self-guided *Tillamook County Barn & Quilt Trail* (tillamookquilttrail.org), which features historic barns mounted with decorative quilt block designs throughout Tillamook County. For other barn quilt trails across the United States, see barnquiltinfo.com.

Linger a while longer on the Tillamook coast region to visit the world's largest clear-span wooden structure at the *Tillamook Air Museum* (6030 Hangar Road, 503-842-1130; tillamookair.com) along with its collection of historic photographs and memorabilia. The building, more than 20-stories high and 0.2-mile long, was the site of a World War II blimp hangar; it was in commission until 1948. Operated in cooperation with the Port of Tillamook Bay, the museum is open daily from 10:00 a.m. to 4:00 p.m. (except major holidays).

It's located 2 miles south of Tillamook, just off US 101. Needless to say, you can't miss spotting it! Amenities at the museum include a number of restored vintage airplanes, theater, gift shop, and the 1940s-style *Air Base Cafe*. Among the collection of some twenty vintage airplanes in the enormous blimp hangar, you'll see a Grumman F-14A Tomcat, a Learjet 24, a 1939 Piper J3 Cub, and a Cessna 180F Skywagon. In addition, you'll see a 1944 Willy's Jeep and a 1931 Ford truck. Don't miss it!

Just a mile north of Tillamook, in a converted dairy barn at 2001 Blue Heron Drive off US 101, the *Blue Heron French Cheese Factory* (503-842-8281; blue heronoregon.com), open daily at 8 a.m., offers visitors a gaggle of small farm animals, including colorful hens and roosters; delicious French-style cheeses; deli fare and tasty sandwiches; and a large selection of wines. You could also stop to visit the splendid *Tillamook Creamery* (503-815-1300) located nearby. A brand-new visitor center opened here in 2018, with viewing windows to the factory floor and tasting stations for cheese and ice cream. A restaurant and coffee bar are here, too; weekdays are less crowded at this popular spot. Then pop across US 101 to *5 Rivers Coffee Roasters & Coffeehouse*, 3670 N. US Highway 101 (503-815-2739; fiveriverscoffeeroasters.com) for steaming lattes, breakfast crois-sants, bagels, pastries, and lunch paninis; it's open daily except Sundays. Come afternoon or evening, stop in at the tasting room at *de Garde Brewing* (503-815-1635; degardebrewing.com), where the brews are fermented with natural yeasts and microflora, and naturally conditioned.

Arrange a ride on the *Oregon Coast Scenic Railroad* located at 306 American Avenue in *Garibaldi* (503-842-7972; oregoncoastscenic.org). The small depot, a green caboose, is located across from the Dairy Queen and next to Lumberman's Park. Excursions include rides with a 1910 Heisler steam locomotive, a 1953 BUDD Rail Diesel Car, and also a Sunset Dinner Train and seasonal events. The Oregon Coast Scenic Railroad's nonprofit museum group operates in conjunction with the Port of Tillamook Bay. Call or check the web-site for current schedules that take visitors railroading several miles between Garibaldi and Rockaway Beach just north of Tillamook.

If you're itching to do a bit of shopping for coastal antiques, stop first in the village of *Wheeler* and find *Wheeler Station Antique Mall* (503-368-5677) just across from the small Waterfront Park and Wheeler Marina on Nehalem Bay. The mall is filled with an eclectic mix of vintage furniture and collectibles. Opens daily at 10:00 a.m. For another antiques shopping foray, trundle into nearby *Nehalem Riverside Trading Company* for collectibles offered by a gaggle of aficionados of more vintage and intriguing stuff. For tasty eats in Wheeler, try *Rising Star Café*, 92 Rorvik Street (541-368-3990) for fresh sea-food and locally grown fruits and vegetables. You're ready for some outdoor activities? You could kayak the calm waters of the Nehalem River and Nehalem Bay by renting crafts at **Wheeler Marina** (503-368-5780; wheelermarina.net).

You also want to try camping on the coast, but you don't have a tent? Well, not to worry, both **Cape Lookout State Park** and **Nehalem Bay State Park** campgrounds near Tillamook offer cozy alternatives to setting up a tent. Try yurt camping in a stationary circular domed tent with a wood floor, structural wall supports, electricity, and a skylight. Your yurt is furnished with a bunk bed, foldout couch, small table, and space heater; bring your own sleeping bags or bedding and your own food and outdoor cooking gear. You'd like your digs a bit more plush? Ask about the state parks that now offer a number of three-room cabins and extra-deluxe yurts that come with small kitchens and bath with shower. For more information, call Oregon State Parks at (800) 551-6949 or go to oregonstateparks.org for general information about these accommodations and locations throughout the Beaver State. Or, rent a tiny home at **Sheltered Nook** on Tillamook Bay (7860 Warren Street; 503-805-5526; shelterednook.com). Six tiny homes are fully furnished with locally made furniture, a TV, and all the cooking utensils you may need during your stay, Sheltered Nook is also nestled in the trees and has a fire pit and community gathering area to enjoy.

US 101 skirts **Nehalem Bay** and wends through the villages of **Nehalem** and **Wheeler**, known for crabbing and clamming and for fine fishing. Angling for silver and Chinook salmon and cutthroat, native, and steelhead trout is among the best along the Nehalem River and bay area; there's a marina here with both free boat launches and private moorages.

Wine lovers can plan a short detour to **Nehalem Bay Winery** located at 34965 Highway 53 in an abandoned creamery refurbished by its owners in the 1970s (503-368-9463; nehalembaywinery.com); the tasting room is open daily at 10:00 a.m.

For information about fishing and crabbing, bicycle and horse trails, and annual festivals, contact the Nehalem Bay Area Visitor Center (877-368-5100) at 425 Nehalem Boulevard (across from Waterfront Park).

Manzanita, Cannon Beach, and Seaside

US 101 now winds north to the small coastal community of **Manzanita**. For fresh scones, muffins, and coffee or lattes, pop into one of the locals' favorite, **Manzanita News & Espresso**, 500 Laneda Avenue (503-368-7450), open daily at 7:30 a.m. Or try **Bread and Ocean Bakery**, 154 Laneda Avenue (503-368-5823; breadandocean.com), for tasty sandwiches and decadent pastries. **Left Coast Siesta**, 288 Laneda Avenue (503-368-7997; leftcoastsiesta.com), offers a fresh take on Mexican food, with big or wet burritos loaded with organic fillings and five different tortilla flavors. **Neah-Kah-Nie Bistro**, 519 Laneda Avenue (503-368-2722; nknbistro.com) delivers gourmet comfort food including fancy fries, which are adorned with garlic, parsley, and truffle oil. Beginning in the late afternoon, visit **MacGregor's Whiskey Bar & Restaurant**, 387 D Laneda Avenue (503-368-2447; macgregorswhiskeybar.com), where over 140 bottles of whiskey are on hand and food comes by way of Scottish favorites and meat and cheese platters. MacGregor's has a second location in Cannon Beach at 100 E. 2nd Street.

Then, continue north on US 101 high atop **Neahkahnie Mountain** and proceed down to one of the north coast's most hidden coves and beach areas, **Short Sand Beach** and **Oswald West State Park**. Here you can explore the agate- and driftwood-strewn cove, snoop into shallow caves and caverns, fish or wade in an icy creek or shallow streams, peer at delicate tide pools, and let the sounds of the surf lull you to sleep on a blanket for a midday beach nap.

The particulars: Park in the large designated parking area on US 101 and walk the easy 0.5-mile trail to the beach, through old-growth Douglas fir, coast pines, salal, salmonberry, and ferns growing in lush profusion along the way. Nicknamed "Shorty's" by locals, **Short Sand Beach** is very popular with surfers and you'll likely see wetsuit-clad visitors toting gear down the trail and catching waves offshore. A section of the Oregon Coast Trail passes through the area as well (oregonstateparks.org).

After a day well-spent exploring Oswald West State Park, plan for a night at one of dozens of motels, cozy bed-and-breakfast inns, and hostelries in **Cannon Beach**, just a few miles north via US 101. For current lodging information, contact the Cannon Beach Visitor Center, located at 2nd and Spruce Streets (503-436-2623; cannonbeach.org).

Park the car in downtown Cannon Beach and pull on tennis shoes and a warm windbreaker for a walk on the beach to nearby **Haystack Rock**, the north coast's venerable landmark that houses colonies of seabirds and myriad tide pools. Then browse through Cannon Beach's main street art galleries, boutiques, and bookshops and then sip hot coffee and steaming lattes over delicious pastries at **Sleepy Monk Coffeehouse**, 1235 S. Hemlock Street (503-436-2796; sleepymonk.com), open 8:00 a.m. daily but closed on Wednesday. Drink or order such tasty blends as Monastery Blend, Gaelic Grounds, Fiddler's Fusion, and Monk's Choice along with local pastries. Enjoy seafood, steaks, clam chowder, and fish and chips at cozy eateries such as **Driftwood Restaurant & Lounge**, 179 N. Hemlock (503-436-2439; driftwoodcannonbeach.com), and Irish favorites at The Irish Table, 1235 S Hemlock Street (503-436 0708; theirishtable.com), which shares a space with **Sleepy Monk Coffeehouse**. Don't miss a visit to **Cannon Beach Hardware & Public House**, 1235 S

Hemlock Street (503-436-4086; cannonbeachhardware.com), where you can shop for tools while sipping a beer (and even dine on food from hot dogs to ahi salads). Poke into **Bruce's Candy Kitchen**, 256 N. Hemlock Street (503-436-2641; brucescandy.com), for a gaggle of saltwater taffy flavors and other treats and then pause at **Icefire Glassworks**, at the corner of Hemlock and Gower (503-436-2359), open Tuesday through Monday at 10:00 a.m. to watch the glass-blowing process and ogle at colorful hand-blown glassware.

At the north edge of Cannon Beach, drive the shaded winding road up to **Ecola State Park** for one of the most dramatic seascape panoramas on the north coast. In the lush 1,300-acre park, you'll see splendid examples of old-growth Sitka spruce, western hemlock forest, native shrubs, and wildflower species. Picnic tables are tucked here and there, many sheltered from coastal breezes. The views are spectacular, particularly on blue sky days; walk the trails along the ledges and remain safely behind the fenced areas. You can spy migrating whales during winter months and ask questions of whale-watching volunteers stationed on the bluff during mid-March (whalespoken.org).

For those who want to plan hikes along the **Oregon Coast Trail**, some of which passes through scenic Ecola State Park and Indian Beach, maps and current information can be obtained from the Oregon Parks and Recreation Department, oregonstateparks.org.

Follow US 101 north to one of Oregon's oldest coastal resort towns, **Seaside**, where families have vacationed since the turn of the twentieth century. For a nostalgic experience, park the car on any side street near the ocean and walk as far as you like on the **Historic Seaside Promenade**—a 2-mile-long sidewalk, with its old-fashioned railing and lampposts restored—that skirts the wide, sandy beach. Benches are available here and there for sitting as you ponder the fact that folks have walked "the Prom" since the 1920s.

The Lewis and Clark expedition reached the Pacific Ocean in 1804, near the Seaside area, and you can see the original salt cairn—just off the south section of the Prom on Lewis and Clark Avenue—where the company boiled seawater to make salt during the rainy winter of 1805–1806.

Standing regally on the corner of Beach Drive and Avenue A is one of Seaside's historic homes, ca. 1890, **The Gilbert Inn**, 341 Beach Drive (800-507-2714; gilbertinn.com). The vintage dowager inn offers travelers ten spacious guest suites. In the Turrett Room on the second floor, for example, you can sleep in a queen-size four-poster amid romantic, country French-style decor.

Also in Seaside is **The Stephanie Inn**, 2740 S Pacific Street (855-977-2444; stephanieinn.com), long renowned as a romantic luxury getaway, with views of Haystack Rock, the Pacific and the Coast range. For good eats in Seaside, don't miss **Norma's Seafood & Steak Restaurant** (20 N. Columbia Street;

503-738-4331; normasoceandiner.com), open daily at 11:00 a.m. For steaming espresso drinks pop into **Seaside Coffee House**, 5 N. Holladay Drive (503-717-0111), open daily at 6:30 a.m.

Astoria

For a close-up look at a fine replica of Lewis and Clark's 1805–1806 winter headquarters, visit **Fort Clatsop National Memorial** (503-861-2471; nps.gov/lewi), about 10 miles north of Seaside, near Astoria. Walk the winding path from the interpretive center to the log replica of the encampment. Here, from June to September, you can watch a living-history program that includes buckskin-clad park rangers, live musket firing, boat carving, tanning, and mapmaking—all frontier skills used by the company during that first, very rainy winter. Within 25 miles are several sites described in the Lewis and Clark journals. The Fort Clatsop brochure, available at the visitor center, gives all the details and a helpful map.

Not far from the Lewis and Clark encampment, enterprising John Jacob Astor founded **Astoria** just six years later, in 1811. Settled for the purpose of fur trading, the bustling seaport at the mouth of the Columbia River grew into a respectable city during the late 1800s. You can take a walking or a driving tour and see some of the 400 historic structures still remaining, including the historic 125-foot **Astoria Column** high atop Coxcomb Hill. Completed in 1925 with fourteen murals etched into the concrete and encircling the tall column, you can climb 164 steps to the top for a panoramic view of the large bay and Pacific Ocean. For comfortable sleeps, consider one of the restored Victorian homes, many now open as bed-and-breakfast inns (oldoregon.com).

For helpful maps, brochures, and current lodging information, stop at either of the Astoria-Warrenton Visitor Centers, located at 111 W. Marine Drive in downtown Astoria (503-325-6311; oldoregon.com) and just off US 101 in nearby Warrenton (503-861-1031), open daily 9:00 a.m. to 5:00 p.m.

Built in 1883 by Capt. George Flavel, the **Flavel Mansion Museum** is one of the finest examples of Victorian architecture in the state. Located at 441 8th Street, between Exchange and Duane Streets, this impressive structure, with its columned porches, carved gingerbread detailing, and tall cupola, is worth a visit. The mansion is open daily. For further information contact the **Clatsop County Historical Society** (503-325-2203; cumtux.org). Also downtown, in the historic Clatsop County Jail, is the **Oregon Film Museum**, 732 Duane Street (503-325-2203; oregonfilmmuseum.org), which celebrates the art and legacy of Oregon films and filmmaking. To browse a fine collection of firefighting equipment that dates from the 1870s, call to arrange a visit to **Uppertown Firefighters Museum** (503-325-2203; cumtux.org) on 30th Street and Marine Drive.

Lewis and Clark at the "Ocian"

On November 7, 1805, some 554 days after departing Camp DuBois in Illinois, William Clark wrote in his journal: "Great joy in camp we are in view of the Ocian." Actually, they didn't reach the mouth of the Columbia River and the Pacific Ocean until November 15 due to lashing storms. By December 7, the party of thirty-one, including Clark's Newfoundland dog, Seaman, had crossed the Columbia River from the Long Beach Peninsula area and arrived at the Fort Clatsop site. By December 26, they had built winter headquarters, several log cabins that protected them from one of the wettest winters on record for the north coast.

Representing Astoria's beginnings, history buffs can also see the partially restored *Fort Astoria*, located on Exchange Street, built in 1811 by John Jacob Astor's Pacific Fur Company. Nearby is the site of the first US post office west of the Rocky Mountains, established in 1847. Pick up a copy of *An Explorer's Guide to Historic Astoria* at the Astoria-Warrenton Visitors Center at 111 W. Marine Drive (503-325-6311; travelastoria.com). Also check out the splendid *Columbia River Maritime Museum*, with its nautical memorabilia, historic ship models, and programs at 1792 Marine Drive (503-325-2323; crmm.org). Just across Marine Drive from the museum at 17th Street, check to see if *Bowpicker Fish & Chips* stand is open (503-791-2942); the awesome fish and chips are served outdoors from a vintage Columbia River gillnet boat.

Good eats, including ocean fish entrees and tasty desserts, great coffee drinks, and casual pub sandwiches and great burgers, can be had at *Astoria Coffeehouse & Bistro* (243 11th Street; 503-325-1787; astoriacoffeehouse.com), open daily at 7:00 a.m.; and *Fort George Brewery and Public House* at 1483 Duane Street (503-325-PINT; fortgeorgebrewery.com), which offers terrific craft brews and delicious food, open daily at 11:00 a.m. Be sure to check out the *Riverwalk Food Carts*, Marine Drive and 6th Street. Visit *Blue Scorcher Bakery & Café* (1493 Duane Street; 503-338-7473; bluescorcher.coop) for tasty espresso drinks along with breads, pastries, and handcrafted seasonal foods using local and organic ingredients.

In Astoria's lively historic downtown area along Marine Drive, be sure to stop by *Coffee Girl* (503-325-6900; thecoffeegirl.com), open daily at 8:00 a.m. on Pier 39 with views of the Columbia River. You can order tasty breakfast bagels, deli-style and grilled panini sandwiches, along with homemade soups, quiche, and espresso and coffee. Or pop into the *Bridgewater Bistro* on the Columbia River and near the bridge (bridgewaterbistro.com) for delicious seafood fare including fresh oysters, fish entrees, and tasty chowders. Visit or book a night at the splendid *Cannery Pier Hotel* at No. 10 Basin Street

(888-325-4996; cannerypierhotel.com), which rests on the 100-year-old pilings that formerly supported the Union Fisherman's Cooperative Packing Company formed in 1897. The hotel offers awesome views of the Columbia River from its public rooms and guest rooms. Nearby, at 1203 Commercial Street, see the ca. 1920 *Liberty Theater* (libertytheater.org), renovated to its former vaudevillian splendor. And pop around the corner to ogle the renovated *Hotel Elliot* at 357 12th Street (503-325-2222; hotelelliott.com), with its comfortable guest rooms, splendid finery, rooftop garden, Cigar Room, and Cellar Wine Bar.

Sneak Over to Long Beach Peninsula

Take the graceful 4.1-mile-long *Astoria-Megler Bridge* across the wide mouth of the Columbia River, where it empties into the Pacific Ocean. It is known as the longest three-span truss bridge in the world. Drive a few miles north to the ocean-side communities of Chinook, Ilwaco, Seaview, and Long Beach. In the early 1900s, the Clamshell Railway at Ilwaco transported mothers, youngsters, and even the family goats, who arrived from the Portland area to summer on the *Long Beach Peninsula*; fathers would join their families on weekends. To plan your own forays to the friendly towns, hamlets, historic sites, and beaches on the peninsula, check out the following destinations, eateries, and resources in Washington's Evergreen State:

Visit busy *Ilwaco Port Marina* and shops, *Ilwaco Historical Society Museum,* and *Lewis and Clark Interpretive Center*, and walk the wheelchair-accessible *Discovery Trail.*

Visit the *World Kite Museum* (303 Syd Snyder Drive in Long Beach; 360-642-4020; worldkitemuseum.com). Fly kites or dig for clams on the nearby wide, sandy beach; walk the boardwalk along the beach (lighted at night); and take in annual music festivals. Sections of the wide beach are allowed for horseback riding and cars at Long Beach.

Check out tasty eateries: In Ilwaco visit *Salt Pub* at 147 Howerton Avenue (360-642-7258; salt-hotel.com) for delicious food with a view of the harbor. In *Long Beach*, try *Lost Roo* at 1700 Pacific Avenue South (360-642-4329; lostroo.com) and *Cottage Bakery & Deli* at 118 Pacific Avenue South (360-642-4441). *42nd Street Café* in Seaview (4201 Pacific Way; 360-642-2323; 2ndstcafe.com) is a local's favorite with terrific seafood dishes and homemade sauces. *The Depot Restaurant*, also in Seaview (1208 38th Pl.; 360-642-7880; depotrestaurantdining.com) serves fine dining and an incredible wine list in a 120-year-old train depot.

Find comfortable lodging in *Long Beach* at friendly *Boreas Inn Bed & Breakfast* (607 Ocean Beach Boulevard North; 360-642-8069, 888-642-8069; boreasinn.com) and at *Klipsan Beach Cottages* in *Ocean Park* (22617 Pacific Way; 360-665-4888; klipsanbeachcottages.com). The Long Beach Peninsula Visitors Bureau in Seaview (360-642-2400, 800-451-2542; funbeach.com) can provide more information about resorts, cozy motels, cottages, and upcoming events in Chinook, Ilwaco, Seaview, Long Beach, Nahcotta, Oysterville, and Ocean Park.

If you travel along the north coast during winter and early spring, visit the *Twilight Eagle Sanctuary*, located just 8 miles east of Astoria and 0.5 mile north of US 30 on Burnside Road. The protected area offers prime feeding and roosting for about 48 bald eagles. You can identify the noble birds by their white heads and tails, large beaks, and yellow legs. Then, too, during all four seasons, bird lovers find that one of the best places on the coast to watch an enormous variety of bird species is from the viewing platform at *Fort Stevens State Park*, located 10 miles west of Astoria near Hammond. Be sure to take along your binoculars or cameras with telephoto lenses. Call (800) 452-5687 or visit oregonstateparks.org to inquire about comfy yurts, RV sites with hook-ups, and shady campsites at Fort Stevens.

To enjoy a day at the beach and do a good deed at the same time, you can participate in one of the twice-yearly *Great Oregon Beach Cleanup* events sponsored by SOLVE, a nonprofit organization that facilitates environmental cleanup projects statewide. The Beach Cleanup is lots of work, but it's great fun for the entire family; and it happens with hundreds of volunteers along the entire coast, from Brookings in the south to Astoria in the north. Folks show up with rubber gloves, comfortable walking shoes, drinking water, and a lunch. Zone captains provide trash bags and directions. Scientists tracked ocean currents for months by following the journey of thousands of tennis shoes! For current information, dates, and numerous ways to volunteer, call the friendly beach cleanup staff at (503) 844-9571 or log onto solveoregon.org.

Places to Stay on the Oregon Coast

ASTORIA–LONG BEACH PENINSULA

Adrift Hotel
409 Sid Snyder Drive
(800) 561-2456
adrifthotel.com

Boreas Inn Bed & Breakfast
607 North Ocean Beach Blvd.
Long Beach, WA

(888) 642-8069
boreasinn.com

Klipsan Beach Cottages
22617 Pacific Way
Ocean Park, WA
(360) 664-4888
klipsanbeachcottages.com

BANDON

Bandon Inn
355 US 101
(541) 347-4417
bandoninn.com

Windermere on the Beach
3250 Beach Loop Drive

(541) 347-3710
winderemereonthebeach.com

CANNON BEACH

Inn at Haystack Rock
487 S. Hemlock Street
(855) 562-2014

The Ocean Lodge
2864 S. Pacific Street
(888) 777-4047
theoceanlodge.com

DEPOE BAY

Whale Cove Inn
2345 US 101
(541) 765-4300
whalecoveinn.com

FLORENCE

River House Inn
1202 Bay Street
(888) 824-2454
riverhouseflorence.com

GEARHART

Gearhart Ocean Inn
67 N. Cottage Avenue
(800) 352-8034
gearhartoceaninn.com

McMenamins Gearhart
Hotel and Sand Trap Pub
1157 N. Marion Avenue
(503) 717-8159
mcmenamins.com/gearhart
-hotel

GOLD BEACH

Gold Beach Inn
29346 Ellensburg Avenue
(541) 247-7091
goldbeachinn.com

LINCOLN CITY

Ocean Terrace
Condominiums
4229 SW Beach Avenue
(541) 996-3623
oceanterrace.com

The Sea Gypsy Motel
145 NW Inlet Avenue
(541) 994-5266

Surftides Resort
2945 NW Jetty Avenue

(541) 994-2191
surftideslincolncity.com

NEWPORT

Agate Beach Motel
175 NW Gilbert Way
(800) 755-5674

Inn at Nye Beach
729 NW Coast Street
(800) 480-2477
innatnyebeach.com

**REEDSPORT-
WINCHESTER BAY**

Loon Lake RV, Cabins,
Yurts, Houseboats
(541) 599-2244
loonlakerv.com

HELPFUL TELEPHONE NUMBERS & WEBSITES FOR THE OREGON COAST

Astoria/Warrenton
Area Visitor Center
(503) 325-6311
oldoregon.com

Bandon Visitor Center
(541) 347-9616
bandonbythesea.com

Brookings-Harbor Visi-
tor Center
(541) 813-2300
brookingsor.com

Cannon Beach Visitor
Center
(503) 436-2623
cannonbeach.org

Cape Perpetua Scenic
Area
(541) 547-3289
fs.usda.gov/siuslaw

Columbia River Mari-
time Museum and
Lightship Columbia
Astoria
(503) 325-2323
crmm.org

Coos Bay/North Bend
Area Visitor Center
(541) 269-0215
oregonsadventurecoast.
com

Florence Area Visitor
Center
(541) 997-3128
florencechamber.com

Fort Clatsop National
Monument
(503) 861-2471
nps.gov/lewi

Friends of Yaquina
Lighthouses
yaquinalights.org

Gold Beach Visitor
Center
(541) 247-7526 or (800)
525-2334
goldbeach.org

Lincoln City Visitor
Bureau
(541) 994-3302
oregoncoast.org

Long Beach Peninsula
Visitors Bureau
(360) 642-2400
funbeach.com

Newport Visitor Center
(541) 265-8801
discovernewport.com

Oregon Coast Scenic Railroad
Garibaldi–Rockaway Beach
(503) 842-7972
oregoncoastscenic.org

Oregon State Parks Campground Reservations
(800) 452-5687
oregonstateparks.org

Port Orford Battle Rock Wayside Visitors Center
(541) 332-4016
enjoyportorford.com

Reedsport–Winchester Bay Visitors' Center and Oregon Dunes National Recreation Area Visitor Center
(541) 271-3495 and (541) 271-6000
reedsportcc.org

Seaside Visitor Bureau
(503) 738-3097
seasideor.com

Visit Tillamook Coast
(503) 842-2672
tillamookcoast.com

Yachats Visitor Center
(541) 547-3530
goyachats.com

ROCKAWAY BEACH

Silver Sands Motel
215 S. Pacific Street
(503) 355-2206

SEASIDE

Ashore Hotel
125 Oceanway Street
(503) 568-7506
ashorehotel.com

Inn at the Prom
341 S Prom
(800) 507-2714
innattheprom.com

Saltline Hotel
250 1st Avenue
(971) 601-1082
Saltlinehotel.com

YACHATS

The Drift Inn
124 US 101
(541) 547-4477
the-drift-inn.com

Places to Eat on the Oregon Coast

ASTORIA

Blue Scorcher Bakery & Café
1493 Duane Street
(503) 338-7473
bluescorcher.coop

Bowpicker Fish & Chips
Vintage gillnet river boat,
Commercial & 17th Street
(503) 791-2942

Buoy Beer Company
1 8th Street
(503) 325-4540
buoybeer.com

Bridgewater Bistro
20 Basin Street on the
Columbia River

(503) 325-6777
bridgewaterbistro.com

Frite and Scoop
175 14th Street
(503) 468-0416
friteandscoop.com

Street 14 Coffee Shop
1410 Commercial Street
(503) 325-5511

BANDON

Bandon Coffee Cafe
365 2nd Street Old Town
(541) 347-1144
bandoncoffee.com

Bandon Brewing Company
395 2nd Street SE
(541) 347-3911
bandonbrewingco.com

Tony's Crab Shack
Bandon's Waterfront
Boardwalk
tonyscrabshack.com

BROOKINGS-HARBOR

Black Trumpet Bistro
625 Chetco Avenue,
Ste. 220
(541) 887-0860
blacktrumpetbistro.net

Oxenfre Public House
631 Chetco Avenue
(541) 813-1985
oxenpub.com

Zola's Pizzaria
16362 Lower Harbor Road
(541) 412-7100
zolaspizzeria.com

CANNON BEACH

**Cannon Beach Hardware
& Public House**
1235 S Hemlock Street
(503) 436-4086
cannonbeachhardware.com

**MacGregor's Whiskey
Bar & Restaurant**
100 E 2nd Street B
(503) 436-0322
macgregorswhiskeybar
.com

Newman's at 988
988 S Hemlock Street
(503) 436-1151
newmansat988.com

**Sleepy Monk
Coffeehouse**
1235 S. Hemlock Street
(503) 436-2796
sleepymonkcoffee.com

DEPOE BAY

Gracie's Sea Hag
US Hwy. 101
(541) 765-2734
theseahag.com

**Tidal Raves Seafood
Grill**
279 N. US 101
(541) 765-2995
tidalraves.com

FLORENCE

**Bridgewater Fish House
and Zebra Bar**
1297 Bay Street
(541) 997-1133
bridgewaterfishhouse.com

Hukilau Pacific Fusion
185 US 101
(541) 991-1071
hukilauflorence.com

GOLD BEACH

Barnacle Bistro
29805 Ellensburg Aveue
(541) 247-7799
barnaclebistro.com

**Port Hole Cafe on the
Waterfront**
29975 Harbor Way
(541) 247-7411

**Rachel's Coffeehouse &
Bakery Cafe**
29707 US 101
(541) 247-7733

LINCOLN CITY

Blackfish Café
2733 NW US 101
(541) 996-1007
blackfishcafe.com

Pacific Grind Cafe
4741 SW Highway 101
(541) 994-8314
pacificgrindcafe.com

Wildflower Grill
4250 NE US 101
(541) 994-9663
thewildflowergrill.com

LONG BEACH PENINSULA

The Depot Restaurant
1208 38th Place
(360) 642-7880
depotrestaurantdining.com

42nd Street Café
4201 Pacific Way
Seaview

(360) 642-2323
2ndstcafe.com

Lost Roo
1700 Pacific Avenue South
(360) 642-4329
lostroo.com

MANZANITA

**Manzanita News &
Espresso**
500 Laneda Avenue
(503) 368-7450

Neah-Kah-Nie Bistro
519 Laneda Avenue
(503) 368-2722
nknbistro.com

NESKOWIN

The Café at Hawk Creek
4505 Salem Avenue
(503) 392-3838
cafeonhawkcreek.com

NEWPORT

Local Ocean
213 SE Bay Boulevard
(541) 574-7959
localocean.net

Nana's Irish Pub
613 NW 3rd Street
(541) 574-8787
nanasirishpub.com

**Rogue Ale Brewers Pub
on the Bay**
Yaquina Bay Marina
(541) 867-3664
rogue.com

NORTH BEND

Pancake Mill
2390 Tremont Avenue
(541) 756-2751
pancakemill.com

PACIFIC CITY

**Grateful Bread
Restaurant Bakery**
34805 Brooten Road
(503) 965-7337

Pelican Pub & Brewery
Cape Kiwanda Drive
(503) 965-7007
pelicanbrewing.com

SEASIDE

Norma's Seafood & Steak Restaurant
20 N. Columbia Street
(503) 738-4331
normasoceandiner.com

Seaside Brewing Company
851 Broadway Street
(503) 717-5451
seasidebrewery.com

TILLAMOOK

Pelican Brewery and Tap Room
1708 1st Street
(503) 842-7007
pelicanbrewing.com/pubs/tillamook

WHEELER-NEHALEM

Rising Star Café
92 Rorvik Street
(503) 368-3990
risingstarcafe.net

YACHATS

The Drift Inn
124 US 101
(541) 547-4477
the-drift-inn.com

Green Salmon Coffee Company
Highway 101 at 2nd Street
(541) 547-3077
thegreensalmon.com

Southern Oregon

Southern Oregon is a pleasant mixture of old ghost towns and historic landmarks combined with white-water rivers, wildlife refuges, colorful caverns, a high-altitude volcanic lake, and national forests and mountain ranges containing some of the least-known wilderness areas in the Beaver State. Spread throughout is a vibrant arts and culture scene and a burgeoning wine community.

Crater Lake and Southern Cascades

In Oregon's only national park, **Crater Lake** shimmers like a crystal blue jewel in the enormous caldera of the former 12,000-foot *Mount Mazama.* More than 6,000 years ago, this peak in the southern Cascade Mountains collapsed with a fiery roar, some forty times greater than the Mount Saint Helens eruption of 1980 in nearby Washington State, and formed a deep basin of 20 square miles. The lake is more than 1,500-feet deep in places, and because of numerous underground thermal springs, it rarely freezes.

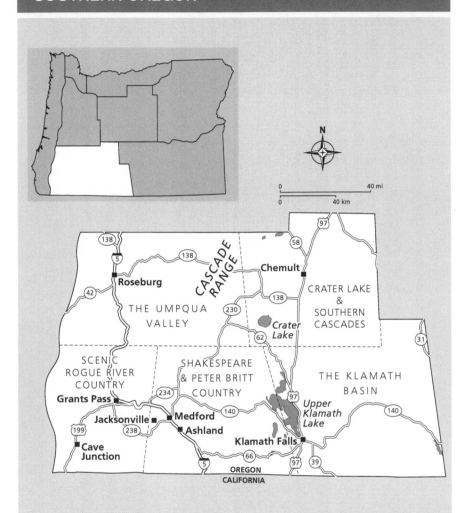

The 33-mile-long *Crater Lake Rim Drive*, encircling the lake at an invigorating elevation of 6,177 feet, can be done in an hour or so, but to savor the 360-degree panorama and succession of splendid changing views, you'll want to plan a longer outing: Spend the whole day there, and then stay overnight in one of the several campgrounds in the area or in the venerable Crater Lake Lodge perched on the south rim.

TOP HITS IN SOUTHERN OREGON

Britt Festivals
Jacksonville

Crater Lake National Park
Highway 138

Chemult Sled Dog Races
Chemult

Grants Pass Grower's Market
Grants Pass

Great Umpqua Food Trail
Roseburg

Jacksonville Pioneer Cemetery
Jacksonville

Klamath Basin National Wildlife Refuge
Klamath Falls

Oregon Caves National Monument
Cave Junction

Oregon Shakespeare Festival
Ashland

Volcanic Legacy Scenic Byway
Highway 62

Wildlife Safari
Winston

You can also take a 6-mile side road from Kerr Notch, at the southeast corner of the rim, down to the *Pinnacles*, 200-foot spires of pumice and tuff (layers of volcanic ash). Within the park are some 85 miles of hiking and nature trails. The 8-mile *Greyback Drive* is unpaved and vehicle-prohibited, making it popular with mountain bikers seeking sights of rock formations, native trees, and wildflowers.

For another panoramic view take the 2-hour boat trip around Crater Lake's 25-mile shoreline, accompanied by a Park Service interpreter. *Note*: The Cleetwood Trail down to the dock at Cleetwood Cove is a very steep, 1.1-mile hike. For an easier scenic trek, try the 1-mile day hike on *Castle Crest Wildflower Trail* near Rim Village. You can hang out afterwards at Rim Village Café for a meal.

Winter brings a sparkling snowy beauty to the lake, along with outdoor activities such as cross-country skiing, snowshoeing, and ski touring. For information about renting snowshoes or cross-country skis, or about winter tours—reservations are required—contact Crater Lake park staff, Crater Lake (541-594-3100; nps.gov/crla).

Built in the early 1900s and opened in 1915, historic **Crater Lake Lodge** underwent a complete renovation in the mid-1990s. Accommodations are available from June to mid-October. Call (866) 292-6720 or visit travelcraterlake.com for room reservations. For current weather and road conditions in the Crater Lake area, see nps.gov/crla. For information about the more than 900 camping sites available in nearby Forest Service campgrounds, call the Rogue-Siskiyou district, Prospect Ranger Station at (541) 560-3400 or log onto fs.usda.gov/rogue-siskiyou.

Mazama Village, located 7 miles south of Rim Village, is also a good alternative for overnight accommodations in cozy cabins (888-774-2728; travel craterlake.com). Dining onsite is at Annie Creek Restaurant and Gift Shop. The nearby **Mazama Campground** offers 200 tent and RV spaces on a first-come, first-served basis; there are public showers, laundry facilities, a convenience store, and a gas station. Located in Fort Klamath about 30 miles south find cozy rooms at **Aspen Inn Motel**, 52250 Highway 62 (541-381-2321; theaspeninn.com), and at **Crater Lake Resort**, 50711 Highway 62 (541-381-2349; craterlake resort.com). Browse additional information about the Crater Lake National Park region at craterlakecountry.com.

Fast Facts about Crater Lake and Crater Lake Lodge

First visited by non-Native settlers in 1853, Crater Lake is the second-deepest lake in North America, behind Canada's Great Slave Lake.

Maximum depth: 1,932 feet

Average depth: 1,500 feet

Elevation at lake's surface: 6,176 feet above sea level

Elevation at Rim Village: 7,100 feet above sea level

Average snowfall: 533 inches

Tourists: 700,000 annually

Rim Drive: 33 miles long; usually clear of snow by July

Crater Lake Lodge: 71 rooms; originally opened in 1915; closed in 1989 for a $15 million rehabilitation; reopened in May 1995

Lodge decor: 1920s mood with Craftsman- and mission-style furnishings; bent twig chairs and hickory rockers; original stone fireplace in the Great Hall

Best time to visit: August and September

Road and weather information in the local area: see nps.gov/crla

Access the Crater Lake area via US 97 from Bend (about 80 miles); US 97 and Highway 62 from Klamath Falls (about 60 miles); Highway 62 from Medford (about 70 miles); or Highway 138 from Roseburg (about 80 miles). This last entrance closes with the first heavy snowstorm, usually in mid-October, and reopens by mid-June or July; the south entrance via Highway 62 remains open year-round.

Just north of Crater Lake National Park, at a lower elevation, is **Diamond Lake**, a smaller jewel nestled within Umpqua National Forest. Rainbow trout season is open year-round here, though before April, you might be ice fishing. During summer season, sailboats, motorboats, and canoes can be rented in advance. Moorage space is available throughout the summer and early fall, and fishing and hunting licenses can be purchased at the tackle shop.

Many campground sites, open from May through October, are found on the lakeshore; Diamond Lake and Broken Arrow Campgrounds have trailer dump stations. At **Diamond Lake Resort** (541-793-3333; diamondlake.net), lakeshore cabins are available as well as motel-style units and large cabins—book well ahead of time to reserve one of the cabins with a fireplace and kitchen. The lodge resort restaurant offers a large, diverse menu from burgers to entrees, and a short distance away is South Shore Pizza, offering a variety of pies as well as roasted chicken.

winteryretreat

Crater Lake National Park is snow-covered from October through June, and with an average annual snowfall of 44 feet, snow can stick around into July. But while the park is dominated by winter, the lake itself very rarely freezes over. Still, even in August, a chill permeates the air on the lake rim. Take a jacket!

Crater Lake: The Early Days

A Portland mountain climber and transplanted Kansan, William G. Steel visited the lake in 1885, some thirty years after it was first seen by non-Native settlers; he then helped lead the crusade to save the area from homesteading. He battled to have the area designated a national park, a measure approved by President Theodore Roosevelt on May 22, 1902. It was the seventh such park to be established in the United States. The first horseless carriage motored up to Crater Lake in 1905, and by 1919 the spectacular Rim Drive, though just a bumpy dirt road, was a standard stop on sightseeing rambles around the state. In July 1920, the steamer *Klamath* began transporting passengers from Klamath Falls to Rocky Point, at the northern end of Klamath Lake, to meet the Crater Lake Stage Line. This new improved service—steamboat and automobile—deposited travelers at Crater Lake (a total of about 65 miles) in the record time of 12 hours!

Today, a journey to the park is much easier, at least during the summer season when the roads are clear and an average car can climb from the highways below to the rim in under an hour. Visit the restored 1934 visitor center near the main headquarters building, open year-round, named in Steel's honor. A smaller visitor center, located between the lodge and the cafeteria and gift shop at Rim Village, is open daily during the summer season.

During winter, snow lovers can take a guided snowmobile tour or arrange for snowcat skiing on nearby Mount Bailey. Call ahead for information and reservations (541-793-3333; diamondlake.net). There are also miles of groomed trails for cross-country skiing as well as a great inner tube sledding hill for families with small children. During summer, visitors enjoy horseback riding—special group rates can be arranged, and guides are also available. Serious snowmobilers can obtain information about the annual *Mt. Bailey Poker Run*, in mid-February, from the Oregon State Snowmobile Association; oregonsnow.org.

In February each year, you can hear the cries of "Mush, you huskies!" at the annual *Chemult Sled Dog Races* (psdsa.org/races/chemult) in Chemult, located on US 97 south of Bend and north of Crater Lake. Events include a mid-distance race; a weight pull; four-, six-, and eight-dog team sprint races; novice-class races; a skijor; and a peewee race for the kids. The races start and finish at the Walt Haring Snopark just north of Chemult, snow conditions permitting. The Chemult Rural Fire Department usually operates a food-and-beverage stand at the sled dog race and also sponsors a mushers banquet at the Chemult Fire Hall. A number of local snowmobile clubs help to groom the snowy trails for the event. To bed down in Chemult, call *Dawson House Lodge* at 109455 Highway 97 North (541-365-2232; dawsonhouse.net) and ask about the cozy rooms with hand-carved burled-pine bed frames and handmade quilts.

For lodging in the southern Oregon Cascades near the Willamette Pass Ski Area, consider **Odell Lake Lodge & Resort** off Highway 58 north of Chemult (541-433-2540; odelllakeresort.com). Rustic and comfortable, the lodge has welcomed travelers since 1903. Facilities include a small cafe, boat docks, boat rentals, and housekeeping cabins. You're breathing crisp mountain air above 4,000 feet elevation in the company of tall firs, soft breezes, and ground critters like squirrels and chipmunks. During snowy winter months, families bring their cross-country skis, sleds, and inner tubes, and they also pack hearty lunches. On the northeast shore of Odell Lake is another lodging and recreation option, **Shelter Cove Resort and Marina** (27600 West Odell Lake Road, Highway 58 Crescent Lake; 541-433-2548; highwaywestvacations.com). Cabins, camping, boat launch, fishing and more are here. In late September and early October, spot spawning kokanee salmon in nearby Trapper Creek.

Another historic retreat within driving distance of Chemult is **Union Creek Lodge** (541-560-3565; unioncreekoregon.com), located on Highway 62 between Crater Lake and Medford. The lodge, built in the early 1900s, is on the National Register of Historic Places and offers travelers rustic cabins, rooms in the main lodge, a country store, and gift shop. Directly across the highway from the lodge, **Beckie's Restaurant** (541-560-3565; unionreekore gon.com) is known for homestyle cooking and tasty pies; open daily at 8:00 a.m. While you're in the area, visit the **Rogue Gorge**—it's definitely worth a stop and several photos. Pack plenty of warm jackets, stocking caps, and warm boots if you travel into the **Cascade Mountains** during the winter months. Take along extra blankets, sleeping bags, and extra food and beverages as well. Traction devices may be required from November through March on snowy mountain passes, depending on weather conditions—many of them are more than 5,000 feet in elevation. Log onto tripcheck.com for road conditions in the Crater Lake area; call (800) 977-6368 inside Oregon and 503-588-2941 outside Oregon. Wilderness seekers, backpackers, and hikers can try climbing 8,363-foot **Mount Bailey**—strenuous but worth the sweat—or the 4-mile trail to 9,182-foot **Mount Thielson**. Both offer superb views of the southern Cascade Mountains, Crater Lake, and Diamond Lake. Rangers caution that summer is quite short at these alpine elevations and urge folks to dress adequately and bring the proper gear, including sufficient food, water, and emergency shelter. For information about the **Pacific Crest National Scenic Trail**, which crosses the west side of the area and winds south through the wooded ridges and plateaus of Mountain Lakes Wilderness, contact the Diamond Lake Ranger District (541-498-2531; fs.usda.gov/umpqua), 59 miles east of Roseburg via Highway 138 and near Toketee Falls, open Monday through Friday at 8:00 a.m.

South of Union Creek and at a lower elevation is the hamlet of **Prospect** (population 500). For a great dinner choice and a historic lodging option in the area, check with **Prospect Historic Hotel, Motel and Dinner House** located at 391 Mill Creek Road (541-560-3664 or 800-944-6490; prospecthotel.com). While in the area, visit Mill Creek Falls, a short hike downhill from the parking lot. For additional information about the Crater Lake National Park region, browse craterlakecountry.com.

The Klamath Basin

Continuing your exploration of southern Oregon, head south via Highway 62 or US 97 toward **Klamath Falls** to see another region of diversity, including one of the largest wildlife and wildfowl refuges in the Northwest. Many of the roads in this area, particularly Highway 66 from "K Falls" to Ashland, were used by early mail and freight stagecoach lines between the Klamath Basin and settlements along the Rogue River, to the west.

When it was the land of the ancient Ouxkanee, or "people of the marsh," the million-acre **Klamath Basin** contained a vast expanse of lakes and marshes ideal for waterfowl courtship and nesting. White settlers nearly drained the area dry for farmland, but beginning in 1908, in an effort aided by the emerging conservation ethic, portions of the Klamath Basin were set aside as wildlife refuges, secure from further encroachment. With the last of the area reserved in 1958, the entire region is now known as the **Klamath Basin National Wildlife Refuge**. Though their domain is much smaller than in the days of the Ouxkanee, birds and waterfowl of all species crowd enthusiastically into what remains: some 83,000 acres of marsh and shallow lakes near Klamath Falls.

For the visitor there are countless opportunities for close-up, unobtrusive viewing of waterfowl, marsh birds, shorebirds, and upland species—along lakes and marshes, near grassy meadows and farms, among the sagebrush and juniper, near ancient lava flows, and in nearby coniferous forests. The great thrill is seeing the early spring or fall migrations, when the sky is dark with wings and the silence pierced by much cacophonous honking—climaxing to some seven million birds en route along the **Pacific Flyway**, which extends the entire length of North and South America. First the ducks—pintails, ruddies, mallards, shovelers, and wigeons—and then the geese—Canada, snow, white-fronted, and cackling—to mention just a few of the more than 270 species recorded here.

In March visitors can welcome the return of the white pelicans, Klamath Falls's feathery mascot; they nest and remain here until November. Link River and Lake Ewauna at *Veteran's Memorial Park* in Klamath Falls are among the most accessible places to see these large, curious birds, with their pouched beaks. And during winter some 500 bald eagles visit from the frozen north, attracting naturalists and bird lovers from all over to count them and observe their nesting habits at the annual *Winter Wings Festival* during mid-February (877-541-2473; winterwingsfest.org).

For current information about the Klamath Basin National Wildlife Refuge, including maps, bird species lists, viewing sites, interpretive sites, canoe trails, and self-guided auto tours on the refuge, drive 25 miles south of Klamath Falls to refuge headquarters at 4009 Hill Road just east of Tule Lake, California (530-667-2231); also browse the refuge website at fws.gov/refuge/Lower_Klamath. Additional information about the Klamath Falls area, including overnight accommodations, can be obtained from the Discover Klamath Visitor and Convention Bureau at 205 Riverside Dr. in Klamath Falls (541-882-1501; discoverklamath.com).

The *Klamath County Museum*, at 1451 Main Street (541-883-4208; co .klamath.or.us/museum/index.htm), offers exhibits and displays on the history, geology, anthropology, and wildlife of the Klamath Basin; it's open Tuesday through Saturday from 9:00 a.m. to 5:00 p.m. Also, part of the museum complex, the four-story *Baldwin Hotel Museum* (541-883-4207), a noted hostelry built in 1906 by state senator George Baldwin, offers a look at the hotel's opulent original furnishings and early history. Located at 31 Main Street, the brick building is open for tours year-round Tuesday through Saturday, from 9:00 a.m. to 5:00 p.m.

oregontrivia

Klamath Falls, named Linkville when founded in 1876, sits atop a geothermal area, and in those early days many businesses and homes were heated by the hot water; the early Native peoples used it for cooking. A number of businesses and the local hospital still use this source for heating.

Maud Baldwin, a well-known photographer at the turn of the twentieth century, followed her father, George, around the county and into the marshes to record on film the area's early farmland reclamation project. More than 2,000 of her vintage photographs are housed at the Klamath County Museum.

For good eats, Klamath Falls offers a number of options. For great soups, tasty sandwiches and bagels, specialty coffees, and fresh pastries, try *The Daily Bagel* at 636 Main Street (541-850-0744), open Monday through Saturday at 6:00 a.m.; or *Nibbley's Restaurant* at 2424 Washburn Way (541-883-2314; nibbleys.com), open daily for tasty breakfasts of stuffed French toast or Nibbley's Omelet along with fresh pastries and lunch with Death by Burger or

Rueben! Rueben! For local ales and casual pub fare, pop into the **Klamath Basin Brewing Brewpub** at 1320 Main Street, formerly the 1935 Crater Lake Creamery building (541-273-5222; kbbrewing.com), open daily at 11:00 a.m. (10:00 a.m. on Sunday for brunch!) and serving lunch, dinner, and those pub favorites. Galleries to visit in Klamath Falls include **Klamath Art Association & Gallery** (120 Riverside Drive; 541-888-1833; klamathartgallery.blogspot .com) and **Favell Museum of Indian Artifacts & Western Art** (125 W. Main Street; 541-882-9996).

If time allows, call and check out the current play or concert offerings at the **Ross Ragland Theater**, housed in a historic Art Deco-style building at 218 N. 7th Street (541-884-5483; rrtheater.org). The **Linkville Theatre Players**, 201 Main Street (541-884-6782; linkvilleplayers.org), offers a season of live theater productions each year.

Just 30 miles north of Klamath Falls via US 97 and located in Chiloquin is **Collier Memorial State Park and Logging Museum** (541-783-2471; oregonstateparks.org), where you can take a gander at one of the largest collections of logging equipment in the United States. Look for the huge steam locomotive—it ran on roads rather than on tracks. Stop at the **Ouxkanee Lookout** for a panoramic view of Spring Creek Valley and for historical information about the region. Collier Memorial State Park offers both RV and tent campsites. Take in the park's annual **Living History Day** in mid-June.

You could also head northwest on Highway 140 for about 30 miles to find lakeside cabins and RV spaces at **Lake of the Woods** (541-949-8300; lakeofthe woodsresort.com). The rustic **Lake House Restaurant** offers views of the lake along with an array of good fare including breakfast, weekend brunch, lunch, and dinner. The lodge's General Store, which dates back to 1924, is well stocked with gourmet foods, fishing gear, and provisions for campers. Known then as Lake O' the Woods, all other buildings and the cabins have been renovated for new generations of families who gather here during the summer months.

Historic Logging Trivia

Both steam-powered machinery and railroads were important to logging. Portable "donkey" steam engines provided power for skidding logs to loading areas; colorful jargon like "high lead," "choker," and "whistle punk" came from this era. Railroads hauled timber from the woods to mills. Four large pieces of railroad equipment can be seen near Chiloquin off US 97 at Collier State Park, including a stiff-boom loader, a log buncher, a swing-boom loader, and a track-laying car; these are mounted on sections of railroad track. Samples of Oregon's tree species can also be seen—Douglas fir, sugar pine, and ponderosa pine, each more than 6 feet in diameter.

For a special outdoor experience, consider exploring the **Upper Klamath Canoe Trail**, particularly the northern section, where you can canoe gently along the 50-foot-wide water trail and often see families of beavers and muskrats. Families of ducks, geese, cormorants, and swans may protest a bit as you paddle along the 9.5-mile water trail. For canoe and kayak rentals, contact **Rocky Point Resort**, north of Klamath Falls (541-356-2287; rockypointoregon .com). Take Highway 140 along the west side of Upper Klamath Lake about 28 miles and turn at the signs to the resort; the put-in spot is nearby. Canoeists can also find good floating and paddling on Crystal Creek and on Lake Ewauna in Klamath Falls.

Covering an area of 133 miles, **Upper Klamath Lake** is Oregon's largest freshwater lake. Located on the Pacific Flyway, the area hosts more than 500 wildlife and bird species, including red-winged blackbirds, bald eagles, beavers, otters, mink, raccoons, deer, Canada geese, trumpeter swans, white pelicans, white-faced ibis, and sandhill cranes. For additional information and maps, contact the US Fish and Wildlife Service (530-667-2231 or 541-883-5732; fws.gov/refuge/upper_klamath).

If you decide to stay overnight in the area, check out the guest rooms, cozy cabins, tent sites, and RV accommodations at **Rocky Point Resort** (28121 Rocky Point Road; 541-356-2287; rockypointoregon.com), located on Upper Klamath Lake near Fort Klamath. Here you can commune with gaggles of wildlife and bird species (klamathbirdingtrails.com) as well as go canoeing or fishing. Guests can explore hundreds of miles of nearby forest trails and backcountry roads, in the winter by stepping into cross-country skis and in the summer atop mountain bikes or on guided horseback rides.

For nearby campgrounds, hiking trails, places to fish, helpful maps, and general visitor information, stop by the Klamath Ranger District office at 2819 Dahlia Street in Klamath Falls (541-888-6714; fs.usda.gov/fremont-winema); Forest Service Ranger District offices are generally open Monday through Friday from 8:00 a.m. to 4:30 p.m.

If you'd like to venture farther off the beaten path, head east into the **Gearhart Mountain Wilderness** environs and arrange a couple of days at **Aspen Ridge Resort** (541-884-8685 or call from outside Oregon at 800-393-3323; aspenrr.com), located northeast of Klamath Falls. This 14,000-acre working cattle ranch, owned by former Californians, is accessed via Chiloquin, Sprague River Road, Highway 140, and, finally, Fish Hole Creek Road just east of Bly. But what's there to do here, you ask? Well, go horseback riding with the cowboys and learn how to manage a herd of cattle; hole up and read; go trout fishing or mountain biking; inhale fresh air and aromatic high-desert smells of sagebrush and juniper; cook your own grub or eat hearty meals at the lodge restaurant prepared by the ranch cook; saunter over to the Buffalo Saloon; then listen to evening sounds, like the howl of coyotes or the bawl of cattle, and gaze at a wide sky jam-packed with glittering stars.

By this time your senses will have become saturated with the wonder of Crater Lake's crystalline waters; the quietness and mystery of the southern Cascade Mountains wilderness areas will have seeped into your bones. Having experienced the breathtaking sight of a half million or so ducks, geese, swans, white pelicans, and other birds, waterfowl, and wildlife congregating along the Pacific Flyway near Klamath Falls, you can now head farther east, via Highway 140, into Oregon's Old West country; north on US 97 into Oregon's high-desert country; or west on Highway 66 toward Ashland, Medford, and Jacksonville.

Shakespeare and Peter Britt Country

Heading west on Highway 66 from Klamath Falls toward Ashland, stock up on groceries and drive along Highway 66, the historic Applegate Trail. Those weary pioneers who detoured from the Oregon Trail along this southern route in the mid-1840s often rested in this area at the 3,600-foot elevation level, near springs and lush meadows.

En route, visit *Green Springs Inn & Cabins* (541-890-6435; greensprings inn.net), located at 11470 Highway 66 (about 25 miles east of Ashland and 10 miles east of Emigrant Lake). Here you can enjoy breakfast, lunch, and dinner daily year-round in a rustic lodge setting at the brisk 4,500-foot elevation in the Cascade Mountains. The inn offers eight guest rooms and several elegant mountain cabins with fully equipped kitchens and outdoor barbeques. The cabins sleep up to six people. Highway 66 between Klamath Falls and Ashland is narrow and winding and is kept open all year; travelers should be prepared for snow conditions during winter months.

Ashland

Highway 66 intersects with busy I-5 near *Ashland*, just north of Mount Ashland and the Siskiyou Pass, which takes travelers to and from the Oregon-California border. Detour at this intersection into the bustling community of Ashland, where you can take in a southern Oregon Shakespeare tradition that dates from 1935. In that year, young professor Angus Bowmer of Southern Oregon Normal School—later renamed Southern Oregon State College and now Southern Oregon State University—conceived the idea of producing Shakespeare's plays by reworking the walls of the town's old Chautauqua Building into an outdoor theater reminiscent of those of Elizabethan England.

Convincing Ashland's city leaders took some time, but with their conditional blessing the first productions—*Twelfth Night* and *The Merchant of Venice*—took place over the Fourth of July in 1935. The deficits from a boxing match that was scheduled to satisfy the Shakespeare skeptics were covered by the resounding success and bulging receipts from the two plays. In 1937, the **Oregon Shakespeare Festival Association** was organized as a nonprofit corporation, and in 1941 the first scholarships for actors were offered. The festival celebrated its eighty-fifth year in 2020.

To complement the splendid outdoor **Elizabethan Theatre**, the indoor **Angus Bowmer Theatre** was built in 1970, the intimate **Black Swan Theatre** was constructed in 1977, and the **Thomas Theatre**, replacing the former Black Swan Theatre, was inaugurated in 2002. The three theaters anchor a large outdoor plaza, a gift shop, and ticket offices. Visitors can also poke into interesting shops and eateries along nearby Main Street. Visit the charming **Tree House Books** (15 N. Main) for children's books and games, **Paddington Station** (125 E. Main) for gifts and clothing, and **Mountain Provisions** (27 N. Main) for outdoor gear.

The Applegate Trail

While motoring along Highway 66 between Klamath Falls and Ashland, you're following the path of early pioneers Jesse and Lindsay Applegate. In 1845, the brothers carved a route through the rugged mountains here as an alternative to the Oregon Trail and the treacherous Columbia River to the north. The Applegates' route, which crossed northern Nevada and California before reaching Oregon, was well traveled, but pioneer families suffered many hardships, including battles with the Modoc Indians who lived in the area. From Ashland the *Applegate Trail* continues along the route of I-5 north toward Roseburg and Oakland. Both the *Southern Oregon Historical Society* in Medford and the *Jacksonville Museum* in nearby Jacksonville (541-773-6536; sohs.org) offer more history, journals, and diaries, and also maps for retracing the pioneers' footsteps.

Lithia Springs

The area surrounding Ashland has long been known for its mineral waters, with Native families using the springs to care for their sick and aged. In 1911, the city began developing lithia water fountains; the lithia spring that presently serves the city is located about 3 miles east. Early pipelines of wood were replaced with cast iron, and this 2-inch line serves public fountains on the downtown plaza, in Lithia Park, and at the library. The water, which has a decidedly mineral-salty taste (try at least one sip!), contains more than twenty different kinds of minerals and acids, including lithium (Li), calcium (Ca), magnesium (Mg), barium (Ba), potassium (K), sulfuric acid (H_2SO_4), and phosphoric acid (H_3PO_4).

Now more than eleven or more plays are staged from mid-February through October; past favorites have included *Hamlet, Romeo and Juliet, The Merry Wives of Windsor, Shakespeare in Love, Guys and Dolls*, and *Peter and the Starcatcher*. For information about the current repertoire of traditional as well as contemporary offerings, contact the Oregon Shakespeare Festival (541-482-4331 or 800-219-8161; osfashland.org). The plays staged at the outdoor Elizabethan Theatre run from June through October.

Ask for a complete schedule, including information about the Backstage Tour and the Green Show, free nightly entertainment held on the bricks outdoors between theaters before each evening's performances. Special festival events are held throughout the nearly year-round season; be sure to check osfashland.org. A traditional, medieval feast officially opens the Shakespeare Festival season in mid-June. Known as the Feast of Will, it's held, amid much music and colorful heraldry, in Ashland's lovely **Lithia Park**. The park, located near the Elizabethan Theatre, includes acres of lawn, shade trees, and mature rhododendrons along with bubbling Ashland Creek. A children's playground, a band shell and miles of trails are within the park, as well.

For a quiet respite be sure to visit the lovely **Japanese Garden**, located on a gentle slope across from the Butler-Perozzi Fountain (access from Granite Street, which skirts Lithia Park's perimeter). Stroll graveled paths and giant stepping stones, perhaps pausing to sit at one of several benches placed to catch the best views of native shrubs, many tree species, and a gently flowing stream.

You've had your fill of William Shakespeare for a day or so? Well, not to worry, you can enjoy lots of smiles and laughs including outrageous characters at times at **Oregon Cabaret Theatre**. Built in 1911, the historic Baptist Church building, including its lovely stained-glass windows, was renovated as a cabaret-style theater in 1982 and is located at 1st and Hargadine Streets (541-488-2902; oregoncabaret.com). Past musicals have included *Sweeney Todd, Steel Magnolias, The Full Monty*, and *The Bachelors*. Call ahead for dinner reservations and for tickets to this popular theater; dinner seating is an hour and a half before curtain time.

Ashland has a terrific dining scene, too, and many places stay open late to accommodate theater crowds. Try the **Brickroom** for modern American small plates and a cool, urban vibe (35 N Main Street; 541-708-6030; brickroomashland.com). **Brothers' Restaurant** is the go-to for brunch, especially if you are a fan of a Bloody Mary (95 N Main Street #2781; 541-482-9671; brothersrestaurant.net). **Larks Home Kitchen Cuisine** delivers lovely fine dining from local meats and produce, in a divine atmosphere in the Ashland Springs Hotel (212 E Main Street; 541-488-5558; ashlandspringshotel.com). **Standing Stone Brewing Company** is an excellent destination for the whole family, with award-winning craft brews and a variety of homemade delicacies from soups to salads to vegan dishes (101 Oak Street; 541-482-2448; standingstonebrewing.com).

Stay in the area long enough to also check out **Camelot Theatre Company** in the nearby community of Talent, at 101 Talent Avenue (541-535-5250; camelottheatre.org), near Ashland, which presents contemporary and classic plays such as *One Flew Over the Cuckoo's Nest*, *Annie*, *Oklahoma!*, and *You Can't Take It with You*. In nearby Grants Pass, you can visit one of the oldest theater groups in southern Oregon, founded in 1952, **Barnstormers Little Theatre**, 112 NE Evelyn Avenue (541-479-3557; barnstormersgp.com). This all-volunteer community theater offers such plays as *It's a Wonderful Life*, *The Lion in Winter*, *Death of a Salesman*, *The Curious Incident of the Dog in the Night-Time*, and *The Fantasticks*.

Cozy Lodgings in Shakespeare Town

Cowslip's Belle Bed & Breakfast, 149 N. Main Street (541-488-2901; cowslip.com), greets guests with teddy bears and chocolates, homemade cookies, sherry, and homemade biscotti. There are three cozy rooms that have outside decks; a separate carriage house offers two small suites.

The Iris Inn, 59 Manzanita Street (541-488-2286; irisinnashland.com), *Oak Hill Bed & Breakfast*, 2190 Siskiyou Boulevard (541-482-1554; oakhillbb.com), and *Coolidge House Bed & Breakfast*, 137 N. Main Street (541-482-4721; coolidgehouse.com), all offer lovely gardens, comfortable guest rooms, generous breakfasts, and innkeepers who enjoy sharing Shakespeare town with out-of-towners.

The Peerless Hotel, 243 4th Street (541-488-1082; peerlesshotel.com), until the late 1920s, rented rooms to Southern Pacific railroad workers in Ashland's Historic Railroad District. It has now been upgraded to a classy European-style hostelry, where travelers also can enjoy an intimate restaurant and bar on the premises.

Other comfortable bed-and-breakfasts include *Chanticleer Inn*, 120 Gresham Street (541-482-1919; chanticleerashland.com); *Romeo Inn*, 295 Idaho Street (541-488-2718; romeoinn.com); and *Lithia Springs Resort*, not far from downtown Ashland at 2165 W. Jackson Road (800-482-7128; lithiaspringsresort.com). Because of the busy theater season, it's best to make lodging reservations early. For helpful brochures contact the Ashland Visitor Information Center, 110 E. Main Street (541-482-3486; ashlandchamber.com). Ask about the self-guided walking-tour brochure and map of historic buildings and homes, the *Inside and Outdoor Activities* guide, and winter sports information for nearby Mount Ashland.

For a retro lodging on the outskirts of Ashland, visit the recently renovated *Ashland Hills Hotel and Suites*, 2525 Ashland Street (855-482-8310; ashlandhillshotel.com). The large property has an outdoor pool, spa, café, bar and meeting rooms, with views of the namesake hills and a cool 1950s-era vibe throughout.

Just off the beaten path—about 16 miles south of town—climb the road up to 7,528-foot **Mount Ashland**. Savor the wide-angle view past tall pines to the verdant slopes of the Siskiyou mountain range, the valley floor, and 14,162-foot snowy **Mount Shasta**, looming some 50 miles to the south in northern California. Take an outdoor stroll or a hike along a section of the **Pacific Crest National Scenic Trail**, which traverses the mountain. The trail angles through groves of ponderosa pine and red-barked manzanita up to lush alpine meadows that burst with colorful wildflowers in mid to late summer. The wild larkspur, blue lupine, and white bear grass usually peak in August at the higher elevations. During winter clamp on cross-country skis and hit the trails, or visit Mt. Ashland Ski Area (mtashland.com) for downhill skiing and snowboarding.

Medford and Jacksonville

Right next door to Ashland is **Medford**, the Rogue River Valley's industrious timber-processing and pear-packing center. Once the home of the Takelma tribe, the region changed drastically when gold was discovered near Jacksonville, just west of Medford, in 1852. Miners invaded the valley in search of fortunes in gold nuggets and were followed by early settlers lured to the valley by its fertile soil and favorable growing conditions. The fortune hunters panned and claimed, the farmers cleared and planted—and both groups displaced the peace-loving Takelma tribe. Of course, in addition to all these events, railroad tracks were laid, and the clatter and whistles of trains were heard.

To recapture some of the nostalgia and history connected with the railroad's reaching into the Rogue River Valley at Medford, visit **Medford Railroad Park** and take in the Rogue Valley Model Railroad Show in late November (541-774-2400; playmedford.com). You and the kids can take a short model train ride April through October on the second and fourth Sunday of the month from 11:00 a.m. to 3:00 p.m. The historic park and its vintage model train are located near Table Rock Road at 799 Berrydale Avenue, off Highway 62 just north of Medford. Turn at the fire station to the parking area.

The **Southern Oregon Historical Society Center** in Medford also contains exhibits and historical collections and is a worthwhile addition to your travel itinerary. The center is located downtown at 106 N. Central Avenue (541-773-6536; sohs.org), and it's open from 12:00 a.m. to 4:00 p.m. Tuesday through Saturday. For additional information about the area, contact the Medford Visitor Information Center, 1314 Center Dr. inside the **Harry & David Country Village**, exit 27 from I-5 (541-776-4021; travelmedford.org).

Medford is loved by bicyclists for its **Bear Creek Greenway**, which meanders nearly 18 miles from Ashland to Central Point, partly along the banks of Bear Creek. Walkers and joggers are also welcome to use the paved trail. The

Old Stage Road to Jacksonville, though heavily used by automobiles, is also popular with bicyclists.

In Medford, you can take exit 27 from I-5 and browse another pleasant country store and gift shop, the well-known *Harry & David Country Village*, 1314 Center Drive (541-864-2278; harryanddavid.com), which offers treats from dried fruit and nuts to chocolates, gourmet popcorn, fresh fruits, and cheesecakes. Call ahead (877-322-8000) to reserve space for you and the kids to join a tour of the food preparation area; four tours are offered daily Monday through Friday. From here a pleasant option is to take the scenic route to the National Historic Landmark community of Jacksonville—the *Old Stage Road* off Highway 99 from the Central Point–Medford area—for a close-up view of tidy pear orchards, open-air fruit stands, and old farmsteads. During early spring, the whole valley adorns a canopy of white pear blossoms. This eye-catching spectacle takes place from mid- to late April.

Stroll and Dine in Medford's Old Town Historic District

When Medford's downtown was designated a National Historic District in 1999 (old-townmedford.com), it sparked renewed interest in preserving the city's historic buildings in the downtown core area. Travelers, visitors, and locals enjoy strolling the area, which is anchored by the ca. 1910 railroad depot now restored as *Porters Dining at the Depot*, 147 N. Front Street (541-857-1910; porterstrainstation.com), open daily at 4:00 p.m. The impressive building with its soaring tile roof, massive beams, and brick exterior is named for the porters who served travelers aboard passenger trains of yesterday and today. Dine inside seated in the train-style curtained banquettes or outdoors sitting on the shaded patio or at the cigar-friendly bar patio.

You can also visit other Old Town eateries nearby including *4 Daughters Irish Pub* at 126 W. Main Street (541-779-4455; 4daughtersirishpub.com), *Elements Tapas Bar & Lounge* at 101 E. Main Street (541-779-0135; elementsmedford.com), *Beerworks* at 323 E. Main Street (541-770-9011), *Over Easy* for brunch at 21 N Bartlett Street (458-226-2659; overeasysouthernoregon.com), and *Auntie Carole Hawaiian Cafe* at 130 E. Main Street (541-245-0555).

Also nearby you can take in performances year round at the splendid *Craterian Ginger Rogers Theater*, 16 S. Bartlett (541-779-3000; craterian.org).

Designated a National Historic Landmark in 1966, the town of *Jacksonville* diligently works to preserve the atmosphere of the mid-1800s. Park on any side street and stroll down California Street for a glimpse into the colorful past. Didn't you and the kids just hear the clump of miners' boots, the crunch of wagon wheels pulled by mules or horses, the laughter of the saloon and dance-hall queens, and the wind echoing around the old iron town water pump next to the 1863 Beekman Bank Building?

To further savor Jacksonville's colorful history, trek from the old depot on C Street up E Street to the *Jacksonville Pioneer Cemetery*. Situated on a small hill shaded by tall oak and madrone trees, the historic cemetery offers quiet paths into the past. Pick up a map and self-guided walking tour and history guide at the visitor information center (jacksonvilleoregon.org). Don't miss this lovely spot, especially from April to June.

Living history programs are offered once a month during summer at

> ## oregontrivia
>
> In 1883, when the Oregon and California Railroad reached southern Oregon, a railroad station was built at Middle Ford on Bear Creek. Later a town site was platted here and the name shortened to Medford. Incorporated in 1885, the town took up its first order of business: to establish an ordinance that discouraged disorderly conduct. A second ordinance prohibited minors from loitering at the railroad depot, and a third solemnly outlawed hogs from running loose within the town.

Beekman House, located on California Street near the restored, ca. 1854 Methodist church. Stroll along the side streets to see more than eighty restored homes and other structures, many dating from the early 1800s, and all labeled; some have their own private gardens, which can be enjoyed from the sidewalk. For information about other living history exhibits and programs, contact the Jacksonville Visitor Information Center, 185 N. Oregon Street (541-899-8118; jacksonvilleoregon.com).

Other old buildings, now restored, house specialty shops and boutiques, ice-cream parlors, bakeries, cafes, small shops, and bed-and-breakfast inns. The 1863 *Jacksonville Inn* (541-899-1900; jacksonvilleinn.com) offers cozy guest rooms and good food in its restaurant, as does the *Bella Union Restaurant & Saloon* (541-899-1770; bellau.com); both are on California Street. Should you be ready for espresso and coffee drinks, along with fresh pastries and an opportunity to meet the locals, stop by *Pony Espresso Cafe* at 545 N. 5th Street (541-899-3757; ponyespressocafe.com) 545 N. 5th Street, or *GoodBean Coffee Café*, 165 S. Oregon Street (541-899-8740; goodbean.com), open at 6:00 a.m. You might try various coffee roasts such as Moka Java, Mary's Morning, Shakespeare, and Cowboy Roast. East of downtown at 525 Bigham Knoll Drive is the German gem *The Schoolhaus Brewhaus* (541-899-1000; theschoolhaus .com), a multi-room establishment in an old schoolhouse with indoor and outdoor seating, a lively atmosphere, plenty of beer on tap and delectable food.

Walk up 1st Street to the *Britt Gardens*, founded in 1852 by pioneer photographer, horticulturist, and vintner Peter Britt. Named in his honor, the *Peter Britt Music and Arts Festival* (800-882-7488; brittfest.org) offers a wide variety of classical, bluegrass, jazz, pop and dance music; the events all taking place outdoors under the stars during June, July, and August. Collect a picnic, blankets, lap robes, pillows, or lawn chairs, and find just the right spot on the wide sloping lawn (reserved seats on several rows of wooden benches are for sale, too) under tall Douglas fir trees for the evening's concert. The festival has hosted such notables as Willie Nelson, Kenny Rogers, Boy George and Culture Club, the Avett Brothers, the Manhattan Transfer, Lyle Lovett and his Large Band, Father John Misty, and Huey Lewis and the News. Several evenings are devoted to classical concerts, and you can also enjoy family concerts as well as participate in a wide variety of music and dance workshops. For the schedule and for ticket information, contact Britt Festivals, brittfest.org.

For other overnight stays in the Jacksonville area, try the romantic **Bybee's Historic Inn Bed & Breakfast** at 883 Old Stage Road (541-899-0106; bybeeshistoricinn.com). With Victorian decor, this inn offers lovely gardens and grounds, along with comfortable guest rooms on the main floor and the second level. Some rooms offer fireplaces and whirlpool tubs. Breakfast is plentiful and delicious. Among the amenable bed-and-breakfast inns near Jacksonville, you'll find **TouVelle House Bed & Breakfast**, a splendid Craftsman-style home located at 455 N. Oregon Street (541-899-8938; touvelle.com).

Note: If you plan to attend the summer Britt Festival events in Jacksonville, to avoid being disappointed, call by March or April to make reservations for your lodgings. For other lodgings contact the helpful staff at Jacksonville Visitor Center (541-899-8118; jacksonvilleoregon.org).

A Much-Loved Pioneer Cemetery

Perhaps you have never entertained the notion of falling in love with a cemetery, but many who visit Jacksonville do just that at the **Pioneer Cemetery** on the small bluff at the western edge of the small town. Only the rustle of leaves or soft breezes blowing through the tall oak and madrone trees disturbs the reverent hush. Its many pathways and byways lead to stories of the past. Granite headstones often drift or lean to one side. Weathered and yellowed, they are carved with intricate patterns of leaves, roses, drapery, and scrolls. Visitors peer at the names of loved ones, the dates, and the fond farewells etched into the stones. Many headstones date from 1859, when the cemetery was first platted. In the spring, you can walk among carpets of colorful wildflowers—the heart-shaped leaves, lavender blossoms, and tendrils of wax myrtle trail about; shooting stars, fawn lilies, and columbine poke up in shady nooks and crannies. Unexpected steps lead to terraced areas throughout the grounds. The jumble of tall trees, the undergrowth and wildflowers, and the old headstones urge one to stay longer and again read their poignant stories. Be sure to visit this special place, one of the quintessential outdoor scrapbooks of southern Oregon's pioneer past. For more historical information and maps, contact the Jacksonville Visitor Center (541-899-8118; jacksonvilleoregon.org).

Scenic Rogue River Country

If time allows, take winding old Highway 99 and US 199 for a leisurely, 25-mile drive along the upper Rogue River to **Grants Pass**. You can also detour at **Gold Hill** to visit the **Gold Hill Historical Museum**, located in the 1901 Beeman-Martine House at 504 1st Avenue (541-855-1182). Containing a collection of southern Oregon mining and historical memorabilia, the museum is generally open Thursday through Saturday, noon to 4:00 p.m. The **Oregon Vortex and House of Mystery** (4303 Sardine Creek L Fork Road; 541-855-1543; oregonvortex.com) are also in Gold Hill. This quirky Oregon curiosity is worth a stop with the kids, to investigate claims of naturally occurring visual and perceptual phenomena reported at the site. Open seven days a week March through October.

If you love old covered bridges, plan to visit **Wimer Covered Bridge**. The original bridge was constructed in 1892; the current covered structure, often called "a barn over water," was built in 1927 by Jason Hartman, a county bridge superintendent. The bridge collapsed in 2003 due to vehicular traffic, but the community rebuilt, and five years later, the bridge stood proudly once more. To find the bridge, detour from the town of Rogue River about 7 miles north on E. Evans Creek Road. For information on other covered bridges in the area, call the Southern Oregon Historical Society library in Medford at (541) 773-6536 or visit sohs.org.

For an alternate route from Jacksonville to Grants Pass, take Highway 238, which winds along the Applegate River, passes the hamlet of Ruch where you'll see **Valley View Winery**—visit the tasting room here, open 11:00 a.m. to 5:00 p.m. daily (541-899-8486; valleyviewwinery.com), and continues past **Historic McKee Covered Bridge**. Continue another 6 miles west of Ruch to reach **Applegate River Lodge & Restaurant,** 15100 Highway 238 (lodge: 541-846-6690 or restaurant: 541-846-6082; applegateriverlodge.com). Of massive log construction, the inn offers seven large guestroom suites using decor that depicts the early pioneer history of the area. Enjoy fine dining in the inn's restaurant, Tuesday through Sunday starting at 5:00 p.m. Many other wineries have popped up in the Applegate Valley; see applegatevalley.wine.

Entering Grants Pass via Highway 238, you'll cross the Rogue River on the ca. 1931 **Caveman Bridge**, which is on the National Register of Historic Places. For helpful visitor information, stop by the well-stocked Grants Pass Visitor Information Center (198 SW 6th Street; 541-476-7574; travelgrantspass.com).

The **Rogue River** is reknowned for fishing, and anglers come in droves to fish its pools and riffles year-round. The best chinook salmon angling is reported to take place from mid-April through September, whereas trout fishing picks up in August and again in December through March. Local tackle shops sell bait, supplies, the required licenses, and salmon/trout tags. Ask about catch regulations.

You can fish from the shore at parks along the river or hire a drift-boat guide for half days or full days—a tradition since the early 1930s, long before an 84-mile stretch of the river between Grants Pass and Gold Beach on the south coast was designated part of the National Wild and Scenic system. More adventurous anglers can check out the three- and four-day guided fishing trips down this section of the Rogue that are offered by licensed outfitters from September 1 to November 15; the Grants Pass visitor information center (541-476-7574) will have current information.

The most common summer white-water trips use large, inflatable oar-and-paddle rafts, inflatable kayaks, drift boats, or the popular jet boats. As you drift along with an expert guide handling the oars, the Rogue River ripples, cascades, boils, churns, and spills over rocks and boulders, through narrow canyons and gorges, and along quiet and peaceful stretches—rimmed on both sides by forests of Douglas fir, madrone, and oak and reflecting sunlight, blue sky, and puffy white clouds from its ever-moving surface.

You can also enjoy a one-day guided raft trip on the Rogue River or a 4-hour, 36-mile jet-boat excursion to **Hellgate Canyon**, stopping at O.K. Corral for a country-style barbecue dinner served on a large deck overlooking all that marvelous river and wilderness scenery. Other trips stop at **Morrisons Rogue Wilderness Lodge** (8500 Galice Road; 800-826-1963; morrisonslodge. com), which also doubles as a charming, if rustic and remote, overnight lodging with excellent dinners, served outdoors family style in summer. For information and reservations contact **Hellgate Jetboat Excursions** (541-479-7204; hellgate.com).

Wine Tasting in Southern Oregon

Bridgeview Vineyard & Winery
4210 Holland Loop Road
Cave Junction
(877) 273-4843, (541) 592-4688
bridgeviewwine.com
Open 11:00 a.m. to 5:00 p.m. daily

Irvine & Roberts Vineyards
1614 Emigrant Creek Road
Ashland
(541) 482-9383

irvinerobertsvineyard.com
Open 12:00 a.m. to 6:00 p.m. Thursday
through Monday

Red Lily Winery
11777 OR-238
Jacksonville
(541) 846-6800
Redlilyvineyards.com
Open daily 11:00 a.m. to 5:00 p.m.

Troon Winery
1475 Kubli Road
Grants Pass
(541) 846-9900
Troonvineyard.com
Open 11:00 a.m. to 5:00 p.m. daily

Valley View Winery
1000 Upper Applegate Road
Jacksonville
(800) 781-9463, (541) 899-8468

valleyviewwinery.com
Open 11:00 a.m. to 5:00 p.m. daily
except holidays

Weisinger's of Ashland
3150 Siskiyou Boulevard
Ashland
(800) 551-9463, (541) 488-5989
weisingers.com
Open 11:00 a.m. to 5:00 p.m. daily May
through October

TOP ANNUAL EVENTS IN SOUTHERN OREGON

JANUARY

Chemult Sled Dog Races
Chemult
(541-408-5729)
chemult.org, sleddogchemult.org

FEBRUARY

Winter Wings Festival
Klamath Falls
(877) 541-2473
winterwingsfest.org

MARCH

Pear Blossom Festival
Medford
pearblossomparade.org

APRIL

Annual Glide Wildflower Show
Glide-Roseburg
glidewildflowershow.org

SUMMER

Britt Festivals
Jacksonville; June–August
(800) 882-7488, (541) 773-6077
brittfest.org

JUNE

Umpqua Valley Roundup
Roseburg
(541) 957-7010
douglasfairgrounds.com

NOVEMBER

Ashland Culinary Festival
Ashland
(541) 482-3486
ashlandchamber.com

YEAR-ROUND

Oregon Shakespeare Festival
Ashland; February–October
(541) 482-4331
osfashland.org

If you'd like to remain a little closer to civilization, consider spending the night at the ca. 1924 *Weasku Inn Historic Lodge*, a historic fishing lodge near Grants Pass located at 5560 Rogue River Highway (541-471-8000; weasku.com). Travelers can choose from cozy rooms in the log lodge, several river cabins, an A-frame river cabin, or a log house with three bedrooms—all of which include fireplaces except for the main lodge rooms. Well-known writers and actors stayed here in early years.

For good eats in Grants Pass, try *River's Edge Restaurant* at 1936 Rogue River Highway (541-244-1182; theriversedge.us) and *Taprock Northwest Grill* at 971 SE 6th Street (541-995-5998; taprock.com). For delicious brunch downtown, visit *Ma Mosa's* (118 NW E Street; 541-479-0236; mamosas.com), where the from-scratch kitchen delivers meals made from local products. If you're in the area on a Saturday during summer months, visit the lively *Grants Pass Grower's Market* at 4th and F Streets (growersmarket.org) open at 9:00 a.m.—the fresh-baked cinnamon rolls, breads, and pastries are to die for, not to mention the farm-fresh fruits, vegetables, and herbs. During the winter, the Saturday Market and Growers Market moves indoors, to the fairgrounds.

Before heading north via I-5 toward Roseburg, or going west via the Redwood Highway (US 199) toward Cave Junction and the south coast, plan a natural history stop at *Wildlife Images Rehabilitation and Education Center* at 11845 Lower Road. Originally, started to nurse injured birds of prey back to health, the center now aids and nurtures all types of injured or orphaned wild animals, from bears and fawns to raccoons and beavers. To arrange a guided tour, call ahead to make a reservation (541-476-0222; wildlifeimages.org).

For another scenic side trip, take the 20-mile, paved, twisting road east of Cave Junction, located 30 miles southwest of Grants Pass via US 199, up to *Oregon Caves National Monument* (541-592-2100 ext. 2262; nps.gov/orca). Located in the heart of the Siskiyou Mountains at an elevation of 4,000 feet, the prehistoric marble and limestone underground caverns were discovered by Elijah H. Davidson in 1874, although Native peoples, of course, knew about the caves for centuries before non-Native people arrived. Although guided walks through the caves can be taken late March through early November, avoid midsummer crowds and long lines by planning a trip in either early spring or late fall, after Labor Day.

The cave tour, somewhat strenuous, lasts about 90 minutes and is not recommended for those with heart, breathing, or walking difficulties; canes and other walking aids are not permitted inside the caverns. Youth who are 42 inches in height or taller may join the cave tour; those fifteen years and under must be accompanied by an adult. *Note*: The caverns are a chilly 41 degrees Fahrenheit inside; dress warmly and wear sturdy shoes.

Then, too, you could arrange to stay the night at the rustic **Oregon Caves Chateau** (541-592-3400; oregoncaveschateau.com), built in 1934 and now on the National Register of Historic Places. It's a handsome cedar structure with twenty-two guest rooms (no telephones or TV), some overlooking a waterfall and pond, and others the Douglas fir-clothed canyon or the entrance to the caverns. The chateau's restaurant serves dinner, offering steak, seafood, chicken, and a selection of Northwest wines, with Cave Creek close by—it bubbles right through the dining room. The old-fashioned coffee shop, Caves Café, is open for breakfast and lunch. The Oregon Caves Chateau operates from mid-May to September.

If you'd like to experience a summer camp for families that also features comfy accommodations in a variety of sturdy tree houses, call **Out 'N' About Treesort**, located near Cave Junction (541-592-2208; treehouses.com). You and your family will climb ladders and sometimes negotiate a short suspension bridge to reach your cozy nest, but it's great fun and the kids love it.

For **Kalmiopsis Wilderness** hiking trails and for maps and additional information, contact the Illinois Valley Ranger District (541-592-4000; fs.fed.us/rogue-siskiyou) or the Illinois Valley Visitor Center, 201 Caves Highway, Cave Junction (541-592-4076; cavejunctionoregon.com). **Coffee Heaven** (541-592-3888), located at 409 Redwood Highway next to the visitor's center, opens for steaming java at 6:30 a.m. daily. For good eats and ales try **Wild River Brewing & Pizza Co.**, 249 Redwood Highway (541-592-3556; wildriverbrewing.com), open daily at 11:00 a.m. and Sunday at noon. Hops lovers can ask about the tasty brews including Jerry's India Pale Ale, Honey Wheat, Nut Brown Ale, Bohemian Pilsener, and Golden Lager. **Taylor's Sausage**, 202 Redwood Highway (541-592-5358; taylorsausage.com/country-store), open daily, is renowned for its freshly made sausages and meats along with great sandwiches, deli items, and dinner service on Friday at 5:30 p.m.

For pleasant lodgings in Cave Junction, check with **Kerbyville Inn Bed & Breakfast**, 24304 Redwood Highway (541-592-4689; kerbyvilleinn.com), or with **Country Hills Resort**, 7901 Caves Highway (541-592-3406; countryhills resort.com), which offers cozy cabins, motel rooms, an ice-cream parlor, and creekside RV and camping sites.

From here continue west on the scenic Redwood Highway (US 199) toward Crescent City, California, and to the heart of **Redwood National Park** and state parks. For helpful maps and information, stop at the Hiouchi Visitor Center (707-458-3294) and Jedediah Smith Visitor Center (707-458-3496) are both on US 199, just 8 miles east of Crescent City. Crescent City Information Center is located at 1111 2nd Street in Crescent City (707-465-7306). Ask about Myrtle Creek Botanical Area, Jedediah Smith Redwoods State Park, and Stout

Grove, as well as Lake Earl Wildlife Area, Point Street George Lighthouse, North Fork Smith River Botanical Area, Rowdy Creek Fish Hatchery, and extensive lily fields, all located near Crescent City in northern California's Del Norte County. From Crescent City it's an easy drive north on US 101 to Brookings-Harbor and Gold Beach on the southern Oregon coast.

The Umpqua Valley

Early travelers in the mid-1800s came through southern Oregon by stagecoach over those rough, dusty, and sometimes muddy roads from central California on their way north to the Oregon country. The trip from San Francisco to Portland took about sixteen days, the fare being about 10 cents a mile. Stage stations were situated every 10 or so miles, and the big crimson-colored stages, built to carry the mail and as many as sixteen passengers, were an important link in the early development of the Northwest.

Completion of the railroad in 1887 through the Willamette and Umpqua Valleys south to California brought a sudden halt to the overland mail stage. Although this marked the end of a colorful chapter in Northwest history, today's traveler can nevertheless recapture a bit of that history. For a look at one of the oldest stage stops in the state, detour from I-5 at **Wolf Creek**, about 20 miles north of Grants Pass. Here you will find the ca. 1883 **Historic Wolf Creek Inn** (541-866-2474; wolfcreekinn.com), a large, two-story, classical revival-style inn that is still open to travelers.

Purchased by the state and completely restored in 1979, the inn is now administered by the Oregon Parks and Recreation Department. Hearty meals are served in the dining room, and guest rooms are available on the second floor. When you walk into the parlor, which is furnished with period antiques, you might notice the sunlight filtering through lace-curtained windows and imagine a long-skirted matron or young lady sipping a cup of tea while waiting for the next stage to depart. The inn's pleasant dining room is open to the public for breakfast, lunch, and dinner most of the year.

Roseburg and Oakland

If time allows, take the Sunny Valley exit from I-5, exit 71, and visit the **Applegate Trail Interpretive Center** at 500 Sunny Valley Loop (541-291-1225; rogueweb.com/interpretive), open Tuesday to Sunday at 10:30 a.m. to 4:30 p.m. (closed during winter months). In this impressive log structure, you and the kids can sample more of the intriguing history of the region, particularly that of the Applegate brothers, Jesse and Lindsay, who in 1846 blazed a new trail to Oregon from Fort Hall, Idaho, entering the Willamette Valley from the south. Hamlets and small communities like Remote, Camas Valley, Days Creek, Tiller, Lookingglass, Riddle, and Glide contain many descendants of both early miners and pioneers. These folks live in the remote areas of the Umpqua River east and west of Roseburg. There are a few Native peoples left, too—a community of Cow Creek Indians. The tribe runs the **Seven Feathers Casino Resort**, at exit 99 off of I-5 (146 Chief Miwaleta Lane, Canyonville; 800-548-8461; seven feathers.com), worth a stop for lodging, dining, or gaming.

Also hidden away on the county roads—look for the bright blue Douglas County road signs with yellow numbers—and in the small valleys near Roseburg are some of the region's first vineyards and wineries. More than thirty years ago the first varietals were planted in southern Oregon by Richard Sommer at **HillCrest Vineyard**, 240 Vineyard Lane (541-673-3709; hillcrest vineyard.com), winery open daily, and from these roots eventually emerged a thriving colony of vintners just west of Roseburg—Giradet Wine Cellars, Delfino Winery, Cooper Ridge Winery, Umpqua River Vineyards, and Reustle Prayer Rock Winery. In town, visit Paul O'Brien Winery, a newer entrant to the scene with an urban vibe.

To reach the wineries, drive through the oak-dotted, rolling hills west of Roseburg. Call ahead to make certain the tasting rooms are open; some of the vineyards are open only by appointment. More wineries are located in town itself, as well as south in Winston and north in Elkton (see umpquavalleywineries.org for lists and maps). The Roseburg Visitor Center, at 410 SE Spruce Street (541-672-9731; roseburgchamber.com), open Monday through Friday 9:00 a.m. to 5:00 p.m., will have helpful maps and brochures.

Wind southwest a few miles from Roseburg to Winston to visit **Wildlife Safari**, 1790 Safari Road (541-679-6761; wildlifesafari.net), open daily. The 600-acre, drive-through wild animal reserve of more than 500 animals represents a hundred different species of animals and birds representing Africa, Asia, and more exotic areas of the world. Among the wildlife living here are the Tibetan yak, wildebeest, eland, lion, elephant, ostrich, hippopotamus, rhinoceros, and cheetah. Ask about special daily close encounters and activities involving some of the animals.

Since 1980, Wildlife Safari has been operated by the Safari Game Search Foundation, a nonprofit organization dedicated to preserving endangered species, conducting animal-related research, providing educational programs for elementary schools throughout the Northwest, and rehabilitating injured wildlife. A world leader in the research on and breeding of cheetahs, the organization has successfully raised more than one hundred cheetah cubs here in the past thirty years and is one of the largest providers of cheetahs to zoos throughout the world.

The Safari Village area offers a petting zoo, gardens, Safari Village Cafe, Village Coffee Hut, gift shop, and the White Rhino Event Center. Visitors also find a small RV park, picnic areas, and self-service kennels for your dog or cat, which are not allowed in the reserve's drive-through areas. Wildlife Safari is about 4 miles west of I-5 from the Winston exit via Highway 42. There is an admission fee.

For exhibits of some of the region's natural history, as well as logging and mining equipment dating from the 1800s, detour from I-5 just south of Roseburg—at the Fairgrounds exit—to visit the **Douglas County Museum of History and Natural History** (541-957-7007; umpquavalleymuseums.org), located in the large contemporary structure next to the fairgrounds. After poking around the vintage logging and mining equipment in the courtyard, be sure to look inside for the fine exhibit of old photographs. Though the photographs are yellowed with age, the weathered faces in them mirror hope and determination as well as hardship and even heartbreak; the exhibit offers a poignant look into Oregon's pioneer past. The museum is open Tuesday through Saturday from 10:00 a.m. to 5:00 p.m. A shady park next door offers picnic tables and parking for recreational vehicles.

If you pass through the community of **Glide**—it's about 17 miles east of Roseburg via Highway 138—the last weekend in April and notice lots of cars parked near the Community Building, be sure to stop to see whether the annual **Glide Wildflower Show** (glidewildflowershow.org) is in progress. At this show, some 300 native plants and flowers from the southern Oregon region are displayed in colorful arrangements by local naturalists and wildflower lovers. Don't miss it; it's great fun and also offers a chance to meet the locals and chat about botanical favorites over a cup of coffee.

OTHER DESTINATIONS WORTH SEEING IN SOUTHERN OREGON

The Butterfly Pavilion and Fort Umpqua
Elkton

Craterian Theater
Medford

Lava Beds National Monument
40 miles south of Klamath Falls

The Parrott House
Roseburg

The ScienceWorks Hands-on Museum
Ashland

Another pleasant side trip from Roseburg weaves farther east on Highway 138 into the southern **Cascade Mountains**. The two-lane asphalt ribbon plays hide-and-seek with the **North Umpqua River** and with many frothy waterfalls carrying names like Toketee, Lemolo, White Horse, Clearwater, and Watson. **Watson Falls** is noted as the second highest in Oregon, a 272-foot drop down a rugged cliff; access is from a well-marked 0.5-mile trail. The falls and nearby parking areas, beginning about 20 miles east of Glide, are well marked. A section of the scenic river, also well marked, is open just to those who love fly fishing; the fly-fishing section between Glide and Steamboat is especially scenic. The 79-mile North Umpqua Trail is popular for hiking and mountain biking, as well as access to fishing spots.

Steamboat Inn at 42705 N. Umpqua Highway 138 (541-498-2230; thesteamboatinn.com) offers rustic but comfortable rooms and a few cozy cabins that overlook the bubbling Umpqua River—you'll likely want to sit on the wide deck for hours and soak in the wilderness. Guests enjoy gourmet fisherman dinners in the knotty-pine dining room.

From here you can continue east on Highway 138 to connect with **Poole Creek Campground** at Lemolo Lake (877-444-6777) and also with nearby **Lemolo Lake/Crater Lake North KOA**. Shady RV and camping spaces are also available at the lodge. Diamond Lake, with its wide range of fishing, camping, and resort facilities, and Crater Lake National Park can be accessed on this route (see the beginning of this chapter for details). Along the route take a break and pull in at the **Dry Creek Store** (541-498-2215) at Dry Creek, off Highway 138, for cold beverages, food supplies, and tips from the locals.

To see another section of the Umpqua River, head north from Roseburg and detour west from I-5 onto Highway 138 at Sutherlin. This meandering rural route carries travelers to **Big K Guest Ranch**, located at 20029 Highway 138 West (541-584-2295; big-k.com) near Elkton on 2,500 acres of rolling Douglas fir forest in the Umpqua River Valley. The guest ranch complex overlooks "the loop," the biggest bend and a scenic stretch of the Umpqua River that is known for good fishing—smallmouth bass, steelhead, shad, and Chinook salmon, depending on the season. The river bubbles and meanders past the ranch, through the Coast Range, and empties into the Pacific Ocean at Reedsport. The Kesterson family offers guests a number of outdoor options. You can go horseback riding, bicycle, hike, try your hand at horseshoes or the sporting-clay range, arrange for a river float trip, go wine tasting, or even go on a fall wild turkey hunt. Home-style fare is offered in the river-rock fireplace dining room in the main lodge; accommodations are in cozy log cabins.

Plan one last detour before entering the lush Willamette Valley region: a stop in the small community of **Oakland** (historicoaklandoregon.com), nestled in the oak-dotted hills just north of Sutherlin. When the area's lumber mill closed, Oakland felt an economic decline common to many timber towns throughout the Northwest. The townsfolk's response, though, was decidedly uncommon—they worked to have their ca. 1852 community designated the **Oakland Historic District** and placed on the National Register of Historic Places, the first such district in Oregon to be so recognized, in 1967.

Begin with a stroll on Locust Street, poking into a few of its antiques shops and boutiques. You can also nip into **Tolly's Grill and Soda Fountain** located in the ca. 1872 building that housed the drug store and mercantile, 115 Locust Street (541-459-3796). Try the historic ca. 1898 **Oakland Tavern** for tasty sandwiches and spirits. Inspect memorabilia and old photographs at the **Oakland Museum** (541-459-3087), open daily from 12:30 to 3:30 p.m. except holidays. Also check out the historic **Stearns Hardware** store, which has been in operation since 1887. Conclude your visit by walking farther up both sides of Locust Street to see vintage commercial structures, art galleries, and Victorian-style houses. Ask about lively performances, vintage melodramas, offered by the **Oakland Community Theater** players and volunteers during summers in the renovated Washington School building at the upper end of Locust Street (541-315-1840; oaklandmelodrama.org).

Places to Stay in Southern Oregon

ASHLAND

Ashland Hills Hotel and Suites
2525 Ashland Street
ashlandhillshotel.com

The Bard's Inn
132 N. Main Street
(541) 482-0049
bardsinn.com

Chanticleer Inn
120 Gresham Street
(541) 482-1919
ashland-bed-breakfast.com

Cowslip's Belle Bed & Breakfast
149 N. Main Street
(541) 488-2901
cowslip.com

The Iris Inn
59 Manzanita Street
(541) 488-2286
irisinnbb.com

BLY

Aspen Ridge Resort
Hwy. 140
(541) 884-8685
aspenrr.com

CHEMULT/CRESCENT LAKE

Odell Lake Lodge & Resort
Highway 58
(541) 433-2540
odelllakelodge.com

Shelter Cove Resort and Marina
27600 W Odell Road
(541) 433-2548
highwaywestvacation.com

GRANTS PASS

Weasku Inn Historic Lodge
5560 Rogue River Highway
(800) 493-2758
weasku.com

JACKSONVILLE

Jacksonville Inn
175 E. California Street
(541) 899-1900
jacksonvilleinn.com

TouVelle House Bed & Breakfast
455 N. Oregon Street
(541) 899-8938
touvellehouse.com

KLAMATH FALLS AREA

Lake of the Woods Lodge, Cabins & RV Resort
950 Harriman Route
(541) 949-8300
lakeofthewoodsresort.com

Rocky Point Resort, Restaurant, and RV Park
28121 Rocky Point Road
Upper Klamath Lake area
(541) 356-2287

MEDFORD

Best Western Horizon Inn
1154 Barnett Road
(541) 779-5085

MERLIN

Morrisons Rogue Wilderness Lodge
8500 Galice Road
(800) 826-1963
morrisonslodge.com

PROSPECT

Prospect Historic Hotel, Motel and Dinner House
391 Mill Creek Drive
(near Crater Lake)
(541) 560-3664
prospecthotel.com

Places to Eat in Southern Oregon

ASHLAND

Brothers' Restaurant
95 N. Main Street
(541) 482-9671
brothersrestaurant.net

Greenleaf Restaurant
49 Main Street
(541) 482-2808
greenleafrestaurant.com

Noble Coffee Roasting
281 4th Street
(541) 488-3288
noblecoffeeroasting.com

Brickroom
35 N Main Street
(541) 708-6030
brickroomashland.com

Standing Stone Brewing Company
101 Oak Street
(541) 482-2448
standingstonebrewing.com

CENTRAL POINT

Rogue Creamery & Cheese
311 N. Front Street
(541) 665-1155
roguecreamery.com

GRANTS PASS

Bluestone Bakery & Café
412 N.W. 6th Street
(541) 471-1922
bluestonebakery.com

Laughing Clam Restaurant
121 SW G Street
(541) 479-1110

Taprock Northwest Grill
971 SE 6th Street
(541) 941-5998
taprock.com

Wild River Brewing & Pizza Co.
595 NE E Street
(541) 471-7487
wildriverbrewing.com

JACKSONVILLE

Bella Union Restaurant & Saloon
170 W. California Street

(541) 899-1770
bellau.com

GoodBean
165 S. Oregon Street
(541) 899-8740
goodbean.com

The Schoolhaus Brewhaus
525 Bigham Knoll Drive
(541) 899-1000
theschoolhaus.com

KLAMATH FALLS AREA

The Daily Bagel
636 Main Street
(541) 850-0744

Klamath Basin Brewing Brewpub
1320 Main Street
(541) 273-5222
kbbrewing.com/brewpub

Lake House Restaurant
Lake of the Woods
(541) 949-8300
lakeofthewoodsresort.com

MEDFORD

Elements Tapas Bar & Lounge
101 E. Main Street
(541) 779-0135
elementsmedford.com

4 Daughters Irish Pub
126 W. Main Street
(541) 779-4455
4daughtersirishpub.com

Porters Dining at the Depot
146 N. Front Street
(541) 857-1910
porterstrainstation.com

The Urban Cork
330 N. Fir Street
(541) 500-8778
theurbancork.com

HELPFUL TELEPHONE NUMBERS AND WEBSITES FOR SOUTHERN OREGON

Ashland Visitor Center
(541) 482-3486
ashlandchamber.com

Britt Festivals
(800) 882-7488
brittfest.org

Grants Pass Visitor Center
(541) 476-7574
travelgrantspass.com

Illinois Valley Visitor Center
Cave Junction
(541) 592-4076

Jacksonville Visitor Center
(541) 899-8118
jacksonvilleoregon.org

Klamath County Visitor Center
Klamath Falls
(541) 882-1501
discoverklamath.com

Klamath National Wildlife Refuge
Klamath Basin
(530) 667-2231 (Tule Lake, CA, office)

fws.gov/refuge/lower_kl amath

Medford Visitor Center
(800) 469-6307
travelmedford.org

Oregon Cabaret Theatre
Ashland
(541) 488-2902
oregoncabaret.com

Oregon Department of Fish and Wildlife
Klamath Falls
(541) 883-5732
myodfw.com

Oregon Shakespeare Festival
(541) 482-2111 (general information)
(541) 482-4331 or (800) 219-8161 (tickets)
osfashland.org

Oregon State Parks and Campgrounds
(800) 551-6949 (general information)
(800) 452-5687 (campground reservations)
oregonstateparks.org

Roseburg Visitor Center
(541) 672-9731
visitroseburg.com

Southern Oregon Historical Society
(541) 773-6536
sohs.org

Oregon Center for the Arts at Southern Oregon University
(541) 552-6101
oca.sou.edu

Weather & Road Conditions
(541) 594-3000 Crater Lake region
(800) 977-6368 (inside OR)
(503) 588-2941 (from outside OR)
tripcheck.com

Southeastern Oregon

Southeastern Oregon is the state's "big sky" country, made up of its three largest and least-populated counties: Harney, Malheur, and Lake. The whole of many states on the East Coast could fit into this wide-open country in the Beaver State's far southeastern corner. In the 28,450-square-mile area containing just Malheur and Lake Counties, there are fewer than ten people per square mile—now, that's elbow room with room to spare.

The Old West

The stark, panoramic landscapes here evoke images of Western movies; one can easily imagine cowboys herding cattle through sagebrush-blanketed valleys and across rushing streams, sending scouts up narrow canyons to flat-topped buttes or along alkali lakes far ahead. The horizon stretches wide in all four directions in this massive high-desert country, broken now and then by shaggy pinnacles, ridged rimrock canyons, and fault-block mountains.

Hudson's Bay Company explorer-trapper Peter Skene Ogden, along with other fur traders who came in the

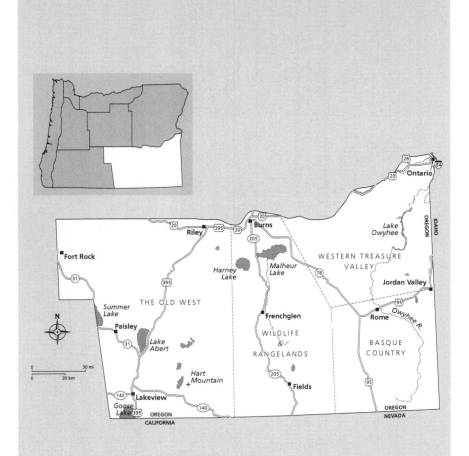

mid-1820s, had a fairly easy trek into the region because resident Native peoples had already carved numerous trails, often following deer and antelope trails. The Paiute Indians hunted, traveled the animal trails, gathered seeds, and dug camas bulbs for centuries before Ogden's party arrived in 1826.

Other non-Native people passed through in the 1850s, during the California gold rush. Early cattle barons then grabbed millions of acres of the southeastern desert country for rangeland in the 1870s and 1880s. The region still contains a number of the old ranches, and raising beef cattle remains one of the primary occupations—along with raising sheep, which was introduced by the immigrant Basques in the 1890s. There is a wonderful **Basque Museum** that history buffs may want to visit; it's located at 611 Grove Street in nearby Boise, Idaho (208-343-2671; basquemuseum.eus), and is open Tuesday through Friday from 10:00 a.m. to 4:00 p.m. and on Saturday from 11:00 a.m. to 3:00 p.m. The annual Basque festival, the **St. Inazio Festival** is held the last weekend in July; call the museum for further information.

In 1843 Capt. John C. Frémont, a topographic engineer, was sent to the territory by the US government to explore the region. He is responsible for naming many of the bold features of Lake County encountered during this winter expedition. You can follow his north–south route on Highway 31, the **Fremont Highway**, which skirts the Fremont National Forest (fs.fed.usda.gov /fremont-winema) and Gearhart Mountain Wilderness and is accessed from Lakeview, near the Oregon-California border, or from US 97 south of Bend and just south of La Pine.

Fort Rock and Summer Lake

If time allows, detour from US 97 at La Pine onto Highway 31 for about 30 miles and follow the signs to the small community of Fort Rock and to **Fort Rock State Park**. You'll get the most dramatic perspective by walking up the path and inside the enormous volcanic remnant, rising 325 feet from the high desert floor and surrounded by miles and miles of pungent sagebrush. It's more than 0.5 mile across inside. If you're lucky, you might spot a baby eagle in its nest. Notice the large wave-cut formations on the east flank, carved by eons-old inland seas that once covered this vast region. **Note**: Although the tiny community of **Fort Rock** offers one gasoline station, a cafe, and a grocery store, it's best to also bring your own supplies such as sunscreen, wide-brimmed hats, and drinking water. The high desert gets very hot and dry during summer months, with temperatures in the high eighties and nineties.

Stay long enough, however, to visit **Fort Rock Homestead Village Museum** (541-576-2251; fortrockoregon.com). Walk around the pathway and snoop into several vintage structures, including cabins, a doctor's office-cabin, and a small church filled with pioneer memorabilia and furnishings that date from those original homestead days. Open mid-April through October, Thursday through Sunday, from 11:00 a.m. to 5:00 p.m. The path is not wheelchair accessible.

To continue exploring proceed south and east from Fort Rock on Christmas Valley Highway, passing miles of lush green irrigated fields, to the community of *Christmas Valley*, which is small but still the largest settlement you'll find for miles in any direction. Call ahead and arrange lodging at *Lakeside Restaurant, Motel* 87275 Spruce Lane (541-576-2309, restaurant: 541-576-2510; lakesideterracecv.com). For evening eats try *Christmas Valley Lodge & RV Park*, 87285 Christmas Valley Highway (541-576-2333). Alternatively, you could check out *Fort Rock Restaurant and Pub* at 64591 Fort Rock Road in Fort Rock (541-947-3988) or continue south from Fort Rock on Highway 31 and pause in Silver Lake for lunch or dinner.

Cowboy Dinner Tree in Southeast Oregon's Outback

You'd like to pause for supper about as far off the beaten path as possible? Not to worry, simply call ahead for reservations at one of the state's most popular eateries, the *Cowboy Dinner Tree*, 50836 E. Bay Road (541-576-2426; cowboydinnertree .net), about 4 miles south of Silver Lake on County Road 4-12/Forest Service Road 28. Don't let the looks of the vintage structure turn you away. Made of rough-sawn lumber, it once housed a whole bunch of cowboys; parts of the structure are well over fifty years old. A lone tall juniper guards the rear of the building. Rusted bridles and bits and old cast iron skillets adorn the walls. Located about 4 miles south of Silver Lake, the eatery is a serious drive from anywhere: about 87 miles from Lakeview, 25 miles from Christmas Valley, 150 miles from Klamath Falls, and 70 miles from Bend. There is no espresso machine here, and no alcohol is served. The menu is set—your only choice is prime beef or chicken. Once seated inside, you dive into bowls of fresh salad greens and hearty soup while the staff grills your 26- to 30-ounce marinated sirloin steak or your whole chicken on a grill out in the lean-to area behind the kitchen. These monster entrees are served with baked potatoes loaded with butter and sour cream and a pan of luscious rolls. Save room for dessert, too. The restaurant is open for dinner at 4:00 p.m. Thursday through Sunday during summer months and offers varying hours during winter months. Don't even think of stopping by without calling first—reservations are a must because of limited seating. Call the hosts at (541) 576-2426 to reserve your table.

Continuing south about 40 miles on Highway 31 from Silver Lake, travelers find *The Lodge at Summer Lake* and *Flyway Restaurant* at 53460 Highway 31 (866-943-3993; lodgeatsummerlake.com, call well ahead for reservations).

It's located across the highway from the Fish and Wildlife ranger station. At the ca. 1940s hostelry, you can choose from seven motel rooms, three cedar cabins at the edge of a large bass pond, and RV spaces. In the main lodge, where the restaurant is located, you'll find a comfy great room and cozy fireplaces. Outside, take in views of this scenic high desert valley that sits at an elevation of about 4,300 feet.

Outdoor activities in the region include fly fishing the Chewaucan River, along with bird and wildlife viewing along the ridges rimmed with fragrant pine, sagebrush, and juniper. Also try backcountry bicycling, rock-hounding, stargazing, or fishing for bass and trout at Ana Reservoir and in the nearby Sycan, Sprague, and Ana Rivers. The lakes in this area along Highway 31 are shallow wetlands often visited by snow geese and sandhill cranes on their spring and fall migrations along the Pacific Flyway.

On the south end of Summer Lake is **Summer Lake Hot Springs** (41777 Oregon 31 Mile Marker 92, Paisley; 541-943-3931; summerlakehotsprings .com). The natural hot springs here have been a gathering place for centuries. Modern-day travelers stop for a day's soak, or choose from a handful of cabins, Airstream trailers for rent, RV sites or tent camping sites. An indoor pool sits in a charmingly ramshackle 1930s-era bathhouse. Three open-air soaking pools are outside under the sky and stars. All in all, the property makes for a peaceful, relaxing and very unique retreat from our usual fast-paced lives. Just a few miles south is the frontier town Paisley, which offers a restaurant, a saloon and services.

Lakeview

On OR 395 just 2 miles north of Lakeview is **Old Perpetual**, a geyser that spouts about 60 feet above the ground. The underground water heats to a temperature of some 200 degrees, erupting in a frothy, billowy column. The geyser spouts once every 60 to 90 seconds in the winter and every 4 to 10 minutes in the summer.

The town of **Lakeview** sits at an elevation of 4,800 feet above sea level and is noted as the tallest town in the Beaver State. Visit a little gem of a museum in Lakeview, **Schminck Memorial Museum** (128 South E Street; 541-947-3134), located in a small bungalow, a half block south of the courthouse. The collection numbers more than 7,000 pieces that were collected over a lifetime by Lula and Dalpheus Schminck. The couple developed the collecting habit and spent many hours recording, labeling, and displaying their finds. You'll see fashions from the 1880s such as bustles, bows, high-button shoes, fancy fans, combs, hats, hatpins, parasols, beads, and bags. One of the splendid collections is composed of more than fifty vintage quilts dating from

1806 to the 1930s. Browsers can also see pipes, canes, spectacles, gold watches, personalized shaving mugs, and tools and tack of the period as well as artifacts and baskets from Lake County. Visit Thursday through Saturday, 12:00 p.m. to 4:00 p.m., May through September. If you trek through the area in September around Labor Day weekend, check out the *Lake County Round-up*, featuring the largest and oldest amateur rodeo in the Northwest, which celebrated its 100th year in 2020.

For eateries in Lakeview try *Burger Queen Drive In* at 109 South F Street (541-947-3677); *Green Mountain Bakery*, 425 North J Street (541-947-4497); or *Jerry's Restaurant*, 508 N. 2nd Street (541-947-2600). *Tall Town Burger & Bakery*, 1028 N. 4th Street (541-947-3521), offers good burgers and tasty bakery selections. Further information on lodging and dining in the Lakeview area can be obtained from the Lake County Visitor Center in Lakeview (877-947-6040; lakecountyor.org). Good overnight accommodations can be found in Lakeview by checking with *Lakeview Lodge Motel* (301 North G Street; 541-947-2181; lakeviewlodgeoregon.com) or *Best Western Skyline Motor Lodge* (414 North G Street; 541-947-2194).

If time allows, head east via Highway 140 to see whether the pelican colony is nesting at *Pelican Lake*, about 28 miles east of Lakeview. Turn north at the hamlet of Adel—a restaurant and a gas station are situated here—and proceed on a paved side road for a mile or so. This road continues another 15 miles to the small ranching community of Plush; along the way you might see deer, Canada geese, and sandhill cranes, particularly during the migrations in late fall.

For an alternate and closer route to Plush, head east from Lakeview on Highway 140 for about 15 miles, passing the small *Warner Canyon Ski Area*. The ski area offers fourteen runs, a 730-foot drop in elevation, and both downhill and cross-country skiing. There are marked trails for snowmobiling enthusiasts as well. You'll reach the top of Warner Pass at 5,846 feet, then turn north and drop steeply into picturesque Warner Valley some 19 miles to *Plush*. You'll find one store, *Hart Mountain General Store* (541-947-2491) with groceries, hamburgers, and gas here. This small ranching community on the edge of Hart Lake serves as the gateway to *Hart Mountain National Antelope Refuge* (fws.gov/refuge/hart_mountain). The 275,000-acre federal wildlife refuge was established in 1930, and the mountain was named for the heart-shaped brand of a former cattle ranch located nearby; the word was apparently misspelled. Along its mountain slopes and canyons clothed with groves of aspen, yellow pine, mountain mahogany, and sagebrush flourishes one of the largest herds of pronghorn antelope in the United States. The larger mule deer, with prominent ears, are seen in the area as well.

Note: The numerous all-weather gravel roads found in this region are often bumpy, steep, and one lane wide; always have a full tank of gas, extra water, and food supplies before heading into the hinterlands. Be prepared to change flat tires as well. Diesel fuel is usually available only in the larger cities and gas stations along remote stretches close at dusk. The high desert is unforgiving regardless of the season; days can be hot and dry, nights chilly or freezing.

Thus, well equipped, and hopefully with a four-wheel-drive vehicle, you can try out your natural-history-exploring persona and enjoy a more relaxed pace while carefully negotiating the narrow all-weather road north of Plush, which climbs very steeply for 27 miles to **Hot Springs Campground** (541-947-2731; fws.gov/refuge/hart_mountain) atop 7,710-foot **Hart Mountain**. You'll pass the refuge headquarters at the top and then continue about 5 miles south to the campground, where you can immerse your road-weary body in a natural hot-water spring right next to the sky. The pool is rimmed with a low lava rock wall—and the night sky is jammed with glittering stars. Pitch your tent, walk the short trail to the summit overlook, and watch for eagles, badgers, sage grouse, and bighorn sheep, as well as the antelope and deer that are protected here (they feed in the early morning and at dusk).

The Hart Mountain National Antelope Refuge area is also well known to rock hounds for its agate nodules, fire opal, crystals, and the Oregon state gemstone, sunstones. For gem-hunting locations open to the public, check with the ranger at the refuge headquarters; or pick up maps and obtain directions from the US Fish and Wildlife refuge visitor information center in Lakeview at 18 South G Street (541-947-3315), particularly if you want to go to the sunstone area. If you want to take home a souvenir without doing the digging yourself, jewelry, raw stones, and gems are for sale at the **Hart Mountain General Store**, as well as other shops in the remote region.

Backtracking to Plush, you can connect with US 395 by heading northwest along the hogback for about 31 miles of good all-weather dirt road. In the distance, you'll see **Coyote Hills** and **Abert Rim** rising 2,000 feet above the plateau, filling the western horizon along the edge of Abert Lake. Abert Rim's 800-foot lava cap ends in a sheer precipice. This 30-mile-long scarp is a nearly perfect fault, one of the largest exposed faults in the world. On huge boulders at the base are pictographs drawn by early Native peoples who lived in the region; arrowheads, rock foundations of primitive huts, and bleached bones have also been discovered in the area.

This southeastern region is dotted with beds of lakes formed thousands of years ago. Some lakes evaporated; others found outlets or were clogged by showers of volcanic ash. Some contain water during the brief rainy season; others are always dry; and still others retain only enough moisture to become meadows. You'll see chalky white alkali around many of the lakes' shores, as the lakes shrink during the summer months.

TOP HITS IN SOUTHEASTERN OREGON

Diamond Loop and Malheur Blitzen Valley Auto Tour Route
south of Burns

Fort Rock State Park and Fort Rock Outdoor Homestead Village Museum
Fort Rock

Four Rivers Cultural Center
Ontario

Harney County Historical Society Museum
Burns

Harney County Migratory Bird Festival
Burns

Jean Baptiste Charbonneau Grave
Danner

Keeney Pass Interpretive Site
Vale

Lake Owyhee and Owyhee River
north of Jordan Valley

Malheur National Wildlife Refuge
south of Burns

Rome Columns
toward Jordan Valley

Schminck Memorial Museum
Lakeview

Summer Lake Hot Springs
Paisley

Vale Murals
Vale

Head north on paved US 395, entering Harney County, passing Wagontire, and stopping at **Riley**, a distance of about 60 miles. Here mule deer share the browse with shaggy range bulls that look the size of locomotives. Gas up at Riley before dark or continue east some 25 miles on US 20, stopping in the larger community of Burns to replenish gas and food supplies.

Just east of Riley you can detour at the state rest area and walk the 0.5-mile *Sagehen Hill Nature Trail* to become acquainted with the native shrubs, plants, and bird species of the high-desert region. At 11 self-guided stations, you and the kids can identify big sagebrush (take a small leaf, rub it between your palms, and sniff the wonderful fragrance); bitterbrush, with its dark green leaves and yellow springtime flowers; western juniper, one of the dominant trees, its blue-green berries loved by many bird species; low sagebrush; and Idaho fescue, an important native bunchgrass that grows on the high desert.

Along the trail you may also see dwarf monkeyflower, western yarrow, blue-eyed Mary, owl clover, lupine, and wild parsley. Keep an eye out for red-tailed hawks, golden eagles, turkey vultures, and prairie falcons, as well as sage grouse, mourning doves, mountain bluebirds, and Oregon's state bird, the melodious western meadowlark.

Look toward the west to spot Wagontire Mountain, Squaw Butte, and Glass Buttes. On a clear day, you can see **Steens Mountain** to the south and east; it's composed of hundreds of layers of basalt lava that were thrust more than 1 mile above the plateau about 15 million years ago. Directly south is **Palomino Buttes**, part of a Bureau of Land Management area for wild horses that covers about 96,000 acres. Often bands of wild horses, each numbering from thirty to sixty, are seen along the roads in the area.

One such area, **Palomino Buttes Horse Management Area**, can be accessed about 0.5 mile east of the Sagehen rest area by turning south on the gravel road labeled "Double-O." The wild horses are wary of humans, however, so binoculars and lack of noise may help you to spot them.

By now even the most confirmed city dweller should have relaxed into the quiet strength of the high desert, and the notion of becoming an amateur geologist or naturalist, even for a brief time, will seem appealing. These wide-open spaces also had an appeal for an eclectic mix of early settlers—first trappers and miners, then cowboys, cattle barons, and sheepherders, each, of course, displacing the Native peoples, many of whom were ultimately sent to reservations.

The cattle barons and sheepherders were on less than friendly terms in those early days, and many bloody skirmishes occurred between the two groups until the federal government intervened. Today, nearly 75 percent of the land in southeastern Oregon is managed by the US Bureau of Land Management.

Wildlife and Rangelands

If your visit to the region coincides with the early spring migration, consider taking in the **Harney County Migratory Bird Festival** in Burns (migratory birdfestival.com). Meet bird lovers from all over the Northwest, participate in guided bird-watching walks, see films and slide shows, and hear interesting lectures given by noted waterfowl experts. You can also take in an auction and a western art show. The festival usually takes place in the second weekend of April—for more details see the event website or contact the Harney County Chamber, 484 N. Broadway (541-573-2636; harneycounty.com).

Burns, Hines, and Frenchglen

Burns, in its earliest years, was the capital of the cattle empire—the surrounding areas were ruled by cattle barons like Peter French and Henry Miller—but by 1889 the town amounted to a straggling frontier village of one dusty main street bordered by wood frame shacks. During the next thirty-five years, the settlers waited for the expanding railroad system to reach their town. A colorful throng gathered to see the first train arrive in September 1924—the cattle ranchers wearing Stetsons, the cowboys sporting jingling spurs on their high-heeled boots, and the Paiute Indians attired in their brightly hued native dress.

While exploring Burns, for good eats try *Broadway Deli*, 530 N. Broadway (541-573-7020), open Monday through Friday at 8:30 a.m.; *Bella Java & Bistro*, 314 N. Broadway (541-573-3077), open every day but Sunday for breakfast and lunch; and *Apple Peddler Restaurant*, 529 US 20 (541-573-2820). You could also head south from Burns on Highway 205 for 25 miles and stop at *Narrows RV Park & Restaurant* (541-495-2006 or 800-403-3294; narrowsrvpark.com) for great homemade soups, hamburgers, and buffalo burgers. Ask if the roomy yurt at the park is available for overnight rental.

From here continue south on Highway 205 to reach Harney and Malheur Lakes on the *Malheur National Wildlife Refuge* (fws.gov/refuge/malheur). The refuge is over 180,000 acres in size—some 39 miles wide and 40 miles long—and is home to more than 300 bird species that soar in and out on the Pacific Flyway. Follow the signs east from the Narrows on Sodhouse Lane to the refuge headquarters located on the south shore of Malheur Lake. The headquarters, its visitor center and nature store (541-493-2612) are open Monday through Thursday from 8:00 a.m. to 4:00 p.m. Be sure to ask the staff about current road, water, and weather conditions on the refuge and which bird species are in residence. *Note*: The only gasoline, lodging, and food services south on Highway 205 from Burns are at the Narrows, at Diamond, at Frenchglen, and at Fields (more than 100 miles south), so be sure to gas up and pack water, food, and snacks in Burns before heading onto the wildlife refuge.

While at the refuge headquarters, stop at the *George M. Benson Memorial Museum*, just next door, where you can see more than 200 beautifully mounted specimens of migratory birds that visit the region every year. The museum is open daily from dawn to dusk.

Use the helpful maps provided by the US Fish and Wildlife Service and the US Department of the Interior obtained at refuge headquarters as you explore this magnificent wildlife sanctuary, which received official approval from President Theodore Roosevelt in 1908. The refuge's lakes, ponds, marshes, mudflats, and grain crops are now managed for the benefit of both resident and migratory wildlife. Prior to this intervention, early settlers had engaged in unrestricted hunting of the birds, and plume hunters had nearly wiped out the swans, egrets, herons, and grebes to obtain and sell their elegant feathers to milliners in San Francisco, Chicago, and New York.

Continue south on Highway 205 to **Frenchglen**, journeying on the two-lane paved road that takes you through the heart of the Malheur National Wildlife Refuge, with its 185,000 acres of open water, marshes, irrigated meadows and grainfields, riparian grassy areas, and uplands. You'll first notice bitterbrush, sagebrush, and aromatic western juniper, followed by quaking aspen and mountain mahogany at elevations above 4,000 feet. The autumn colors in this region are outstanding.

About 40 miles south of Malheur and Harney Lakes, continuing on Highway 205 and in the shadow of a commanding 9,670-foot, 60-mile-long fault block known as Steens Mountain, ca. 1870s **Frenchglen Hotel State Heritage Site** (541-493-2825; frenchglenhotel.com) sits like a miniature sentinel reminding visitors of the pioneer past. Built by the early cattle baron Peter French, the hotel is now owned by the state and managed by the Oregon Parks and Recreation Department (oregonstateparks.org). Along with other bird-watchers and photography buffs, you can reserve one of the eight postage stamp-size guest rooms. The evening meal is served family style, accompanied by lively exchanges between guests, who compare fishing exploits, bird-watching areas, wildflower finds, and ghost towns discovered in the area. Next morning the aroma of freshly brewed coffee will lure you downstairs to an enormous breakfast of such delights as blueberry pancakes, eggs, sausage, and fresh seasonal fruit. For information—reservations are a must, especially for meals—call the innkeepers at (541) 493-2825. The hotel is open March 15 through October.

Workshops and Seminars on the Malheur National Wildlife Refuge

When travelers visit the **Malheur National Wildlife Refuge** and arrange to stay at the nearby **Malheur Field Station** campus, they easily move into the slow lane and learn that the pace here is set by the high desert weather and their desire to learn and explore. Check the website, malheurfieldstation.org, to see the current array of workshops offered including those on birding, geology, entomology and butterflies of the Great Basin. You're inspired by the high desert, the wetlands, and multitudes of bird species on the wildlife refuge, and also by the distant mountains. You find the night skies jam-packed with glittering stars. You can spend a few days with friends or with other wilderness seekers in lodgings that are rustic but comfortable. You bring your own bedding and towels. There are no espresso machines or spas here; you can arrange for meals or cook your own grub. This nonprofit education and research center is supported by a number of regional colleges and universities in both Oregon and Washington State. Outdoor classes for students of all ages from all over the region, including programs for folks 55 and older, are held here year-round. For more information and reservations—the latter are a must, especially during spring and autumn bird migration seasons—contact the staff at Malheur Field Station (541-493-2629).

Quiet Evenings in Fields

You'd like to venture even farther off the beaten path on the high desert? It's easy—just head 50 miles south on Highway 205 from Frenchglen to the hamlet of *Fields*, located on the southern edge of the Alvord Desert. Fields Station was established in 1881 as a roadhouse on the stagecoach line between Burns and Winnemucca, Nevada. The old stone roadhouse, now remodeled, houses the *Fields Station Café, Store and Motel* (541-495-2275). The eatery offers breakfast and lunch and is well known for its juicy hamburgers and old-fashioned thick milk shakes. Gasoline is available here, and then not again for miles, so fill the tank if you're running low. Being far off the beaten path, you'll find one lodging here, the small motel and quantities of quiet on the scenic Alvord desert.

If you have a hardy vehicle, preferably with four-wheel drive, and want to take in spectacular vistas way off the beaten path, drive east on the 52-mile *Steens Mountain National Backcountry Byway*, which begins just 3 miles south of Frenchglen. Allow 2 to 3 hours for this panoramic loop drive on an all-weather unpaved road. There are two campgrounds for tent campers on the north section of the loop. *Steens Mountain Wilderness Resort* (541-493-2415; steensmountainresort.com), also on North Loop Road, offers RV hookups, small cabins, a bunkhouse, and tent space. For most of the lodgings here, guests bring their own tents, bedding, food, and supplies.

Check with the Bureau of Land Management visitor information trailer in Frenchglen for current road conditions—don't attempt the one-way gravel road to the top of Steens Mountain in rainy or icy weather. On this route, the steep climb through sagebrush to juniper, through groves of quaking aspen, and into alpine wildflower-strewn meadows is deceivingly gradual. Then you are suddenly next to the sky, at nearly 10,000 feet above the desert floor, and are pulling off at *East Rim Viewpoint* to gaze at ancient glaciated valleys and down at the Alvord Desert, more than a mile below. Keep an eye out for kestrels, golden eagles, bald eagles, prairie falcons, bighorn sheep, and deer during summer months—and black rosy finches at the summit.

If the **Steens Mountain Loop Drive** seems a bit strenuous for your automobile (again, it's best to have a sturdy four-wheel-drive vehicle), consider the easier 26-mile **Diamond Loop**. This loop trek is located about 18 miles north of Frenchglen; follow the signs to the **Blitzen Valley Auto Tour Route** as you depart the Malheur National Wildlife Refuge headquarters, where you can pick up a brochure for this self-guided auto tour. Again, check with the refuge staff about road conditions and directions.

While you're driving the Diamond Loop, stop at **Diamond Craters Outstanding Natural Area** for a self-guided hike through lava cones, ropy lava flows, cinder cones, spatter cones, and other unusual volcanic remnants scattered over several square miles. (**Note**: Drive only on the firmly packed roadway to avoid getting stuck; more than one vehicle has sunk to the hubs in the tephra—decomposing volcanic ash that is found in several areas near the roadway.) If you'd like current regional maps, auto guides, and hiking information before leaving Burns, contact the Harney County Visitors Center, 484 N. Broadway (541-573-2636; harneycounty.com) or the Burns District Bureau of Land Management office, 28910 Highway 20 West, in nearby Hines (541-573-4400; blm.gov/or).

Tips for Successful Bird Watching at the Malheur National Wildlife Refuge

Stay in your vehicle; it makes an excellent observation and photography blind.

Drive slowly and remain on posted roadways; the wildlife and waterfowl will be less frightened and more inclined to remain where they can be observed.

Use binoculars and telephoto lenses; take black-and-white as well as color photos.

Go on your own or join a naturalist-guided tour; get current information from refuge headquarters (541-493-2612). Bring water and beverages, sandwiches for the kids; pack out your own litter.

Enjoy and identify the types of bird talk: gabbles, honks, whistles, twitters, low quacking, rattle-honks.

Encourage the kids to take their own photos, and keep a journal or natural history diary.

Waterfowl Species Galore on the Malheur National Wildlife Refuge

Although the largest concentration of migratory birds usually occurs in March and April, many waterfowl species can be seen throughout the year on the Malheur National Wildlife Refuge including:

Common loons, grebes, swans, and many duck species
Canada geese and osprey
Greater sandhill cranes and great blue herons
White pelicans and trumpeter swans
Long-billed curlews
Great egrets and snowy egrets
Avocets, terns, and white-faced ibis
Browse comprehensive bird lists at fws.gov/malheur.

At the northeast corner of Diamond Loop, you can visit one of the state's oldest, most unusual structures, *Peter French Round Barn State Historic Site*, 51955 Lava Bed Road, Diamond (541-932-4453; oregonstateparks.org), a round barn built more than a hundred years ago by cattle baron Peter French. It was used for breaking horses during winter months. You can also browse in the well-stocked Round Barn Visitor Center (888-493-2420) and gift shop and see the historic *P Ranch* location near Frenchglen.

From 1872, when he arrived with a herd of cattle and several Mexican vaqueros, until 1897, Peter French expanded his holdings and cattle operation to the point where he controlled nearly 200,000 acres, ran some 45,000 head of cattle and more than 3,000 horses, and built a dozen ranches encircling his domain on the west side of Steens Mountain. (Rulers of the enormous areas to the north and east were cattle barons John Devine and Henry Miller.) Historical accounts tell that Peter French and his partner were fatally shot by disgruntled neighboring ranchers on the day after Christmas in 1897.

If you're into interesting old *ghost towns*, the kind that offer weathered structures like schools, stores, dance halls, saloons, and houses, you can snoop about and have fun photographing such places of the past as *Narrows* (1889), *Blitzen* (late 1800s), *Stallard Stage Stop* (from 1906 to 1913), *Ragtown Townsite*, and *Alberson Townsite* (1907). *Andrews* (from 1898 to 1918), once known as Wildhorse, sits on the Alvord Desert at the eastern base of Steens Mountain, and all that's left of this once-popular haven for ranchers and sheepherders is a weathered structure that served as a dance hall; the old saloon stood nearby but it was destroyed by fire in the mid-1990s. Ask for maps and directions to these sites at the Harney County Visitor Center in Burns, 484 N. Broadway (541-573-2636; harneycounty.com).

For another comfortable overnight stay a bit closer to civilization, find the hamlet of *Diamond* located off Highway 205 at the south end of the Diamond Loop Drive. Historic *Hotel Diamond* (541-493-1898; historichoteldiamond .com) offers comfortable places to sit in the cozy common area as well as five comfortable bedrooms on the second floor with baths down the hall. The hostelry does extra duty as general store, deli, and post office for Diamond's 6 or so enthusiastic residents. Hearty dinners are served to hotel guests and to travelers in the hotel's small restaurant (reservations are required). The hotel is open April through October and is located about 50 miles south of Burns. Call well ahead for reservations to ensure that rooms are available.

Kiger Mustangs Roam Free in Oregon's Outback

No other horse in the United States is quite like the striking *Kiger mustang.* Dating to the early 1800s in Oregon, these mustangs show many characteristics of the original Spanish mustangs, which helped to settle the west. A large herd of these now-wild horses roams in the far southeast corner of the Beaver State south of the Burns-Hines area. They can often be spotted in the *Kiger Mustang Viewing Area*, located a few miles east and south of Highway 205. On Bureau of Land Management–managed rangelands in Oregon and in nine other western states, it is estimated that more than 30,000 wild horses and also more than 5,000 wild burros are allowed to roam free in outback sections of these states. Every three to four years, a number of these animals are rounded up by BLM personnel to thin the herds. These animals are offered for adoption as part of the national *Adopt-a-Horse* program. Oregon's Kiger mustang adoption events take place at the *Oregon Wild Horse Corral* facility in the Burns-Hines area (541-473-4400; blm.gov/or). For more information about the nation's wild horses and the Wild Horse & Burro adoption program, see blm.gov/programs/wild-hor se-and-burro/adoptions-and-sales.

The *Harney County Historical Society Museum* in Burns contains many informational displays and vintage photographs that allow a peek into this fascinating Old West section of Oregon. The museum, located in a charming vintage house at 18 West D Street (541-573-5618; hchistoricalsociety.com), is open Tuesday through Saturday, from 8:00 a.m. to 4:00 p.m.

If your travel schedule or the weather prevents a trip from Burns into the Malheur National Wildlife Refuge and Peter French's historic Blitzen Valley, try the shorter *Lower Silvies River Valley Drive*, via Highway 78, just southeast of Burns in the scenic Harney Valley. Here you can see ducks, geese, and sandhill cranes in March and April and avocets, ibis, terns, curlews, and egrets through July.

A scenic overnight option is **Lone Pine Guest Ranch**, located on Lone Pine Road just 3 miles east and north of Burns via US 20. Here the Davis family shares their spectacular view from the lodge on the edge of a wide rim that overlooks Steens Mountain, the Silvies River and Five Mile Dam area, and the Harney Valley—the high desert at your feet. Each suite is fully self-contained with private bath, kitchenette, cozy sitting area, and wide deck. For reservations see lonepineguestranch.com or call (541) 573-7020.

From Burns you can head east on US 20 toward Ontario and the Oregon-Idaho border, west on US 20 toward Bend and central Oregon's high-desert country, north via Highway 395 to John Day, southeast via Highway 78 toward the town of Jordan Valley, or continue south via Highway 78 and US 95 to the Oregon-Nevada border. **Note**: Remember that distances in this remote section of the Beaver State are deceiving and that food and gasoline services are also remote and many hours apart. Always have current state maps, keep track of distances and the time of day, refill your gas tank before heading into the sagebrush and alkali desert country, and arrange well ahead for overnight lodgings (unless you are camping).

Basque Country

At Burns Junction, about 92 miles southeast of Burns, turn east on US 95. After roughly 15 miles, turn north on a gravel-surfaced road just beyond the hamlet of Rome (gas, groceries, and RV campsites here) and opposite the Owyhee Canyon road sign. The intriguing **Rome Columns** can be seen about 3.5 miles down the dusty road. The columns are huge formations of sandstone and fossil-bearing clay from Oregon's prehistoric past that jut some 1,000 feet into the intense blue sky. Surrounded by yellow-blooming sagebrush, the creamy-colored battlements, stained with rich browns and deep reds, overlook the peaceful ranch and farm valley of the nearby Owyhee River.

Eons ago this high-desert area was actually a lush tropical paradise, as evidenced by many species of shell and animal fossils found throughout the layers of ancient riverbeds and lake beds. Those emigrant pioneers who detoured south through this region in the early 1840s carved their names in the soft sandstone; later the area also served as a stage stop.

Just north of the bridge, across the Owyhee River, you could turn right to the Bureau of Land Management guard station, which has a small grassy area, picnic tables, potable water, a restroom, and public boat ramp. The vintage **Rome Station Cafe**, 3605 US 95 (541-586-2295), offers eats, small cabins, RV spaces, gasoline, and conversation with local folks. It's a casual diner in the out-back with not only tumbleweeds blowing about but also the only place to get a few gallons of gasoline, a burger, and a cup of coffee within about 50 miles.

TOP ANNUAL EVENTS IN SOUTHEASTERN OREGON

APRIL
Harney County Migratory Bird Festival
Burns
(541) 573-2636
migratorybirdfestival.com
harneycounty.com

MAY
Jordan Valley Big Loop Rodeo
Jordan Valley
(208) 586-2551
biglooprodeo.com

JULY
Japan Nite Obon Festival
Ontario
(541) 889-8691
4rcc.com

Thunderegg Days
Nyssa
(541) 372-3091

SEPTEMBER
Lake County Fair and Round-up
Lakeview; Labor Day weekend
(541) 417-0476
lakecountyroundup.org

Just 33 miles east of Rome, the pleasant community of *Jordan Valley* sits at a high elevation of 4,389 feet, practically on the Oregon-Idaho border. This small town became the unlikely home of a band of Basque immigrants who, in the 1890s, left their homelands in the French and Spanish Pyrenees Mountains of southern Europe. The Basques, being sheepherders, also brought lambs and ewes to the Jordan Valley. By the turn of the twentieth century—and after countless bloody skirmishes—sheepherding replaced cattle ranching in this far southeastern corner of the Beaver State.

Originally an important way station on a supply line between the mining camps of California and Idaho, Jordan Valley soon became a major sheep-trading center and the home of the Basque settlers and their families. Near the old Jordan Valley Hotel in the center of town, you can see remnants of a hand-hewn stone court where early Basque townspeople played pelota, an energetic game similar to handball. Call ahead to ask about the *Jordan Valley Heritage Museum*, 502 Swisher Avenue (541-586-2100), usually open summer season, Wednesday through Saturday from 12:00 p.m. to 4:00 p.m.

Jordan Valley Cafe (701 Main St.; 541-586-2922) opens daily for breakfast, lunch, legendary marionberry pie, and good java. Don't miss *Rockhouse Coffee* for luscious cinnamon rolls and pastries, legendary huckleberry milkshakes, and tasty coffee drinks. For an overnight stay, try the **Basque Station Motel** (541-586-9244). Check with the City of Jordan Valley (cityofjordanvalley.com) for other lodgings available in the area. **Note**: Call well ahead for accommodations, there are a minimal number of beds available in this remote corner of Oregon. For current information about the annual **Jordan Valley Big Loop Rodeo**, held each May, browse the website biglooprodeo.com.

Western Treasure Valley

From Jordan Valley head north on US 95 about 18 miles, turning onto an all-weather gravel road that angles northwest toward Leslie Gulch–Succor Creek. The rugged road—accessible to all but low-slung automobiles, which won't do so well—drops into a canyon where sandstone cliffs seem to loom higher, as well as hover closer together. Their deep pinks, flamboyant purples, vibrant oranges, and flaming reds splash across the brilliant blue sky, the stark landscape littered here and there with pungent sage and bitterbrush.

Viewing Wildlife in the Owyhee Wild River Area

By visiting where animals hunt, feed, rest, nest, and hide you can almost always find them, but you'll have the best chance if you move very slowly, whether walking or driving. When walking, wear clothing that blends with the surrounding habitat colors. Sunrise and sundown are the best times to watch for wildlife, which is when they most actively look for food and water. The federal lands of the Owyhee Canyon from the dam to the mouth of the canyon have been designated as a Watchable Wildlife Area, part of a national program to foster appreciation of America's wildlife heritage. Bring binoculars and a good field guide.

ANIMAL SPECIES IN THE AREA (YEAR-ROUND)

Wild horses, bighorn sheep, deer, coyote

River otters, long-tailed and short-tailed weasels, mink, beaver

Bobcat, jackrabbit, porcupine, marmot, striped skunk

BIRD SPECIES IN THE AREA (MOST YEAR-ROUND)

Black-crowned night heron, great blue heron, American kestrel (sparrow hawk)

Long-eared owl, great horned owl, common nighthawk, golden eagle

Killdeer, spotted sandpiper, nighthawks, chukar, northern bald eagle (winter visitor)

For wildlife and bird lists, maps, camping, and other information, contact the BLM Vale District Office, 100 Oregon Street (541-473-3144; blm.gov/or).

Miles of dirt roads and trails are available to hikers, backpackers, and off-road vehicles in the **Leslie Gulch** area, managed by the Bureau of Land Management. If you move quietly and carefully, you may see wild horses (mustangs) and bighorn sheep roaming through the canyons, as well as chukars (small partridges) dashing across dusty roadbeds and up steep talus slopes. Look for thunder eggs—oblong rocks, rough on the outside but usually containing beautiful crystal formations on the inside—at nearby **Succor Creek Canyon**, and look for agates along the banks of the Owyhee River. The best time to visit is April through June, although snow is possible in early May. Summers are hot and dry, with temperatures of 90 degrees and above; by late September the nights are frosty. **Note**: Check for ticks after hiking—they can carry Lyme disease.

There are primitive campsites and restrooms at the **Succor Creek State Natural Area**, and at Slocum Creek Campground. For maps and current information, contact the Vale District Office of the Bureau of Land Management, 100 Oregon Street, Vale (541-473-3144).

A better alternative is the campground just south of Owyhee Dam at **Lake Owyhee State Park**, on the shores of Lake Owyhee—about 23 miles from Adrian, off Highway 201 (Adrian is about 20 miles north of Succor Creek State Recreation Area). There are twenty-nine electrical hookups at Lake Owyhee State Park's McCormack Campground and twenty-two at Indian Creek Campground, as well as a public boat ramp. For campground reservations, call the Oregon State Parks reservation center at (800) 452-5687 or visit oregonstate parks.org. **Note**: If you plan a trip into this remote area, be sure to have a full tank of gas, plenty of food and beverages, extra containers of water, sturdy shoes, and camping gear.

Be sure to stop and see the imposing **Owyhee Dam**, located north of the campground. Begun in 1926 and completed in 1932, the dam rises 405 feet from bedrock, is 255-feet thick at its base in the sandstone and basalt canyon, and is 30-feet thick at the top. The structure represents one of the largest and most important irrigation developments in the state, for the Owyhee River waters stored in the large lake behind the dam are used not only for year-round recreation but also to irrigate an extensive area of high desert that would otherwise remain an arid wasteland.

Nyssa, Vale, and Ontario

Near the communities of Nyssa, Vale, and Ontario—located on the Oregon-Idaho border about 25 miles north of Owyhee Dam and Lake Owyhee—you can see evidence of the Owyhee River waters bringing life to lush fields of sugar beets, potatoes, onions, and alfalfa. Notice the tall green poplars and shaggy locust trees around homesteads, then rows of fruit trees gradually giving way to wheat and grazing lands.

In *Nyssa*, a thriving community for the dairy and poultry industries, a large beet-sugar refining plant also produces and ships many tons of sugar each day. Between the three communities of Nyssa, Vale, and Ontario, you can see broad fields of blooming zinnias, bachelor buttons, and other flowers grown for the garden seed market; vegetables are grown here, too. Midsummer is a good time to see the fields of flowers in gorgeous bloom—and you might also smell the pungent, dark-green peppermint plants that cover large fields as well. Pop into *Thunderegg Coffee Co. Café*, 125 Main Street (541-372-3545), for tasty scones, bagels, muffins, and more or *Bob's Steak N' Spirits*, 207 Main Street (541-372-4262), for great breakfasts, tasty lunch, or dinner of premium steaks from the local Double R Ranch.

In the sagebrush-covered rimrock hills above these fields, a number of Basque sheepherders still sing and echo their distinctive native melodies while they and their sheepdogs tend large flocks. Many Mexican-American families also live in the area, as do a large number of Japanese Americans.

The *Four Rivers Cultural Center*, located at 676 SW 5th Avenue in *Ontario* (541-889-8191; 4rcc.com), celebrates the heritage of four rivers important to the vitality and growth of this region: the Malheur, Payette, Owyhee, and Snake. The 10,000-square-foot museum also features a comprehensive look at the variety of cultures that live in the Treasure Valley area. A walk through the museum introduces visitors first to the Paiute Indians, who lived off the land for thousands of years until they were displaced by miners, ranchers, and settlers. Next, you'll learn about the Basques, who came from Spain and started out as sheepherders; many Basque families still live in the area. Then there are the Mexican vaqueros, who brought the western buckaroo tradition to the area; other Hispanic families followed in the 1930s and 1940s.

Perhaps the most poignant story depicted at the museum, however, is that of the Japanese-American families who found new homes on Oregon's far eastern border. Many of these families were released in the early 1940s from World War II internment camps on the West Coast because they were willing to relocate and work on farms in Ontario, Vale, and Nyssa. The beautiful Japanese Garden at the Cultural Center is a memorial to those Japanese Americans interned in the Ontario region during World War II and to the many Japanese Americans who fought for the United States during the war in both the Atlantic and Pacific theaters. After the war many of these families chose to remain here in Ontario. An annual summer event, *Japan Nite Obon Festival*, celebrates the Japanese-American culture, costumes, food, and traditions. The Four Rivers Museum complex also contains a 640-seat performing-arts theater, meeting spaces, cafe, and gift shop. The center is open Monday through Friday from 9:00 a.m. to 5:00 p.m., as well as 10:00 a.m. to 5:00 p.m. Saturday April through October. For information and dates for other annual ethnic festivals and lodgings in the area, contact the Ontario Chamber of Commerce, 251 SW 9th Street, Ontario (541-889-8012; ontariochamber.com). There is also a well-stocked State Welcome Center at the Ontario rest area on I-84 (I-80 North) about 0.5 mile from the Oregon-Idaho border.

For eateries in Ontario try *Casa Jaramillo*, 157 SE 2nd Street (541-889-9258; casajaramillo.com), which opens at 11:30 a.m. for tasty Mexican fare; and *Sorbenots Coffee*, 213 W. Idaho Avenue (541-889-3587), which opens 5:30 a.m. daily for great espresso drinks. *Brewsky's Broiler* (23 SE 1st Street; 541-889-3700) offers great sandwiches, burgers and nachos. For huge breakfasts, diner-style, visit the *Country Kitchen* (1249 Tapadera Avenue; 541-889-3941)

Located in downtown Ontario, *Jolts & Juice Coffee House*, 298 Oregon Street (541-889-4166; jjccoffee.com), is situated in a beautifully restored ca. 1899 bank building on the corner of SW 3rd Avenue and Oregon Street. Settle at a table for java brewed from their fabulous fresh roasted coffee beans, espresso drinks, and coffee-based smoothies made by the barista, and always, luscious freshly baked pastries. At lunchtime you can order tasty sandwiches the size of hubcaps! Jolts & Juice expanded their operations to include Tandem Brewing Co., and now craft beer is part of the appeal, too. Try their brews such as Coffee Porter, Tandem Amber, and Chocolate Peanut Butter Stout. Open Monday through Friday at 6:00 a.m. and weekends at 7:00 a.m.

From nearby Nyssa, located just south of Ontario, travel west and north on Enterprise Avenue, which is actually a section of the Oregon Trail. Stop at the *Keeney Pass Interpretive Site* and look up and down the draw at the deep wagon ruts cut into the soft clay. Here you can also read about some of the hardships experienced. From Amelia Knight's diary entry dated August 5 through 8, 1853, for example, you'll read this: "Just reached Malheur River and campt, the roads have been very dusty, no water, nothing but dust and dead cattle all day."

For the pioneers, the hot mineral springs near *Vale* were a welcome stop for bathing and washing clothes. At the *Malheur Crossing* marker, located between the bridges on the east edge of Vale, notice the deep ruts left by the heavy wagons pulling up the grade after crossing the river. Also, while in town, notice the *Vale Murals*. Painted on buildings throughout the community, the large and colorful murals depict poignant scenes from the Oregon Trail journey. Make a stop at *The Rinehart Stone House* (283 Main St S). Built in 1872, it's one of the oldest buildings in Malheur County and in Eastern Oregon, and periodically open to the public.

The pioneers actually entered what is now Oregon at old Fort Boise—in Idaho, just a few miles east of Nyssa—a fur-trading post established in 1834 by the British Hudson's Bay Company. Here the wagons forded the Snake River, the settlers often having to remove the wheels before the wagons could float across. From Malheur Crossing, where the pioneers enjoyed a welcome soak in the hot springs, the wagon trains continued northwest, met the Snake River again at Farewell Bend, and then made their way northwest toward The Dalles and the most difficult river passage, on the mighty Columbia River, from there downriver to Fort Vancouver.

History buffs can also walk a 1-mile trail to view wagon ruts at the *Oregon Trail Reserve* in nearby Boise, Idaho, or, better yet, head east about 65 miles farther on I-84 to visit the splendid *Oregon Trail History and Education Center* at Three Island Crossing State Park in Glenns Ferry, Idaho (208-366-2394; parksandrecreation.idaho.gov). The state of Idaho boasts a large section of clearly visible ruts carved by thousands of those horse- and oxen-drawn wagons during the 1840s migration from Independence, Missouri, to the Oregon country.

An alternate route, the old *Central Oregon Emigrant Trail*, is followed rather closely by US 20 west from Ontario and Vale, just north of Keeney Pass. In 1845, a wagon train of some 200 pioneers, led by Stephen Meek, first attempted this route. Unfortunately, about seventy members of the group died from hardship and exposure when the wagon train wandered for weeks on the high desert, bewildered by the maze of similar ridges, canyons, and washes. Meek was attempting to find a shortcut to the Willamette Valley. The survivors finally reached the Deschutes River, near Bend, and followed it to the Dalles.

Take US 20 toward Burns for a nostalgic look at more of the wagon ruts, as well as a view of the vast sagebrush desert those first pioneers struggled to cross. Later, between 1864 and 1868, the *Cascade Mountain Military Road* was laid out following the route of the Central Oregon Emigrant Trail. This new road connected with the old Willamette Valley Road, which brought travelers across the central Cascade Mountains to Albany, in the lush central and northern Willamette Valley.

In those days wagon trains, some 0.5-mile long, carried wool and live-stock from the eastern Oregon range country to the Willamette Valley, returning with fruit, vegetables, and other food supplies. Stagecoaches, conveying both mail and passengers, added their own dramatic chapter to the history of the Cascade Mountain Military Road. Every settlement on the route drew all or part of its livelihood from this transportation link. From historians we learn that the first automobile to cross the United States was driven over this route in June 1905.

As you speed along modern US 20 between Ontario, Vale, and Burns, a drive of about 2 hours, note that this same trip took two full days and one night for the stagecoaches to complete. The trip was hot and dusty, with a change of horses taking place every 15 miles. Images of a Roy Rogers or a John Wayne western movie come to mind, with a stagecoach pulled by a team of horses bumping across the sagebrush desert.

About midway between Vale and Burns, you'll pass through *Juntura*, a poplar-shaded village nestled in a small valley where the North Fork of the Malheur River joins the South Fork. Stop to see the lambing sheds near the railroad tracks. This was long a major shipping point for both sheep and cattle; the entire valley and surrounding range country were once dominated by the legendary Henry Miller, one of the powerful cattle barons of the late 1800s.

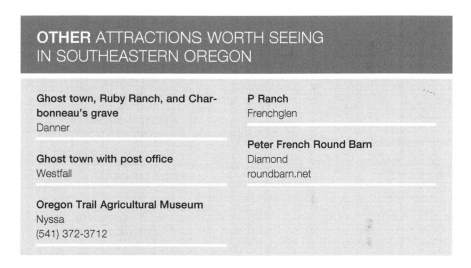

OTHER ATTRACTIONS WORTH SEEING IN SOUTHEASTERN OREGON

Ghost town, Ruby Ranch, and Charbonneau's grave
Danner

Ghost town with post office
Westfall

Oregon Trail Agricultural Museum
Nyssa
(541) 372-3712

P Ranch
Frenchglen

Peter French Round Barn
Diamond
roundbarn.net

You can see a shearing and dipping plant by turning south from Juntura on an all-weather gravel road and then proceeding for about 4 miles, toward the tiny community of Riverside. For camping or a late-afternoon picnic, head north from Juntura to *Beulah Reservoir*. The Bureau of Land Management's *Chukar Park Campground*, situated on the North Fork of the Malheur River, has 18 sites with vault toilets and drinking water available; the county has a primitive campground on the lake as well.

About 4 miles north of the campground is a good area for day hikes at *Castle Rock*, an extinct volcano cone that rises to an elevation of 6,837 feet. For maps and further information about Chukar Park Campground, day hiking, and fall hunting in the area, contact the BLM's Vale District Office (541-473-3144; blm.gov/or).

Tired of camping? Well, not to worry, call the staff at ***Crystal Crane Hot Springs*** near Burns, at 59315 Highway 78 (541-493-2312; cranehotsprings.com). You'll have your choice of lodgings here including cabins, tepees with tubs, and cozy rooms in the Sage Inn, the Cowpoke Inn, and the Ranch House. You could even camp or bring your RV. You'll sink into the soothing mineral waters here, with temperatures of about 102 degrees. The minerals come from an ancient lake bed in the area and include sodium, magnesium, silica, potassium, and iron. Guests have the use of the camp kitchen, which is equipped with a stove, refrigerator, microwave, sink, and dinnerware. Bring your own food and supplies. Coffee and wireless Internet are available in the common area.

Places to Stay in Southeastern Oregon

BURNS-HINES

Best Western Inn
534 US 20 North
(541) 573-5050

Crystal Crane Hot Springs
59315 Highway 78
(541) 493-2312
cranehotsprings.com

Lone Pine Guest Ranch
HC 71-51 Lone Pine Road
(541) 573-7020
lonepineguestranch.com

CHRISTMAS VALLEY

Lakeside Restaurant, Motel & RV Park
87275 Spruce Lane
(541) 576-2309
lakesideterracecv.com

DIAMOND—FRENCHGLEN—FIELDS

Frenchglen Hotel State Heritage Site
Highway 205
Frenchglen
(541) 493-2825
oregon.gov

Hotel Diamond
10 Main Street
Diamond
(541) 493-1898
historichoteldiamond.com

Narrows RV Park & Restaurant
Highway 205 at Sod House Lane
(541) 495-2006
narrowsrvpark.com

LAKEVIEW

Best Western Skyline Motor Lodge
414 North G Street
(541) 947-2194

ONTARIO

Best Western Inn & Suites
251 Goodfellow Street
(541) 889-2600

Super 8 by Wyndham Motel
266 Goodfellow Street
(541) 241-8516

SUMMER LAKE

The Lodge at Summer Lake
53460 Highway 31
(541) 943-3993
lodgeatsummerlake.com

Summer Lake Hot Springs
41777 Highway 31
(541) 943-3931
summerlakehotsprings.com).

Places to Eat in Southeastern Oregon

BURNS

Apple Peddler Restaurant
540 US 20
(541) 573-2820

Bella Java & Bistro
314 N. Broadway
(541) 573-3077

Broadway Deli
530 N. Broadway
(541) 573-7020

Narrows RV Park & Restaurant
33468 Sod House Lane
US 205 South
(541) 495-2006
narrowsrvpark.com

FORT ROCK– CHRISTMAS VALLEY

Lakeside Restaurant, Motel & RV Park
87275 Spruce Lane
Christmas Valley
(541) 576-2510
lakesideterracecv.com

Rockhouse Coffee
(541) 586-2326

LAKEVIEW

Burger Queen Drive In
109 South F Street
(541) 947-3677

Dinner Bell Cafe
930 South F Street
(541) 947-5446

Tall Town Burger & Bakery
1028 N. 4th Street
(541) 947-3521

NYSSA

Bob's Steak N' Spirits
207 Main Street
(541) 372-4262

Thunderegg Coffee Co. Café
125 Main Street
(541) 372-3545

ONTARIO

Casa Jaramillo
157 SE 2nd Street
(541) 889-9258
casajaramillo.com

Jolts & Juice Coffee House
2953 Oregon Street
(541) 889-4166

SILVER LAKE
Cowboy Dinner Tree
50962 E. Bay Road
County Road 4-12 and
Forest Service Road 28
(541) 576-2426
cowboydinnertree.net

HELPFUL TELEPHONE NUMBERS & WEBSITES FOR SOUTHEASTERN OREGON

BLM Campground Information
Bureau of Land Management (BLM)
(541) 573-4400
blm.gov/or/districts/burns

Fremont National Forest
Lakeview Ranger District
18049 Highway 395
(541) 947-3334
fs.usda.gov/fremont-winema

Harney County Visitor Center
Burns
(541) 573-2636
harneycounty.com

Lake County Examiner
(since 1880) published every Wednesday
(541) 947-3378
lakecountyexam.com

Lake County Chamber
126 North E Street
Lakeview
(877) 947-6040
lakecountyor.org

Malheur National Wildlife Refuge
(541) 493-2612
fws.gov/refuge/malheur

Ontario Visitor Center
(888) 889-8012
ontariochamber.com

Oregon Natural Desert Association
50 SW Bond Street, Ste. 4
Bend
(541) 330-2638
onda.org

Central Oregon

Carpeted with pungent sagebrush, juniper, and ponderosa pine, Oregon's central high desert country offers generous amounts of sunshine and miles of wide-open spaces at elevations of 3,000 feet and higher. Where ancient Indian fires once blazed on the shores of volcanic lakes and long-ago hunters left tracks and trails through pine and juniper forests, both Oregonians and out-of-staters now come to fish, hunt, camp, hike, and golf. Climbing high rocks and mountains, spelunking in lava-tube caves, and going Alpine as well as cross-country skiing offer even more adventures. The region's hub, Bend, has become a modern boomtown that draws visitors and new residents from around the globe.

Lava Lands

The high desert region was long populated by the Paiute tribe, and the first non-Native people to venture into central Oregon were hunters who trapped beavers for their lush pelts. Capt. John C. Frémont, a topographic engineer, was sent from the East Coast to map the region in the 1840s, although both Peter

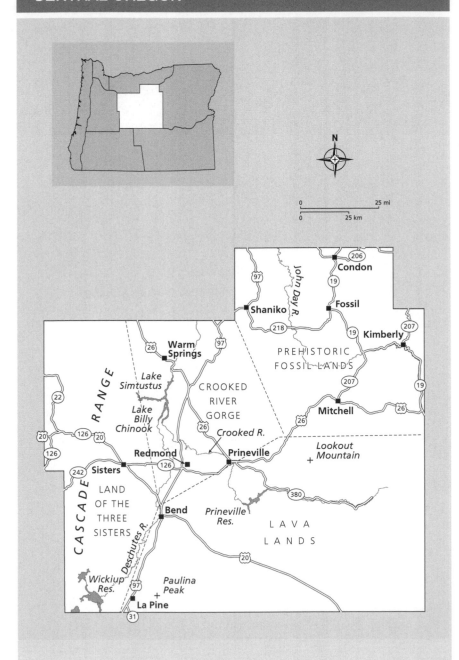

Skene Ogden and Nathaniel Wyeth traveled through the area before Frémont's trek.

Tempted by luxuriant meadows and grasses, the first emigrants to settle in the region raised cattle and sheep, and many ranches still operate in the area. Although Indian chief Paulina and his Paiute tribe fought against white settlement, peace eventually won out. Named for the old chief, the **Paulina Mountains**, rising south of Bend, offer a reminder of an important chapter in the area's colorful history.

Bend and La Pine

To get your bearings when arriving in **Bend**—the largest city and hub of the central Oregon region—start from the downtown area and drive on Greenwood Avenue/US 20 to the top of nearby **Pilot Butte**, at an elevation of more than 4,000 feet. Here you'll have a panoramic view of this sprawling mountain resort community and a dozen gorgeous snowcapped volcanic peaks to the west, in the Cascade Range.

The mountain peaks rise along the western horizon. From north to south, spot Ollalie Butte, Mount Jefferson, Mount Washington, Broken Top, North, Middle and South Sister, and Mount Bachelor. Dusty and tired members of the pioneer wagon trains, as they lumbered across the harsh, unforgiving high desert, would sight on Pilot Butte so as to maintain their bearings after having crossed the Snake River near the present communities of Ontario, Nyssa, and Vale in the eastern section of the state. Today the road to the top of Pilot Butte is paved, and the viewpoint area is wheelchair accessible. A popular trail leads to the summit as well, if you'd rather earn your views on foot.

Sip Along a Brew Tour

In the late 1980s, Deschutes Brewery opened for business in downtown Bend. Since, the town has become a craft brew Mecca, with over thirty breweries spread throughout the Central Oregon region today. The beers are creative and tasty, the brewpubs a variety of interesting destinations in and of themselves. Many also serve terrific food, ranging from traditional pub food to more creative options from vegetarian to gourmet. Grab a Bend Ale Trail guide and passport at the Visit Bend office in downtown Bend to navigate the city's best brews and pubs. Collect stamps on your passport to earn prizes back at Visit Bend (750 NW Lava Road, Suite 160; 877-245-8484; visitbend.com/bend-ale-trail).

Views into the Geological Past from Atop Lava Butte

The road leading up to 500-foot *Lava Butte*, the extinct, reddish brown volcanic cone looming above the visitor center, is steep but paved with red cinder rock, and there's a large parking area at the top. With camera or binoculars in hand, walk the easy self-guided trail around the top of the butte for spectacular views of ancient lava fields to the north and south and of those ever-present stunning mountain peaks.

You're now gazing at a vast area in which folks have lived for more than 9,000 years. The earliest visitors probably came from the Great Basin area of Idaho and Utah to hunt and gather food. About 7,000 years ago the eruptions of Mount Mazama—now Crater Lake, to the south—and nearby Newberry Volcano produced about 200 times the amount of ash, pumice, and debris created by the eruption of Mount Saint Helens in Washington State in 1980. As you continue walking around the rim of Lava Butte, you can also see Paulina Peak and the rim of Newberry Crater. From inside the look-out, peak finders identify mountains even further afield, including Mount Thielsen, the Ochocos and the rim of Crater Lake.

For one of the best introductions to the natural history of this vast, unique region, visit the **High Desert Museum**, just 5 miles south of Bend via US 97 toward Lava Butte. On the 150-acre site, you can investigate a rimrock canyon, a marsh area, meadows, a flowing stream, a prehistoric cave, and other natural habitats for plants, birds, and wildlife native to the high desert. Self-guided interpretive paths shoelace in and around each life zone. Watch mischievous river otters frolic in their indoor-outdoor pool; say hello to porcupines; and peer into the trunk of a ponderosa pine to learn about its growth. Visit a high desert homestead, learn about the effects of fire on the landscape, and watch a live birds of prey show.

Indoors, visitors enjoy a nostalgic dawn-to-dusk walk through eight historic scenes portraying the sights and sounds of the settling of the West with the help of authentic memorabilia. You'll hear desert bird songs, wind and rain, and water rushing through an old mine sluice; you'll see the glow of a blacksmith's fire; and you'll smell the wood and leather in the saddlery. Study contemporary Native American life and artistry, see snakes, fish and owls in the Desertarium, and visit changing exhibits, too.

A Walk on the Deschutes River Trail

Is the weather nice enough for a stroll? You're in the right place. The Deschutes River Trail is over 20 miles of varied pathway, along both sides of the Deschutes River in Bend. Some stretches are dirt, rugged and climbing into gorgeous rimrock canyons. Others are paved and wheelchair and stroller accessible. You can easily walk from downtown Bend to the Old Mill District, with kids and dogs and buggies in tow, in under an hour, passing parks, wildlife, a wave park, and interpretive signs. Grab maps of the trail's various sections from Bend Park and Recreation District at bendparksand rec.org.

The Old Mill District

Upriver from downtown Bend is the site of what were once the two largest lumber mills in the world, Brooks-Scanlon and Shevlin-Hixon. Today the parcel along both sides of the Deschutes River with views of the distant Cascade Range is a bustling commercial district with shops, restaurants, an outdoor concert venue, hotels, and open spaces. The Old Mill District (oldmilldistrict.com) is dotted with interpretive signs revealing the history of the mills and of Bend; three smokestacks remain as iconic towers on the horizon. As a destination, today, the Old Mill District is utterly modern and well worth a visit.

For a schedule of workshops, lectures, traveling exhibits, and special events offered year-round, contact the museum (59800 S. US 97; 541-382-4754; highdesertmuseum.org). The museum is open daily, except major holidays, from 9:00 a.m. to 5:00 p.m. Enjoy, too, browsing in the **Silver Sage Trading Store** and having a snack in the **Rimrock Cafe**.

For another panoramic view of the region, continue south from Bend along US 97 for about 10 miles to **Lava Butte**, stopping first at the Lava Lands Visitor Center (541-593-2421; open daily May to October) at its base for an intriguing look at the region's volcanic past. Colorful, animated displays simulate natural phenomena such as a volcanic eruption and an earthquake. Outdoors you can also walk the **Trail of the Molten Land** or the **Whispering Pines Trail**, both short self-guided tours near the visitor center.

If time allows, continue a few miles south on US 97 and take the 10-mile side trip into **Lava Cast Forest**, winding east through ponderosa pine, bitterbrush, and manzanita on a red cinder gravel road into the high desert hinterlands. Access it from US 97, turning east on the Forest Service Road, just opposite the Sunriver Resort turnoff. Pick up an illustrated guide at the beginning of the paved trail and enjoy twelve descriptive stops along the easy 1-mile route. As you walk the path, notice the characteristic cinnamon-colored bark of the tall ponderosa pine; then, as you reach the sunny, open lava plain, notice the smaller version of the pine, nature's own bonsai, or dwarf, trees.

Though short and stunted—struggling to grow in the volcanic lava, with its rough, jagged, and clinker-like surfaces—the trees may actually be very old, their root systems enlarged to help fight the extreme environment. You'll also see dead trees bleached white by the desert weather, stark skeletons hunched in the black lava. During spring, flowering wild currant and bitterbrush ornament the volcanic landscape with pale pinks and yellows. Look, too, for red Indian paintbrush and rock penstemons blooming in crevices and crannies.

Peer into vertical and horizontal tree casts that about 6,000 years ago were enormous pines engulfed by slow-moving molten lava from **Newberry Volcano**. At station 9 along the trail, you can actually see the source of the lava flow, toward what remains of the mountain, to the southeast. Station 11 offers another grand view of the other snowcapped peaks in the Cascade Mountain Range, to the west.

Although there is no potable water at Lava Cast Forest, there are a couple of picnic tables, as well as an outdoor restroom, in the shade of tall ponderosa pines. You'll also find a few benches along the trail, affording sunny spots for a picnic lunch. Be sure to pack drinking water or canned beverages, especially on warm summer days, when temperatures can climb to the eighties or nineties.

Further information about this geologic phenomenon can be obtained from the Lava Lands Visitor Center (541-593-2421; fs.usda.gov/deschutes). The center is open daily from May to October, and interpretive specialists are on duty.

For a closer look at Newberry Volcano, drive inside of it. Turn east off of Highway 97, just 8 miles south of the Lava Cast Forest and Sunriver Resort turnoffs, and wind about 15 miles up to Paulina and East Lakes. When 9,000-foot Newberry Volcano collapsed in a fiery roar thousands of years ago, a large caldera, 4 to 5 miles across, was formed; it was blocked by further eruptions over the next million or so years, creating two lakes, Paulina and East, rather than the single lake exemplified by, say, Crater Lake to the south.

Both lakes have campgrounds and boat docks, and both offer fishing boats and motors for rent. **East Lake** is known for producing some of the largest trout ever caught in the United States; both German brown and eastern brook trout weighing in at more than 25 pounds have been reeled in here by dedicated anglers. **East Lake Resort** offers rustic accommodations (541-536-2230; eastlakeresort.com), and the lakeside campground for tents here offers great views. At **Paulina Lake**, there is also a rustic lodge and small cabins (pauli nalakelodge.com), as well as rowboats and fishing equipment for rent. Because legal seasons, bag limits, and types of tackle are highly variable, anglers who want to get licenses to fish the many lakes and rivers in central Oregon should obtain current copies of the official regulations from the Oregon Department of Fish and Wildlife located in Bend (541-388-6363; dfw.state.or.us).

Although the first non-Native person to see the two lakes was explorer Peter Skene Ogden, in 1826, he didn't find those wily trout. Fish were introduced into both lakes years later by the state's Fish and Game Department; the fish hatchery is on the Metolius River in Camp Sherman near Sisters and Black Butte. The mountain was named for John Strong Newberry, a physician and noted geologist who, in 1855, accompanied the Williamson expedition to explore possible railroad routes through the central section of the state.

As you bask in the warm sun on the boat dock at Paulina Lake at a level of 6,331 feet, inside Newberry's crater, notice the large peak looming some 2,000 feet higher into the deep blue sky—that's **Paulina Peak**, also named for the Paiute Indian chief. During the summer, drive up to Paulina Peak on the hard-surface gravel road for stupendous views. If you're itching to bring your horse to the high desert, you'll find riding trails here, too, and you can bunk at the nearby **Chief Paulina Horse Camp** (877-444-6777; fs.usda.gov for current information). For a bit more comfortable lodging, you can stay at **Paulina Lake Lodge** (541-536-2240; paulinalakelodge.com), in one of a dozen rustic knotty-pine, housekeeping cabins. The lodge restaurant serves lunch and dinner and a Saturday-night barbecue. The lodge opens in late April for the summer season and December through March for snowmobiling and cross-country skiing.

Before retracing your route back to US 97, detour on the marked Forest Service side road located between the two lakes to see the **Big Obsidian Flow** of glassy black obsidian used by Native peoples to fashion arrowheads and other implements; lovely **Paulina Creek Falls** is close by as well. During winter the main paved road into the lakes is plowed for the first 10 miles to the Sno-Park parking area, allowing for backcountry snowmobiling and cross-country skiing; Sno-Park permits can be purchased in Bend or La Pine. This entire 56,000-acre geologic area has been designated the **Newberry National Volcanic Monument**.

Summer campers, those without horses, can try the campground along East Lake, but if these sites are full, try larger **La Pine State Park** along the Deschutes River just a few miles south and west of US 97, in the La Pine Recreation Area. For campground reservations call the state toll-free number, (800) 452-5687, or check oregonstateparks.org.

While exploring Oregon's high desert country, you and the kids must go spelunking in a lava cave. Many are closed to the public, some are visited by paid tour, but the most accessible is **Lava River Cave**, in **Lava River Cave State Park**, just off US 97 north of Sunriver Resort and Lava Cast Forest. With lantern in hand—lanterns are available for a nominal fee at the park entrance station—and dressed warmly and with sturdy shoes on your feet, proceed toward the cave's yawning entrance. The trail drops over volcanic rocks, bridged by stairs, leading to the floor of the first large, cool chamber. There you might see stalactites and stalagmites of ice, which often don't melt completely until late June or early July.

Negotiate another stairway up to the main tunnel and walk the winding passageway, your lantern reflecting ghostly shadows all along the way. The enormous cave is nearly 60-feet high and 50-feet wide in places, larger than the tunnels beneath New York's Hudson River. Conversations echo from the cave's farthest recesses, as you walk the narrow pathway.

Geologists explain that the great cavernous tunnel, which runs for about 5,000 feet through solid lava, was once the course of a molten lava river. Along the walls are remnants of the lava current—slaggy crusts in some places, rounded and overhanging cornice-like shelves in others—marking the various levels of old volcanic streams. Notice where the walls are coated with a glaze of varying smoothness, while from the ceiling hang "lavacicles," volcanic stalactites formed by dripping lava.

Lava River Cave, located about 12 miles south of Bend, is open seasonally, usually May through September, with varying hours (see fs.usda.gov). Picnic facilities are available in the park, but no drinking water is provided. (**Note**: Temperatures inside the lava caves range from 30 to 45 degrees Fahrenheit, so be sure to dress warmly.)

If you have junior naturalists in your travel party, you could also check on nature programs for youngsters at the **Sunriver Nature Center and Observatory** (541-593-4394; snco.org), located nearby at Sunriver Resort (sunriver -resort.com). Sunriver is also your destination for lodging options of all kinds, from condominiums to lodge rooms to houses big enough for the whole family. Shops, restaurants, bike rentals and more are also found here.

For another spectacle, this one next to the nighttime sky at a brisk altitude of 6,300 feet, head east from Bend via US 20 about 25 miles to **Pine Mountain Observatory** (pmo-sun.uoregon.edu), where you can snoop at the moon, the planets, star clusters, nebulas, and galaxies through a 15-inch research telescope managed by students and instructors from the University of Oregon. In addition to the 15-inch telescope are two other Cassegrain telescopes, with mirrors of 24 and 32 inches, which are used by the staff to collect data on the planets and stars.

To reach the site, just beyond the Millican gas station, turn south off High-way 20 on the all-weather gravel road, take the right fork near the base of the mountain, and wind 9 miles up to the parking area next to the sky. Though the Pine Mountain Observatory is usually open Friday and Saturday, late May through September, with viewing at dusk, visitors are asked always to call ahead—(541) 382-8331—to make arrangements before driving out to the obser-vatory. Stargazers are advised to wear warm clothing, bring flashlights with red bulbs or red coverings (so as not to interfere with the visibility of the stars), and dim their cars' headlights as they approach the parking area.

While exploring Bend, have lunch or dinner at one of the city's oldest eateries, the ca. 1936 *Pine Tavern Restaurant* (541-382-5581; pinetavern.com), overlook-ing Mirror Pond on the Deschutes River near Drake Park. One 125-foot ponderosa pine grows right in the middle of the pondside dining room. A mere 260 years old, the cinnamon-barked tree blends nicely with the room's rustic decor and has been growing through the roof for over eighty years, since the establishment began welcoming diners in 1936. Especially tasty are the warm sourdough scones, similar to Indian fry bread, delicious with honey butter. Located downtown, at 967 NW Brooks Street, the restaurant is open for every day 11:30 a.m. to close.

You'd like a shot of really good espresso? Just next door you can pop into *Looney Bean Coffee House*, 961 NW Brooks Street (541-323-6418; looney bean.com), for your favorite espresso drink along with yummy pastries and good conversation with locals. On the other side of the Pine Tavern is *Bend Brewing Co.* (1019 NW Brooks Street; 541-383-1599; bendbrewing.com), Bend's second-oldest brewery and a delicious destination for beer and pub food, as well as lawn games overlooking the pond in nice weather.

While in the downtown area, stop by the *Deschutes Historical Museum* at 129 NW Idaho Avenue (541-389-1813; deschuteshistory.org) in the ca. 1914 Reid School building, which was placed on the National Register of Historic Places in 1979. Among the fine displays are old farm tools; well-used pioneer crockery; native arrowheads; thunder eggs, Oregon's state rock; and a 530-page chronicle of the region's early history, which was compiled by sifting through old family records and census data. The center is open Tuesday through Satur-day from 10:00 a.m. to 4:30 p.m.

If you have a canoe or kayak, save time for a leisurely paddle with a gaggle of swans, mallards, and Canada geese on *Mirror Pond* at lovely *Drake Park*. You could also contact the staff at Bend Park and Recreation (541-389-7275; bendparksandrec.org) for information about canoeing classes, held during spring, summer, and fall. In the summer, visitors flock to the river to float on tubes and other floatation devices from the Old Mill District to downtown, through the gentle waves of the water park.

TOP HITS IN CENTRAL OREGON

Bend Ale Trail
@BendAleTrail, visitbend.com

Black Butte Ranch
Sisters

Cascade Lakes and Century Drive
(mid-June through Oct or until first
snows), Bend

High Desert Museum
Bend

**John Day Fossil Beds National
Monument**
John Day

Lava Cast Forest
La Pine

The Museum at Warm Springs
Warm Springs

**Newberry National Volcanic
Monument**
La Pine

The Old Mill District
Bend

Pine Tavern Restaurant
Bend

Sunriver Resort
Sunriver

For delicious baked goodies, and for breakfast or lunch, be sure to stop at the ca. 1916 *McKay Cottage Bakery Café*, a charming Craftsman-style bungalow, located at 62910 O. B. Riley Road (541-383-2697; themckaycottage.com) at the north edge of Bend. House specialties include fabulous cinnamon rolls and other delicious pastries plus tasty breakfasts and weekend brunch. You could also have a meal at one of Bend's downtown eateries such as *The Lemon Tree* (718 NW Franklin Avenue; 541-241-5306; lemontreebend.com) renowned for amazing brunches Tuesday through Sunday 8:00 a.m. to 3:00 p.m. and *Joolz* (916 NW Wall St.; 541-388-5094; joolzbend.com) for incredible Middle Eastern food. If you're into delicious waist-bulging breakfasts, head to *Jake's Diner*, 2210 NE Highway 20 near Pilot Butte (541-382-0118; jakesdinerbend.com). Visit *Jackson's Corner* at 845 NW Delaware Avenue (541-647-2198; jacksonscorn erbend.com) for tasty sandwiches, pizzas and pastas in a renovated former corner grocery. At *Big-O-Bagels*, 1032 NW Galveston Street (541-383-2446), try the yummy bacon cheddar breakfast bagel. Located near Drake Park and Mirror Pond is the ca. 1910 *Lara House Bed and Breakfast*, located at 640

NW Congress Street (541-388-4064; larahouse.com). This handsome Craftsman-style home offers six guest rooms that come with private baths. Your morning breakfast is often served in the solarium, which overlooks the landscaped grounds and Drake Park.

For helpful information about the local Bend area, you can contact the Visit Bend Visitors Center at the corner of NW Oregon and Lava Streets, 750 NW Lava Road (877-245-8484; visitbend.com); take the Hawthorne exit off Highway 97 just south of the Highway 20 intersection to the downtown area. You can also obtain information about the larger central Oregon region from the Central Oregon Visitors Association, 57100 Beaver Drive #130 in Sunriver (800-800-8334; visitcentraloregon.com).

Your visit to the high Cascades wouldn't be complete, however, without including the 87-mile *Cascades Lakes Scenic Byway*, which meanders along the same routes traversed by the Native peoples, botanist David Douglas, and explorers like John Frémont, Nathaniel Wyeth, Peter Skene Ogden, and Kit Carson. Designated a National Forest Scenic Byway in 1989, this nearly 100-mile highway loop from Bend south to the Wickiup Reservoir is more commonly called Century Drive by most of the locals. In 1920, the original Indian trails, horse trails, and wagon roads were finally replaced by a main wagon road from Bend to Sparks Lake and the Elk Lake area.

During summer and early fall, before snow season, take the well-paved cinder road to wind your way through ancient lava beds to 6,000-foot *Mount Bachelor* and down through pine forests, skirting more than a dozen alpine lakes—Sparks, Elk, Big Lava, Little Lava, Cultus, Little Cultus, Deer, North Twin, and South Twin—on whose shores are many campgrounds and places from which to fish. Fly-fishing-only waters include Davis and Sparks Lakes and the Fall River. A quiet spot, much loved by serious fly fishers, is *Davis Lake*, at the far south end of Century Drive, beyond Wickiup Reservoir. At *Cultus Lake* and *Little Cultus Lake*, an interesting mixture of ponderosa pine, Douglas fir, white fir, white pine, sugar pine, and spruce grows along the road into the lake area; here, too, are some of the few places along the drive that offer shallow sandy beaches. Cultus Lake allows motorboats and offers some of the best waterskiing and Jet Skiing in the area. Family-friendly *Cultus Lake Resort* (541-408-1560; cultuslakeresort.com) offers cozy cabins, a marina, and a restaurant and is open from May through October; the resort also offers canoe and rowboat rentals.

Fast Facts About Mount Bachelor

- **Elevation:** 5,700 feet at base, 9,065 feet at summit
- **Acres of skiing:** 4,318
- **Vertical drop:** 3,365 feet
- **Number of Alpine ski runs:** 101
- **Maximum Alpine ski-run length:** 1.5 miles
- **Ski season:** Generally November through April
- **Alpine terrain ratings:** 15 percent novice, 25 percent intermediate, 35 percent advanced intermediate, 25 percent expert
- **Chairlifts:** 14, including 8 express chairs
- **Average annual snowfall:** 462 inches; average snow base is 150–200 inches
- **Day lodges:** 6, including Sunrise Lodge, mid-mountain Pine Marten Lodge, and the Cross-Country Lodge
- **Cross-country skiing:** 12 trails with more than 35 miles of machine-groomed tracks
- **Ski report, recorded:** (541) 382-7888 and mtbachelor.com
- **Information and reservations:** Ski school, equipment rental, winter activities, including dogsled rides (800) 829-2442, mtbachelor.com
- **Number of skiers and snowboarders served every season:** 400,000
- **How to beat the crowds:** Plan to stay during the week or on Sunday, ski early or late in the day, avoid holiday weekends and spring break weeks; also, try out other winter activities such as horse-drawn sleigh rides, Alaskan husky dogsled rides (from Sunrise Lodge), tobogganing, inner tubing, snowshoeing (some walks are led by members of the Forest Service), snowmobiling, and ice skating.

There are summer hiking and camping areas at most of the lakes, as well as winter cross-country ski trails along the route; during winter, hardy visitors may enjoy cross-country skiing the 11 miles to *Elk Lake*, where rustic *Elk Lake Resort* (541-480-7378; elklakeresort.net) remains open year-round. *Note*: If you have confirmed reservations for one of the cabins, you can pull in to *Dutchman Flat Sno Park* for the 11-mile ride in SUVs turned snow-cats on Friday afternoons to the resort and back to the Sno Park on Sunday. Bring your own cross-country ski gear, there are no ski rentals at the lodge. The lodge does rent snowshoes. Eat at the small cafe or bring your own food and supplies. Good sources for maps and information are the Ranger District Station in Bend (541-383-5300; fs.usda.gov/deschutes), the Sisters Ranger Station in Sisters (541-549-7700; fs.usda.gov/deschutes), and Visit Bend in Bend (877-245-8484; visitbend.com).

During summer months, visitors can ride one of the Mount Bachelor chairlifts for grand top-of-the-mountain views of more than a dozen snowy peaks, shaggy green forests, and sparkling mountain lakes. It's a stunning panorama. On select nights, the Pine Marten Lodge is open for sunset dinners (mtbachelor.com for information).

Located just west of Elk Lake and directly south of McKenzie Pass, the 247,000-acre *Three Sisters Wilderness* offers more than 250 miles of trails that skirt alpine meadows, sparkling streams, glittering patches of obsidian, ancient lava flows, old craters, and dozens of small lakes, as well as glaciers at higher elevations. About 40 miles of the *Pacific Crest National Scenic Trail* runs through this vast region, which in the late 1950s was set aside as a wilderness. Check with the Sisters Ranger District in Sisters (541-549-7700; fs .usda.gov/deschutes) for current maps and information about backcountry hiking and camping. *Note*: Backcountry hikers need to be prepared for all types of weather and terrain as well as having ample water, food, and good equipment for hiking and camping outdoors. Carry a cell phone if possible, but don't count on a signal at all times. It is always best to hike and camp in a group and to leave your itinerary with family members or friends at home. Do not hike alone into the wilderness areas.

Protected by the National Wilderness Preservation Act of 1964, the Three Sisters Wilderness—along with more than 15 million acres of other land so designated across the United States—permits visitors to travel only by foot or by horse; no vehicles are allowed in the wilderness areas. Oregon has set aside thirteen such wilderness areas, seven of them located from south to north in the Cascade Mountains.

Like the early mountain men of the 1800s, explorers, naturalists, and well-equipped backpackers will often stay out for four or five days at a time in the high country, letting the wilderness saturate every pore. The Three Sisters Wilderness is accessible from mid-July through October for hiking and from November through June for snow camping and cross-country skiing. Snow often reaches depths of 20 feet or more at the higher elevations, and hikers may encounter white patches up to the first week of August.

The Three Sisters

The three mountains—**North Sister**, **Middle Sister**, and **South Sister** (with elevations of 10,085, 10,047, and 10,358 feet, respectively)—are climbed by experienced climbers, with North Sister requiring the most advanced physical preparation and skills, including rock climbing and snow climbing. South Sister is the most accessible, climbable by strong hikers in summer months. Climbers also carry and know how to use ice axes and crampons. All climbers participate in regulation classes before attempting to climb any mountain in the Cascade Range. The USDA Forest Service Sisters Ranger Station (541-549-7700 fs.usda.gov/deschutes) in Sisters administers this area and is open Monday through Friday from 8:00 a.m. to 4:30 p.m.

Most of the high mountain lakes are stocked with eastern brook, rainbow, and cutthroat trout. From many points along the Cascade Lakes Scenic Byway, you can access trails into the Three Sisters Wilderness, walking just a short distance if time doesn't allow an overnight trek with backpacks and tents.

Land of the Three Sisters

Heading west from Bend on US 20, you'll find that the **Three Sisters**—South Sister, Middle Sister, and North Sister—form a stunning mountain backdrop against the deep blue sky of central Oregon as you make your way to Sisters, Black Butte, and the headwaters of the Metolius River.

If you haven't yet had supper, you could stop by the **Tumalo Feed Co. Steakhouse** (541-382-2202; tumalofeedcosteakhouse.com), a Western-themed family restaurant and old-fashioned saloon. The eatery is located at 64619 Highway 20 in Tumalo, about 4 miles northwest of Bend, and is open seven days a week for dinner opening at 4:30 p.m.

Sisters

The community of **Sisters**, transformed into an Old West tourist town with wooden boardwalks and western-style storefronts, is filled with interesting shops, lovely boutiques, and old-fashioned eateries. **Hotel Sisters** is one of the few early structures remaining, now restored as an 1880s-style restaurant and saloon, **Sisters Saloon and Ranch Grill** (541-549-7427; sisterssaloon.net).

In mid-June hang out with cowboys and cowgirls at the **Sisters Rodeo**; contact the rodeo office (541-549-0121; sistersrodeo.com) for current information. **Creekside City Park** (541-323-5220; ci.sisters.or.us) offers tent and RV spaces during summer months; it's close to downtown shops and eateries. For current information about visiting the Sisters area, contact Sisters Visitor Center (541-549-0251; sisterscountry.com) or browse the *Nugget* newspaper (nugget news.com).

Check out several good eateries in Sisters, one longtime favorite, **Depot Cafe** (541-549-2572; sistersdepot.com) in the center of town at 250 W. Cascade Street, which has great sandwiches, soups, and pastries. The deli also serves great breakfasts on weekends. For tasty made-daily pies (especially the marionberry pie), doughnuts, breads, and pastries, stop by **Sisters Bakery** at 251 E. Cascade Avenue (541-549-0361; sistersbakery.com). For great coffee and espresso, in addition to freshly roasted coffee beans, stop by **Sisters Coffee Company**, 273 W. Hood Avenue (541-549-0527; sisterscoffee.com). And just for fun take in a current film at *Sisters Movie House and Movie House Café* (541-549-8800; sistersmoviehouse.com), where you can order meals and beverages and eat in the cafe or have your fare delivered to your theater seat. Right next door to the theater is *Five Pine Lodge* (1021 E. Desperado Trail; 541-549-5900; fivepinelodge.com). This luxurious lodging has an outdoor pool, lodge rooms, and dozens of romantic cabins overlooking the woods and the lovely landscaped grounds. It's a popular place for weddings and events. The greater Five Pine campus is also home to a spa, the *Three Creeks Brewing Company* (541-549-1963; threecreeksbrewing.com), a Mexican restaurant called *Rancho Viejo* (ranchoviejosistersoregon.com) and the *Sisters Athletic Club*.

For comfy lodging on the other end of town, check out *Best Western Ponderosa Lodge* on Main Street (541-549-1234; bestwesternsisters.com). A herd of llamas is often kept in the field next to the hotel, providing visual entertainment for the kids.

TOP ANNUAL EVENTS IN CENTRAL OREGON

JUNE
Sisters Rodeo
Sisters
(541) 549-0121
sistersrodeo.com

JULY
Deschutes County Fair & Rodeo
Redmond

(541) 548-2711
expo.deschutes.org

Sisters Outdoor Quilt Show
Sisters
(541) 549-0989
sistersoutdoorquiltshow.org

The Rain Shadow Effect

The **Cascade Mountains** form an effective weather barrier, with their forested foothills, sparsely clad higher slopes, and snowy volcanic peaks extending down the midsection of the Beaver State and siphoning those heavy rain clouds from the Pacific Ocean to the west. Most of this moisture falls as snow in the high Cascades from November through April, leaving less moisture for the high desert regions east of the mountains. This phenomenon is known as the rain shadow effect and accounts for the fact that the west side or Oregon may get upwards of 80 inches of rain a year, while locations on the eastside of the Cascades may only see 11 inches in the same annum. In the spring, snowmelt gurgles from the mountains into hundreds of lakes, creeks, and streams, tumbling down to larger rivers that find their way nearly 250 miles to the Pacific Ocean, completing the eternal cycle.

If time allows, drive about 5 miles west of Sisters via Highway 20 and turn north another 5 miles to Camp Sherman to see the headwaters of the **Metolius River**, bubbling directly from the lower north slopes of Black Butte. At the **Wizard Falls Fish Hatchery**, a few miles downriver from Camp Sherman, you can see where those wily trout are raised to stock the more than one hundred lakes in the high Cascades. The Metolius is well known to fly fishers for its enormous wild trout, and nearby **Lake Billy Chinook**, behind Round Butte Dam, offers some of the best kokanee—or landlocked salmon—troll fishing in the region. Walk along the 7.3-mile **Metolius River Trail** near Camp Sherman to see native plants and wildflowers thriving in a lush, spring-fed oasis that contrasts with the dry, open forest floor strewn with long pine needles and ponderosa pinecones the size of softballs. Peer over the footbridge at Camp Sherman to spot some of the largest trout you've ever laid eyes on, playing hide-and-seek in the clear waters of the Metolius. Near the bridge is the vintage **Camp Sherman Store & Fly Shop** (541-595-6711; campshermanstore.com) where you can find just about anything, including a small deli and fresh-baked muffins in the morning.

You and the kids would like to sleep outdoors under the fragrant ponderosa pines and near the chortling Metolius River? It's easy, you can pitch your tent or park your RV at the more than a dozen Forest Service campgrounds located nearby. Before departing Sisters, stop by or call the Sisters Ranger Station (at the west edge of town) for maps and information, (541) 549-7700. On busy summer weekends plan to choose your campground and set up your camping spot early in the day. For sleeping indoors close to a crackling fire, try the vintage 1920s-style **Metolius River Lodges** (800-595-6290; metoliusriver lodges.com) for rustic cottages on the banks of the river or the mid-1930s **Lake Creek Lodge** (800-797-6331; lakecreeklodge.com), which has a dozen-plus pine-paneled cabins with fireplaces, restaurant, heated outdoor pool, tennis court, and stocked fishing pond and creek.

If you're looking for a quiet retreat a bit closer to civilization, consider **Black Butte Ranch Resort** (866-901-2961; blackbutteranch.com), located about 8 miles west of Sisters via Highway 20. Nestled on some 1,800 acres of ponderosa pine forest and meadows at the base of 6,436-foot Black Butte—a volcanic cone with a trail to the top offering amazing views—the area was, from the late 1800s to about 1969, a working cattle ranch and stopping-off place for sheep and wool coming from eastern Oregon across the Cascade Mountains to the Willamette Valley. Today you can stroll or bicycle along paths that wend around guest quarters, condominiums, and private vacation residences. If you play golf or tennis, you can choose from two eighteen-hole golf courses and nineteen open-air tennis courts. Or you can paddle a canoe on the small lake just beyond the restaurant and dining room; nestle in front of a friendly fire and watch busy squirrels dash about the ponderosa pines just outside a wide expanse of windows; or curl up for a snooze amid the utter quiet in this peaceful spot. During winter, you can bring Nordic ski gear and enjoy cross-country treks on those flat meadows, which are often covered with snow from November through March.

Bring your tents or a self-contained RV and check out instead the three scenic lakeside campgrounds at **Suttle Lake**—Blue Bay, South Shore, and Link Creek—located about 15 miles west of Sisters via US 20 (check hoodoo.com or call 877-444-6777 for Forest Service campground reservations). Enjoy walking the trail around the lake as well as boating, fishing, sunning, and swimming. **The Suttle Lodge and Boathouse** (541-638-7001; thesuttlelodge.com) offers lodge and cabin accommodations, a cocktail lounge, a restaurant and gear rentals from the dock.

During summer and fall, horse lovers will enjoy visiting the high mountain country on horseback, just as explorers like Lewis and Clark, John Frémont, and Kit Carson did in the early 1800s. The **Metolius-Windigo Trail**, built in the 1970s by horse lovers in cooperation with the Sisters, Bend, and Crescent ranger districts staff, offers a network of riding trails, as well as campsites with corrals. The Metolius-Windigo Trail runs through the spectacular alpine meadow and high backcountry from Sisters toward Elk Lake and then heads south, following Forest Service roads and sections of the Old Skyline Trail, toward Crescent Lake and Windigo Pass, located off Highway 58, about 60 miles south of Bend.

If you're itching to mount a horse and ride into the ponderosas, check with the folks at **Black Butte Stables** at 13892 Bishop's Cap located behind the General Store at **Black Butte Ranch Resort** (541-595-2061; blackbuttestables .com). Half- or full-day rides, and several shorter rides, will take you and the kids over the age of 7 into high pine forests and meadows and offer great views of the snowcapped mountains.

For folks who can bring their own horses, there are a number of high-country campgrounds available with horse facilities along the Windigo Trail, including **Cow Camp Horse Camp** and **Graham Corral Horse Camp**, both at 3,400-foot elevation; **Sheep Springs Horse Camp**, at 3,200-foot elevation; **Whispering Pines Horse Camp**, at 4,400-foot elevation; and **Three Creeks Meadow Horse Camp**, at 6,350-foot elevation. Maps and additional information can be obtained from the Sisters Ranger Station in Sisters (541-549-7700; fs.usda.gov/deschutes).

To try your hand at high-altitude camping without a horse but with suitable camping gear, warm sleeping bags, warm clothing, and plenty of food and beverages, take Forest Service Road 16 south via Elm Street from Sisters for 18 miles to a gem at about 6,000 feet elevation, ***Three Creek Lake Campground***. There is no piped-in water, there are restrictions on boats with motors, and there are only ten campsites in this pretty forest campground. For current information check with the Sisters Ranger District (541-549-7700; fs.usda .gov/deschutes) in Sisters. At this altitude it will be chilly at night and in the early morning, even during the summer months. If season and energy allow, try the amazing hiking trails that begin at Three Creek Lake and climb onto Tam McArthur Rim and the lap of the Cascades. Within just a few miles, you'll be treated to stunning views.

Quilts, Quilt Walks, and Quilter's Affairs

In mid-July, the second Saturday of the month, don't miss the spectacular one-day **Sisters Outdoor Quilt Show** (sistersoutdoorquiltshow.org). It's been a tradition in Sisters since 1975. Folks can also enjoy browsing intriguing hand-designed fabrics, sewing projects, quilts, and quilt designs at **The Stitchin' Post**, located at 311 W. Cascade Avenue (541-549-6061; stitchinpost.com). On the day of the outdoor quilt show, volunteers carefully hang over 1,000 quilts outdoors at shops and other locations all over town starting at 5:30 a.m.! And then, before sunset the same day, all the outdoor quilts are carefully taken down and packed to be returned to their owners. For several days before and after the outdoor show, see lots of quilts displayed on walls inside shops along Cascade Avenue. Arrive early to find parking places close to the downtown area. Also call well ahead for lodgings if you plan to stay overnight in the area.

Crooked River Gorge

About a million years ago, lava spilled into the Crooked River canyon upriver near the community of Terrebonne and flowed nearly to Warm Springs. As you drive though this area, stop at ***Peter Skene Ogden Wayside***, just off US 97. Stand at the low stone wall and peer into a 300-foot-deep rocky chasm where the ***Crooked River***, at its base, is still searching for that old canyon. It is more than an awesome sight. ***Note***: Keep close watch on children here and keep all pets on a leash.

Prineville and Redmond

If time allows, drive into the ***Crooked River Gorge*** via Highway 27 from Prineville to the large ***Prineville Reservoir State Park***—a gorgeous drive into the heart of the gorge and, at its base, the ancient river. There are campgrounds on the lake, which offers fishing throughout the year, including ice fishing in winter. For more information contact the Prineville–Crook County Visitor Center (185 NW 10th St.; 541-447-6304; prinevillechamber.com). And if you're a rock hound, ask about the annual **Thunderegg Days** held during midsummer.

The **Juniper Golf Club** just south of **Redmond**, and not far from the Redmond Airport, welcomes travelers who enjoy the game. Call ahead for a tee time (541-548-3121; playjuniper.com) for either nine or eighteen holes of golf under a vibrant blue sky and with lush green fairways lined with ponderosa pine, pungent juniper (one of the aromatic cedars), and yellow flowering sagebrush. For a complete list of public golf courses, contact the Redmond Visitor Center, 446 SW 7th Street (541-923-5191; visitredmondoregon.com).

While cruising through Redmond pop into **Pig & Pound Public House**, 427 SW 8th Street (541-526-1697); or, **Black Bear Diner**, 429 NW Cedar Avenue (541-548-5969; blackbeardiner.com); **Wild Ride Brewing,** 332 SW 5th Street (541-516-8544; wildridebrew.com); and **Green Plow Coffee Café,** 436 SW 6th Street (541-516-1128).

North of Redmond a few miles is the small community of Terrebonne, home to spectacular **Smith Rock State Park** (541-548-6949; oregonstateparks .org). Take a look at this amazing volcanic formation from the parking lot or hike into the gorge. You'll find shady places to picnic here, as well as an easy, 10-minute trail you can walk down to the meandering Crooked River. Then cross the footbridge for a close encounter with those enormous, almost intimidating vertical rocks that nature has painted in shades of deep red-orange, vibrant browns, and pale creams. The rock climbing at Smith Rock is considered some of the best and most challenging anywhere in the world. Free climbing, the most popular form of rock climbing, allows only the use of the rock's natural features to make upward progress; however, safety ropes are allowed, to stop a fall. You'll notice climbers on the ascent using just their hands and feet to perch on small outcroppings or to clutch narrow crevices as they carefully negotiate a route to the top; the object is to climb a particular section, or route, "free" without using the safety ropes. Be sure to stay a safe distance from the climbers, because loose chunks of rock can dislodge and plummet to the ground. The best picture-snapping view of Smith Rock and the Crooked River, by the way, is from the far end of the parking area, near the turnaround—an absolute showstopper at sunrise or sunset. As you crane your neck upward to watch the men and women scale the steep red-rock inclines, you may hear words of encouragement in more than a dozen languages—from English, French, and Italian to Swedish, German, and Japanese.

After your hike, pop into *The Pump House Bar and Grill* (541-548-4990) or *The Terrebonne Depot* (541-527-4339; terrebonnedepotrestaurant .com), a lovely spot in a former train station that serves pub food, cocktails and craft beer on tap with a view of Smith Rock and the trains that still whizz by several times a day.

For another eighteen holes of golf on your journey north towards Madras, Warm Springs and Mt. Hood, head to *Crooked River Ranch Golf Course, Cabins and RV Park*, north of Redmond and Terrebonne (541-548-8939; crookedriverranch.com). The high desert scenery along the golf course is awesome. See the cozy cabins on the website. Eateries nearby include the *Big Dog Saloon, Sandbagger Saloon*, and the Snack Shack.

Hotshots Rule: Smokejumpers Ready for the Next Call!

Nearly 300 highly trained smokejumpers, often called *Hotshots*, help fight forest fires in remote areas that cannot be accessed by Forest Service roads. The hotshots on duty fly out of Forest Service smokejumper bases located in Redmond, Oregon, as well as in six other similar bases in Idaho, Montana, California, and Washington State. The Bureau of Land Management (BLM) coordinates two additional smokejumper bases, one in Boise, Idaho, and the other in Fairbanks, Alaska. Aircraft used in smokejumper operations include most often turbine engine DC-3s and Twin Otters. There is always a spotter on board who communicates critical information to the pilot and to the jumpers about wind conditions, the forest fire activity below, and the terrain they will face while parachuting and also when they hit the ground. This is not work for the faint-hearted. For more information about this hazardous and arduous work, call and inquire about visiting the *Redmond Smokejumper Base* located at the Forest Service Redmond Air Center, 1740 SE Ochoco Way (541-504-7200), off US 97 just south of downtown Redmond and just beyond the Redmond Airport. You and the kids may get to watch hotshot trainees jump from the practice tower in their full smoke-jumping regalia as well as see how the parachutes and harnesses are repaired, rebuilt, and repacked. Spring and fall are the best times to arrange a visit; the center may be closed to guests if a summer fire emergency occurs.

Stargazing: From Castor and Pollux to Regulus and Orion

In the wide, unpolluted skies of central Oregon, one's view of the heavens—with or without a telescope—is amazing. With the magnification of a telescope lens, the likes of star clusters, nebulae, and galaxies come into view, and the past, present, and future seem to merge in time. But even without the aid of a telescope you can easily see the high desert sky jam-packed with glittery stars—from low on the horizon to far overhead—and the sight is truly awesome. Most of us having lived in the city most of our lives, we don't realize how star-deprived we may be; the lights of most cities prevent one from seeing this marvelous nighttime show. So, your assignment is to get yourself off to the hinterlands of the high desert and to lie down after dark on a pile of sleeping bags, blankets, and pillows. Take the kids, take the grandkids, take the grandparents—everyone deserves to see this glittery spectacle!

Learn about the mysteries of the night sky through these helpful sources:

Mount Hood Community College Planetarium Sky Theater
Gresham
mhcc.edu/planetarium

Oregon Star Party
Offers a mid-August weekend held under the stars in central Oregon for amateur astronomers
oregonstarparty.org

Rose City Astronomers
rosecityastronomers.org
Do-it-yourself star-viewing spots in central Oregon: Haystack Reservoir State Park, the Cove Palisades State Park, Prineville Reservoir State Park, Ochoco State Park (oregonstateparks.org). All are located in the Redmond and Prineville areas north and east of Bend, and all offer tent camping and RV sites.

Located in the heart of the Warm Springs Reservation, with a massive stone entry shaped like a tribal drum and brick walls fretted with a traditional native basket pattern, **The Museum at Warm Springs** (541-553-3331; museum atwarmsprings.org) resonates with the cultural past and present of the three Native American tribes—Wasco, Warm Springs, and Paiute—who live in this spectacular rimrock canyon near the Deschutes River. The museum is one of the premier tribal-owned museums in the United States, and visitors can see one of the most extensive collections of Native American artifacts on a reservation. From late spring through early fall, enjoy living history and dance presentations, storytelling, and craft demonstrations of basketry, beadwork, and drum making. Be sure to stand in the song chamber, where you can hear traditional chanting. Many Indian elders hope that the museum will be an important link to the younger members of the Confederated tribes, teaching them, as well as visitors, about their languages, religions, and cultures. Located just off US 97 in Warm Springs, on Shitake Creek, the museum is open Tuesday through Saturday from 9:00 a.m. to 5:00 p.m.

Prehistoric Fossil Lands

Shaniko, located at the junction *of US 97 from the Bend-Redmond-Madras* area and Highway 218 from the John Day area, was an important shipping point for wheat, wool, and livestock at the turn of the twentieth century. The bustling town at the end of the railroad tracks was filled with grain warehouses, corrals, loading chutes, cowboys, sheepherders, hotels, and saloons. Known as the Wool Capital, the town was named for August Scherneckau, whom the Native Americans called Shaniko and whose ranch house was a station on the old stage route from the Dalles to central Oregon.

Mostly a Ghost Town

Although Shaniko is mostly a ghost town today, a few energetic citizens have worked to breathe new life into the old frontier village. The *Historic Shaniko Hotel*, no longer tired and weather-beaten, was renovated in the mid-1980s (shaniko.com). A wide plank porch once again wraps around both sides of the redbrick hotel, graceful arched windows reflect the morning sun, and oak doors with glass panels open into a lobby that holds one of the original settees and an antique reception desk. The oak banister still winds up to the second floor. The hotel is closed as of this writing, but you can stop by *Goldie's Ice Cream Shoppe* on 4th Street (541-489-3443) for updates and for delicious ice cream; open April to October.

What's there to do in Shaniko? Well, you can mosey over to the gas station and buy a soft drink; capture with a camera or paintbrush the weathered romance of the old school, jail, and city hall or the water tower and the vintage hotel; peer into old buildings and wonder who lived there; or just reflect about the days when Shaniko bustled with cowboys, ponies, sheepherders, sheep, train whistles, and steam locomotives. Check with the friendly folks at the Madras Visitors Center (541-475-2350; madras chamber.com) to ask about the Shaniko Preservation Guild and its efforts to help Shaniko become less of a ghost town.

From Shaniko, continue east on Highway 218, driving into the *John Day Fossil Beds National Monument* area (nps.gov/joda). Stop to see the palisades of the *Clarno Unit*, just east of the John Day River. This unit comprises about 2,000 acres. Not only the leaves but also the limbs, seeds, and nuts of the tropical plants that grew here 40 to 50 million years ago are preserved in the oldest of the Cenozoic era's layers, the Clarno formation, named for Andrew Clarno, an early white settler who homesteaded here in 1866. The formation is a mudflow conglomerate that has been battered by eons of weather; you'll notice the unusual leftovers—eroded pillars, craggy turrets, top-heavy pedestals, natural stone bridges, and deep chasms. Walk up the slope from the picnic area to stand amid these intriguing shapes and notice pungent-smelling sagebrush and junipers dotting the otherwise barren hills where a tropical forest once grew. *Note*: There is no fresh drinking water here. And although the western Pacific rattlesnake usually hides in rock crevices, keep an eye out for them while you're in this area. Be sure to fill your gas tank before leaving Madras.

According to analysis of the bone and plant fossils unearthed here, first by a cavalry officer and then by Thomas Condon, a minister and amateur paleontologist who settled in the Dalles in the 1850s, an ancient lush tropical forest once covered this region. This humid life zone of eons past contained ferns, hydrangeas, and palm, fig, cinnamon, and sequoia trees, together with alligators, primitive rhinoceroses, and tiny horses. As you walk along the interpretive *Trail of the Fossils*, notice the many leaf prints in which every vein and tooth has been preserved in the chalky-colored hardened clays.

When Condon first learned of the area, through specimens brought to the Dalles, he explored it and found other hidden clues to Oregon's past. In 1870, he shipped a collection of fossil teeth to Yale University, and during the next thirty years, many of the world's leading paleontologists came to Oregon to study the John Day Fossil Beds. The three large units in the region, encompassing more than 14,000 acres, were designated a national monument in 1974 and are now under the direction of the National Park Service. The digging and collecting of fossil materials are coordinated by two Park Service paleontologists, and evidence of new species of prehistoric mammals continues to surface as the ancient layers of mud, ash, and rock are washed and blown away by rain and wind each year.

Wheeler County Is Fossil Country

You've had your fill of civilization for a bit? Maybe have the urge to be alone with just your own thoughts? Two excellent choices come to mind: the scenic *John Day River*, which flows through Wheeler County, and the *John Day Fossil Beds National Monument*, all 14,000 acres of it scattered about the 1,713 square miles of one of the state's the state's least-populated counties.

The first time you visit the John Day area, you'll be unprepared for the *Clarno Unit*'s oddly shaped and deeply weathered spires and palisades; the *Sheep Rock Unit*'s bluish green cliffs; and then the low, rounded *Painted Hills*, with their bands of colors that looked like softly running watercolors.

You'll be unprepared for the solitude and peacefulness of the place. The sky goes on forever. You'll notice a soft breeze blowing through the sagebrush and scattering the dry tumbleweeds about. You and the kids often will hear the distinctive call of the *meadowlark* (the Beaver State's bird). Even snapping photos may seem too jarring a noise for this peaceful place, so far off the beaten path. But you'll find the long light of early morning is a wonderful time to shoot photos of the Painted Hills. The warm light of evening is an equally good time to take pictures here. Early spring and fall are good times to visit; summers are normally quite hot and very dusty. Always bring fresh water when you travel in this area. Don't miss this scenic spot, you'll find it not far from Prineville and Mitchell.

If you discover some interesting fossil remains while exploring the area, the park staff encourages reporting their locations so that the findings can be identified and catalogued into the computer.

To visit the *Painted Hills Unit*, 3,000 acres in size, continue on Highway 218 to Fossil, head south past *Shelton Wayside and Campground*—a lovely oasis and good picnic spot—and turn onto Highway 207 toward Mitchell, a total of about 60 miles. Find the turnoff to the Painted Hills just a few miles west, then continue 6 miles north to the viewpoint.

The vast array of cone-shaped hills you'll see here are actually layer upon layer of volcanic ash from those huge mountains, such as Newberry and Mazama, once looming to the south, which collapsed in fiery roars thousands of years ago. Some of the layers of tuff are stained a rich maroon or pink, others are yellow-gold, and still others are black or bronze. The colors are muted by late afternoon's golden light and at sunset turn a deep burgundy. As you gaze on this barren, surrealistic landscape, you'll blink and wonder whether you aren't really looking at a marvelous watercolor or oil painting.

For a closer view of the brilliantly colored bands of tuff, walk along the 0.5-mile trail from the overlook or drive to nearby *Painted Cove Trail*. *Note*: Remember to take plenty of fresh drinking water with you into both the Clarno and the Painted Hills Units.

Later, returning to Mitchell, you might plan a coffee break at *Bridge Creek Cafe* (541-777-7132), located right on US 26. Here friendly conversation is offered along with tasty espresso drinks. The place is open daily from 8:00 a.m. to 4:00 p.m. daily, offering burgers, sandwiches, and absolutely divine homemade pie. *Tiger Town Brewing Co.* (541-462-3663; tigertownbrewing .com) is a newer addition to Mitchell. Fresh craft beers are served alongside chicken wings, sandwiches and more daily.

Continuing east on US 26 about 30 miles, stop at *Picture Gorge* before turning north on Highway 19 for a couple of miles to visit the ca. 1910 *Cant Ranch Historical Museum*. At Picture Gorge, you can easily see the oldest to youngest major formations, all marching across the landscape in orderly layers of mud, ash, and rock—the Picture Gorge Basalt, about 15 million years old; Mascall Formation, about 12 million years old; and the narrow ridge on top, named the Rattlesnake Formation, about 3 million years old. You can easily see where the two oldest formations were tilted southward together and eroded before the Rattlesnake Formation was laid down across them, horizontally.

Located just across Highway 19 from Cant Ranch Historical Museum is the splendid *Thomas Condon Paleontology Center* (541-987-2333; nps.gov/joda), where fossil replicas and actual specimens from the three units are displayed and identified. You can also watch park staff prepare the fossils for exhibiting, and you can ask questions about the specimens you find and report. In the orchard nearby a collection of farm implements from the Cant Ranch is being restored, and in the main ranch house one of the rooms has been set aside to look just as it did some sixty years ago, complete with original furnishings and an arrangement of Cant family photos. Cant Ranch is open sporadically in the summertime only, but the grounds are open to visit year-round. The paleontology center is open daily from 9:00 a.m. to 5:00 p.m. Drinking water is available at Cant Ranch and also at the Foree Deposit area in the nearby *Sheep Rock Unit*; both facilities are also wheelchair accessible. At this unit, which is 9,000 acres in size, you can walk along self-guided nature trails along the base of blue- and green-tinged cliffs.

Additional information and maps are available from the John Day Fossil Beds National Monument, located at 32651 Highway 19 (541-987-2333; nps.gov/joda). Campgrounds in the area include those at Shelton Wayside State Park (oregonstateparks.org); the Clyde Holiday Wayside on US 26 near Mt. Vernon, about 30 miles east of the Paleontology Center; and the primitive camping areas in the Strawberry Mountain Wilderness, south of John Day and Canyon City. Current camping information is also posted in each unit of the park.

OTHER ATTRACTIONS WORTH SEEING IN CENTRAL OREGON

City of Fossil Museum
Fossil

Forest Fire Hot Shots Memorial
Ochoco Creek Park, Prineville

Metolius River Headwaters
Camp Sherman

Deschutes Historical Museum
Bend

Oregon Observatory
Sunriver

Dayville & Fossil

The **Fish House Inn & RV Park** (541-987-2124; fishhouseinn.com) in nearby **Dayville** offers RV spaces, tent sites, a charming 1908 bungalow, and a small cottage that sleeps four. Within walking distance is the John Day River, a city park with a tennis court, a small cafe, **Dayville Café** (541-987-2122), and several country stores. Bring your own food and groceries; there is an outdoor barbecue for use at the inn.

There are a limited number of hotels, motels, and restaurants in Mt. Vernon and Mitchell; more can be found in Prineville or in John Day, the latter about 5 miles east of Mt. Vernon. For current information, contact the Grant County Chamber of Commerce, 301 W. Main Street, John Day (541-575-0547; gcoregonlive.com).

Because you are also in the middle of Oregon's high desert fossil country, and especially if the kids and or grandkids are with you, plan to head west on Highway 19 for about 45 miles to the community of **Fossil** and plan an expedition to the public fossil beds. One such fossil-digging site, open to the public, is found on the exposed bank directly beyond the Fossil High School football field. Here you and the kids will find many species of fossilized plants and trees imprinted in small and large pieces of shale, such as dawn redwood, pine, alder, and maple. It's a wonderful geology lesson for everyone. **Note**: Bring your own container and small shoe boxes for the kids in which they can collect a few fossils. Again, this is a public fossil bed and open to travelers and locals alike. For good eats in Fossil try **Korner Café** on First Street (541-763-3333) and **Service Creek Stage Stop**, 38686 Highway 19 (541-468-3331).

By now, however, you may be hankerin' for a horse-and-cattle ranch experience. There's one to be had, not far from Fossil. At **Wilson Ranches Retreat Bed & Breakfast**, 15809 Butte Creek Road (866-763-2227; wilsonranchesretreat.com), the Wilson family offers seven comfortable rooms in the large renovated bunkhouse. Mornings bring hearty breakfasts served around a big knotty-pine table; expect sausages or bacon, scrambled eggs, and biscuits for guests, family, and the wranglers. You can go hiking, tour in a four-wheel-drive truck, or even saddle up and rent a gentle steed for riding on the ranch trails. Or you could just lean on the fence and watch the process of branding the calves, which happens three times a year.

If you head west from Mitchell toward Prineville and Redmond, completing the western loop into high desert fossil country, plan to picnic or camp at **Ochoco Lake State Park**, just on the western edge of the Ochoco National Forest. Notice the stands of western larch, often called tamarack, a tall graceful conifer with lacy needles that turn bright lime green in the fall. An interesting side trek is the 10-mile drive on a mostly gravel-surfaced Forest Service road to see **Stein's Pillar**. The basalt pillar rises some 250 feet from the forest floor, ancient layers of clay jutting into the deep blue sky. For information about hiking and camping in the area, contact the Ochoco National Forest Ranger District in Prineville, 3160 NE 3rd Street (541-416-6500; fs.usda.gov/ochoco). Access the road to Stein's Pillar just across the highway from the Ochoco Lake State Park turnoff.

For information about other accommodations in the area, contact the Prineville–Crook County Visitor Information Center, located in Prineville at 185 NE 10th Street (541-447-6304; visitprineville.com). You can also continue east from here via US 26 to access Baker City, LaGrande, and the northeastern section of the Beaver State.

Lonerock's Outdoor Post Office

Tucked at the bottom of a deep canyon at the edge of the Blue Mountains, **Lonerock**, population hardly seventy, is framed by tall ponderosa pines and western junipers. Perched on a wood fence, some nineteen mailboxes await circulars, junk mail, and first-class mail. It's said there's room for two more mailboxes should you want to move there—it's 25 miles from Fossil, 34 miles from Heppner, and 22 miles from Condon. If you'd prefer to just stay overnight, there are swell digs at the historic **Hotel Condon** (800-201-6706; hotelcondon.com). Enjoy lunch and espresso at **Darla's Country Flowers Coffee Shop & Deli** (541-384-4120) or **Condon Cafe** (541-384-2244) at Murray's Pharmacy. They're located on Main Street in Condon; you can't get lost.

Places to Stay in Central Oregon

BEND

Lara House Bed and Breakfast
640 NW Congress Avenue
(541) 388-4064
larahouse.com

Mt. Bachelor Village Resort
19717 Mt. Bachelor Drive
(888) 752-2220
mtbachelorvillageqbac

Riverhouse on the Deschutes
3075 N. US 97
(541) 389-3111 or (866) 453-4480
riverhouse.com

Sunriver Resort and Sunriver Lodge
17600 Center Drive
south of Bend via US 97
(800) 547-3922
sunriver-resort.com

DAYVILLE

Fish House Inn & RV Park
US 26
(541) 987-2124
fishhouseinn.com

FOSSIL

Wilson Ranches Retreat Bed & Breakfast
15809 Butte Creek Road
(866) 763-2227
wilsonranchesretreat.com

LA PINE

East Lake Resort
South of Bend via US 97
(541) 536-2230
eastlakeresort.com

MADRAS & CULVER

Cove Palisades State Park
On Lake Billy Chinook near Madras

(800) 452-5687 (state park reservations)
oregonstateparks.org

Panacea at the Canyon
15580 SW FS 5480 Road
(541) 604-6158
panacearesort.com

PRINEVILLE

Rustlers Inn
960 NW Third Street
(541) 447-4185
rustlersinn.com

REDMOND

SCP Hotel Redmond
521 SW 6th Street
(541) 508-7600
scphotel.com

SISTERS

Best Western Ponderosa Lodge
Main Street/Highway 20
(541) 549-1234 or (888) 549-4321
bestwesternsisters.com

Five Pine Lodge
1021 E Desperado Trl.
(541) 549-5900
fivepinelodge.com

Suttle Lake Forest Service Campgrounds
14 miles west of Sisters via US 20
recreation.gov
for Forest Service campground reservations

The Suttle Lodge
13300 US Highway 20
(541) 638-7001
thesuttlelodge.com

Places to Eat in Central Oregon

BEND

Goody's Ice Cream
957 NW Wall Street
(541) 389-5185
goodyschocolates.com/locations

Greg's Grill on Deschutes River
Old Mill District
395 Powerhouse Drive
(541) 382-2200
gregsgrill.com

Jackson's Corner
845 NW Delaware Avenue
(541) 647-2198
jacksonscornerbend.com

Joolz
916 NW Wall Street
(541) 388-5094
joolzbend.com

Pine Tavern Restaurant
967 NW Brooks Street
(541) 382-5581
pinetavern.com

Worthy Brewing
495 NE Bellevue Drive
(541) 639-4776
worthybrewing.com

CONDON

Darla's Country Flowers Coffee Shop & Deli
201 S. Main Street
(541) 384-4120

FOSSIL

Korner Café
First Street
(541) 763-3333

Service Creek Stage Stop
38686 Highway 19
(541) 468-3331

PRINEVILLE

Barney Prine's Steakhouse and Saloon
389 NW 4th Street
(541) 447-3333
barneyprines.com

Friends Espresso
655 NW 3rd Street
(541) 447-4723

Tastee Treet
493 NE 3rd Street
(541) 447-4165

REDMOND

Bogey's Burgers & Ice Cream Parlor
655 NW Greenwood Avenue
(541) 316-1786
bogeysburgers.com

Green Plow Coffee Café
436 SW 6th Street
(541) 516-1128
greenplowcoffee.com

Pig & Pound Public House
423 SW 8th Street
(541) 526-1697

SHANIKO

Goldie's Ice Cream Shoppe
Main Street
(541) 489-3392

SISTERS

Angeline's Bakery & Cafe
121 W. Main Street
(541) 549-9122

Depot Cafe
250 W. Cascade Avenue
(541) 549-2572
sistersdepot.com

Sisters Coffee Company
273 W. Hood Avenue
(541) 549-0527
sisterscoffee.com

Sno Cap Drive-In
380 W. Cascade Avenue
(541) 549-6151

Three Creeks Brew Pub
721 Desperado Ct.
(541) 549-1963
threecreeksbrewing.com

HELPFUL TELEPHONE NUMBERS AND WEBSITES FOR CENTRAL OREGON

Central Oregon Visitor Center
Sunriver
(800) 800-8334
visitcentraloregon.com

John Day Fossil Beds National Monument
(541) 987-2333
nps.gov/joda

Madras Chamber of Commerce
274 SW 4th Street
Madras
(541) 475-2350
madraschamber.com

Mount Bachelor Ski Report
(541) 382-7888
(recorded)
mtbachelor.com

Oregon Natural Desert Association
50 SW Bond Street, Ste. 4
Bend
(541) 330-2638
onda.org

Oregon Road and Mountain Pass Reports
(800) 977-6368 inside Oregon
(503) 588-2941 outside Oregon
tripcheck.com

Oregon State Parks
campgrounds, yurts, houseboats, cabins, tepees and RVs
(800) 551-6949 (general information)
(800) 452-5687 (reservations)
oregonstateparks.org

Oregon State Snowmobile Association
oregonsnow.org

Prineville/Crook County Visitor Information
185 NW 10th
(541) 447-6304
visitprineville.com

Redmond Area Visitor Information
446 SW 7th Street
Redmond
(541) 923-5191
visitredmondoregon.com

Sisters Area Visitor Information
(541) 549-0251
sisterschamber.com
sistersoregonguide.com

USDA Forest Service
Sisters Ranger District Station
(541) 549-7700
fs.usda.gov/deschutes

Visit Bend
750 NW Lava Road
(877) 245-8484
visitbend.com

Northeastern Oregon

The far northeastern section of Oregon includes sizable wheat farms, numerous cattle ranches, and wide-open skies, as well as high mountain vistas, wilderness areas, and a deep gorge in the farthest corner. Prior to reaching Hermiston, Stanfield, and Pendleton via I-84 from the western Columbia Gorge, drivers will notice a distinct climate change. The vegetation turns to sage and bitterbrush and the trees change from dense stands of Douglas fir to Ponderosa pine, yellow pine, and juniper. You'll see brownish hills hunched on the horizon. Then, continuing east from Pendleton the elevation gains over the Blue Mountains as the interstate continues toward LaGrande, Baker City, the Wallowa Mountains, Hells Canyon National Recreation Area, and the Oregon-Idaho border.

Ranch Country

Long before reaching Pendleton via I-84, you'll begin to see western-style hats on the heads of folks in cars and pickups that pass. You most likely won't see new lizard-skin cowboy boots on their feet, however, because well-worn leather ones are the norm here. Extremely well-worn. As in southeastern

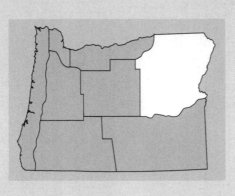

Oregon, travelers find themselves usually above 3,000 feet in elevation, even above 4,000 and 5,000 feet, and, at one viewpoint, a whopping 6,982 feet above sea level.

Pendleton

For a close-up encounter with the not-too-distant past, pause in **Pendleton** to trek back in time to one of the city's unusual historic places, the **Pendleton Underground**. You'll walk through a section of the underground, located beneath the downtown area, where scores of Chinese laborers lived during the early days of this Wild West town. Because of the negative feelings against those of Asian backgrounds, the men rarely came above these dimly lit caverns except to work on the construction of the railroad; even their own businesses and services were located in the tunnels. The 90-minute guided tour starts from the renovated **Shamrock Card Room,** 37 SW Emigrant Street, formerly one of the wild-and-woolly honky-tonks that flourished in the early 1900s. Reservations are required and tours run at intervals between 9:30 a.m. and 4:00 p.m.; call (541) 276-0730 or visit pendletonundergroundtours.org.

Each year the **Pendleton Underground Comes to Life** is held the third weekend in May, with local folks dressing the part and reenacting colorful scenes of a hundred years ago in the now lighted underground tunnels—the Shamrock Card Room, Hop Sing's Laundry, the Empire Ice Cream Parlor, the Empire Meat Market, the Prohibition Card Room, and, upstairs in the nearby old hotel, the Cozy Rooms Bordello. Tickets go like hotcakes so call early (541-276-0730; pendletonundergroudtours.org). Check with the Pendleton Visitor Center, 501 S. Main Street (541-276-7411; pendletonchamber.com), for information about other current tours of the area, which may include vintage barns, ghost towns, and colorful tales about Pendleton's rambunctious early days including gambling, girls, and gold.

Folks have wrapped up in Pendleton blankets since 1909, and you can watch them being woven during tours offered at the ca. 1909 **Pendleton Woolen Mill**, 1307 SE Court Place (541-276-6911; pendleton-usa.com). You can also visit the mill store, where robes, shawls, and blankets are for sale. Mill tours are offered on a first-come basis Monday through Friday, 9:00 and 11:00 a.m. and 1:30 and 3:00 p.m.

You can also visit a well-known saddle-making establishment, **Hamley & Co.**, at 30 SE Court Avenue (541-278-1100; hamleywesternstore.com). Family-owned and creating western gear since 1883, Hamley & Co. underwent a major renovation and expansion to the registered historic site on Court Street. You can watch the saddle makers at work and also browse the well-stocked saddlery and western-wear emporium. Open Monday through Saturday, 10:00 a.m. to

6:00 p.m.; Sunday 10:00 a.m. to 5:00 p.m. Also, on Court Street and within walking distance of the saddlery, *Hamley Steak House & Saloon* features polished handcrafted woodwork and historic artifacts, fine dining for the whole family and also offers the Slick Fork Saloon for large events and the Pendleton Room, Cattle Baron Room, and Wine Cellar for small events. Check the website for upcoming western-style entertainment and musical events, hamleysteakhouse.com.

Although there are plenty of comfortable motels in Pendleton, one terrific option is the splendid Italianate-style *Pendleton House Bed and Breakfast* located at 311 N. Main Street (541-276-8581; pendletonhousebnb.com). Breakfast is served in the grand dining room or by the fireplace and may include such tasty fare as cheese and shallot quiche, Dutch baby (a type of pancake) with rhubarb banana sauce, or Winter Berry French Toast. The inn is located one block from downtown and its many services.

TOP HITS IN NORTHEASTERN OREGON

DeWitt Depot & Sumpter Valley Railway Museum
Prairie City

Frazier Farmstead Museum and Gardens
Milton-Freewater

Geiser Grand Hotel
Baker City

Hells Canyon Mule Days
Enterprise

Hells Canyon National Recreation Area

National Historic Oregon Trail Interpretive Center
Flagstaff Summit near Baker City

Baker Heritage Museum
Baker City

Pendleton Underground Tours
Pendleton

Sumpter Valley Railroad
Sumpter

Union County Museum
Union

Valley Bronze Foundry
Joseph

Wallowa Lake Tramway
Wallowa Lake

The vintage *Working Girls Hotel*, 17 SW Emigrant Avenue, offers a suite with private bath and several comfy rooms with shared bath along with Victorian decor and cozy sitting areas that take you back in time to the late 1800s. It's located near Pendleton's Underground and historic downtown area and not far from the Umatilla River walkway. For another comfortable overnight option, check with the friendly staff at **Rugged Country Lodge Motel**, 1807 SE Court Avenue (541-966-6800; ruggedcountrylodge.com), which feels like an authentic roadside motel from years past.

For eateries in Pendleton, try the 1950s-style **Main Street Diner** at 349 Main Street (541-278-1952) for breakfast and lunch including juicy hamburgers, and **Virgil's at Cimmiyoti's**, 137 S. Main Street (541-276-1350), which offers steak, pasta, and a fine dining atmosphere. **Roosters Country Kitchen** (541-966-1100; roostersdining.com) offers breakfast, lunch, and dinner. Further information about eateries and overnight accommodations can be obtained from the Pendleton Visitor Center (541-276-7411; pendletonchamber.com).

North of Pendleton, the **Frazier Farmstead Museum and Gardens** (541-938-4636; frazierfarmsteadmuseum.org), at 1403 Chestnut Street in Milton-Freewater, seems preserved in time, resembling a slice of small-town America at the turn of the twentieth century. The 6-acre farmstead, with its large ca. 1892 Craftsman-style house, splendid gardens, and outbuildings, is located near downtown Milton-Freewater.

William Samuel Frazier and his wife, Rachel Paulina, bought a 320-acre land claim here, near the Walla Walla River, and built a cabin in 1868. The family, including seven children, had left Texas in the early spring of 1867 in three wagons and arrived in the valley at the base of the Blue Mountains in late autumn of that year. A plain pine secretary desk transported in one of the wagons is one of the prized pieces you can see in the house. When the farmstead was willed to the Milton-Freewater Area Foundation in 1978, to be maintained as a museum, volunteers from the local historical society cataloged more than 700 items and memorabilia, including vintage farm equipment, old photographs, heirloom linens, and family letters from the Civil War. The museum is open April through December; visitors are welcome Thursday through Saturday from 11:00 a.m. to 4:00 p.m. Don't miss the wonderful perennial gardens behind the farmhouse.

If you hanker after a good cup of java or a tasty meal before leaving Milton-Freewater, stop at **Burger Hut**, 5 South Main Street (541-938-6226) for old-fashioned burgers and tasty milkshakes; for good Mexican fare pop into **La Ramada Restaurant**, 6 South Main Street (541-938-3508), for homemade salsa, fajitas, and camarones. Milton-Freewater has an enclave of wineries and vineyards, many of which you can visit. In downtown, try **Watermill Winery** (235 E. Broadway; 541-938-5575; watermillwinery.com), in a former 1940s era fruit-packing plant. **Tero Estates Winery** (52015 Seven Hills Road; 541-203-0020; trwines.com) has a quaint and rustic-tasting room on a historic property just west of town.

It's time to head into the heart of northeast Oregon's ranch country, driving south via US 395 past McKay Creek National Wildlife Refuge, past **Battle Mountain State Park** (where you can camp at a brisk 4,300-foot elevation; oregonstateparks.org; 541-555-6949), and toward Ukiah, Lehman Springs, and the Umatilla National Forest.

Mt. Vernon, John Day, and Canyon City

US 395 connects with US 26 at Mt. Vernon, which then meanders east to the communities of John Day, Canyon City, and Prairie City in the **John Day Valley**, where vast cattle ranches spread to the east and where yellow pine is logged in the Malheur National Forest to the south and north. Native peoples roamed for thousands of years in this region, hunting in the same mountains and fishing the rivers and streams. Many features in the area were named for John Day, the Virginia pioneer, explorer, and trapper who in 1812 traveled through the area with the Overland Expedition of the Pacific Fur Company, on his way to the mouth of the Columbia River and the new fur-trading settlement of Astoria on the Oregon coast. Throughout this region also live mule deer, Rocky Mountain elk, antelope, mountain sheep, and many species of upland game.

At the **Grant County Historical Museum** (grantcountyhistorical museum.org) on South Canyon Boulevard, US 395, in nearby **Canyon City** (you're at an elevation of 3,197 feet here), you'll see a number of vintage horse-drawn vehicles, an old jail from a nearby ghost town—Greenhorn, located just northeast of John Day—and a cabin that reportedly once belonged to poet Joaquin Miller. In its heyday, Canyon City bulged with more than 10,000 miners and gold prospectors; gold was discovered here in 1862 by several miners who were on their way to the goldfields in Idaho. Whiskey Gulch, Canyon Creek, and nearby streams produced several million dollars' worth of gold before the turn of the twentieth century. The museum is open May through September from 9:00 a.m. to 4:30 p.m. Tuesday through Saturday.

Also located nearby at 303 S. Canyon Boulevard., US 395, be sure to stop at the **Oxbow Trade Company** (541-575-2911; oxbowwagonsandcoaches.com) to see a large collection of horse-drawn vehicles along with the building and restoration processes of new and vintage horse-drawn vehicles. From buckboards, buggies, and surreys to carriages, hearses, and chuckwagons, folks get a good look at horse-drawn vehicles from the 1700s and 1800s. The Oxbow website includes a helpful list of links to carriage collections throughout the United States, Canada, and Europe.

From Canyon City you can detour south about 20 miles on US 395 to the small community of **Seneca**. Here you'll find the **Bear Valley Roadhouse**

Restaurant, 209 Barnes Avenue (541-602-2612), which offers prime steaks and juicy burgers. If you like fresh oysters perhaps take in the annual spring *Seneca Oyster Feed* (541-542-2161) mid-May in the city park, which includes a golf tournament and an afternoon softball game.

South of Seneca 6 miles is *The Retreat, Links and Spa at Silvies Valley Ranch* (10000 Rendezvous Ln.; 541-573-5150; silvies.us), a longtime working cattle ranch transformed to boutique eco-retreat. Four award-winning golf courses, luxury accommodations, gourmet food, and a full-service spa are on site. The Dining Room serves huge Western dinners family-style, and Egan's Hideout offers more casual fare as well as to-go lunches. This high-end rural retreat offers log cabins and Ranch House rooms for cozy and quiet nights' sleep on a vast parcel of land under wide-open high desert skies.

Year-round activities in the nearby *Strawberry Mountain* area include hunting, hiking, backcountry camping, fishing on the Malheur River, snowmobiling and cross-country skiing, and spying wildlife such as deer, elk, and antelope. Mountain goats can often be seen up at Strawberry Lake in the Strawberry Mountain Wilderness. For current information on hiking trails, contact Blue Mountain Ranger District, 431 Patterson Bridge Road, John Day (541-575-3000; fs.usda.gov/malheur). Snow lovers can find a good sledding hill, cross-country ski area and snowmobile trails at *Dixie Butte*, located about 12 miles east of Prairie City via US 26 toward Sumpter. Stop by the Grant County Visitor Center, 301 W. Main Street, John Day (541-575-0547; gcoregonlive.com), to pick up current maps and brochures about the area. Ask about the *Strawberry Mountain Scenic Route* and about the *Kam Wah Chung State Heritage Site* (541-575-2800). This unusual small museum, located at 125 NW Canton Street in John Day City Park, is the former home of Chinese herbal doctor Ing Hay, who served Chinese immigrants who worked in the gold mines in the late 1800s. Guided tours of the museum, ten persons per group, start on the hour from 9:00 a.m. until 5:00 p.m., except the noon hour, and allow one to vicariously imagine the distant past—you can smell the aroma of dried herbs and the wood-smoky scent of an evening fire, and even see the black soot on the ceiling of the apothecary where Dr. Hay mixed and brewed his herbs and potions. The site is open May 1 through October 31.

Saddle Up!

The busier modern life gets, the more popular authentic Western ranch retreats become. If you're hankerin' for an out-west experience complete with cowboy or cowgirl boots, fishing gear, great photo ops, well-worn jeans, and a western-style hat, you'll find many options in Oregon to satisfy the urge to get away from it all. Try riding horses, rounding up cattle, photographing a Western-style horse drive, or angling a river for the big ones at these spots, with wide-angle mountain, river, or high desert vistas along with friendly hosts, comfortable guest rooms, and great eats.

Aspen Ridge Resort
Bly
(541) 884-8685
aspenrr.com
travelklamath.com

Big K Guest Ranch
Elkton
(541) 584-2295
big-k.com
visitroseburg.com

Flying M Ranch
Yamhill

(503) 662-3222
flying-m-ranch.com

Long Hollow Ranch
Sisters
(541) 923-1901
lhranch.com

Wilson Ranches Retreat Bed & Breakfast
Fossil
(866) 763-2227
wilsonranchesretreat.com

For good coffee, espresso, and lunch eats in the John Day area, try *Java Jungle*, 142 E. Main Street, John Day (541-575-2224); *Log Cabin Espresso*, 821 W. US 26, John Day (541-575-5778); and *Chuck's Little Diner*, 142 W. Front Street in nearby Prairie City (541-820-4353). For good dinner eateries, check out *Grubsteak Mining Company Bar and Grill* (541-575-2714) on Main Street in John Day, and *The Snaffle Bit Dinner House*, 830 S. Canyon Boulevard (541-575-2426), with a lively western theme, located on US 395 just south of the traffic light in John Day. The town craft brewpub is *1188 Brewing* (141 E Main Street; 541-575-1188), serving microbrews, cider and pub fare.

A few miles east, near the small community of Prairie City, travelers may book a stay at *Riverside School House Bed & Breakfast*, 28076 N. River Road (541-820-4731; riversideschoolhouse.com). Nestled near the headwaters of the John Day River, the structure, an early schoolhouse, dates back to sometime between 1898 and 1905. Guests enjoy a comfortable suite in the renovated schoolhouse that comes with cozy sitting areas and a private bath.

While you're in the Prairie City area, be sure to plan a visit to the *DeWitt Depot & Sumpter Valley Railway Museum* (541-820-3300) located in the historic railroad depot in Depot Park. The museum contains fascinating memorabilia from Grant County's early pioneer days. The depot was the end of the line when the Sumpter Valley Railway was extended from Baker City to Prairie City in 1910. It served as the economic lifeline for logging companies, mining outfits, and families for some fifty years before this section of the rail line was finally closed. Rail buffs and volunteers are in the process of reclaiming a section of the rail line in the Sumpter area. The museum is open Wednesday through Sunday from mid-May to October.

Highway 26 winds north and east over 5,279-foot Dixie Mountain Pass to Austin Junction, continues south toward Unity, and then descends some 50 miles to connect with the Vale-Ontario-Nyssa communities on the Oregon-Idaho border. If you take this route, you could consider detouring at Unity and camping out at *Unity Lake State Park* on the Unity Reservoir. From here you could access Baker City via Highway 245, connecting with Highway 7 between Sumpter and Baker City. If time allows you can pull in at the *Water Hole Café*, 224 Main Street (541-446-3492), in the small community of Unity for enormous hamburgers and other tasty meals, starting daily at 11:00 a.m.

Sumpter

Before continuing to Baker City, detour to *Sumpter* (historicsumpter.com) on Highway 7 for a nostalgic train ride on the *Sumpter Valley Railroad* (541-894-2268; sumptervalleyrailroad.org). Board the train on weekends from May through September at the *Sumpter Valley Dredge State Heritage Area* (541-894-2486; friendsofthedredge.com, historicsumpter.org), then ride behind the puffing, wood-burning 1914 Heisler steam locomotive Stumpdodger for about 8 miles through the scenic pine-, fir-, and tamarack-forested valley etched with piles of dredge tailings. The old train once transported gold ore and logs from the hard-rock mountain mines and pine-dotted Sumpter Valley. During the hour-long ride, watch for geese, herons, beavers, deer, and coyotes, and at occasional special events, be visited by honest-to-goodness train robbers.

A live ghost town, Sumpter is home to about 140 residents, several restaurants, two stores, and a restored ca. 1900 church and offers every year three gigantic flea markets, a winter snowmobile festival, and more than 200 miles of cross-country ski trails. While eating huge ice-cream cones and juicy burgers at *The Log Cabin Restaurant* (541-894-2236) or vittles at *Elkhorn Saloon and Restaurant* (541-894-2244), you just might encounter an old-timer and hear a yarn or two about the 1800s gold rush days and how the town was destroyed by fire in 1917. Snoop into more Sumpter history at the *Sumpter Municipal Museum* on Mill Street (541-894-2253). The folks at the *Historic Sumpter Dredge Interpretive Center* (541-894-2472; historicsumpter.com) can offer more information about the area, including hunting and fishing regulations, and offer a wonderful inventory of books, maps, and souvenirs.

Ghost Towns Galore

Weathered storefronts, sagging porches and partial fences, breezes rattling through rusted hinges and blowing through falling-down rafters and roofs? Ghost locomotives that run on old tracks through the valleys and mountains? Tales of lost ghost locomotives in the thick pine, fir, and larch-tamarack forests in the Sumpter area west of Baker City have circulated for years. Such characters as Skedaddle Smith, One-eyed Dick, and '49 Jimmie reportedly lived in Granite in the old days. Travelers can visit this and other remnants of once-thriving mountain towns of northeastern Oregon's gold country. Maybe you'll spot one of the ghost locomotives along the way.

Check out these ghost town sites:

Whitney: 14 miles southwest of Sumpter in the scenic Whitney Valley
Bourne: 7 miles up Cracker Creek north from Sumpter
Auburn: 10 miles south of Baker City
Flora: north of Joseph and Enterprise via Highway 3
For current information and maps, call the volunteers at Sumpter Valley Railway at (541) 894-2268.

Although you won't find overnight accommodations in any of the abandoned ghost towns in the area, you can find comfortable lodgings in Sumpter at *The Depot Inn*, 179 S. Mill Street (541-894-2522); at *Lazy Moose Cabin* (541-296-1057); and at *Sumpter Bed & Breakfast* at 344 NE. Columbia Street (541-894-0048; sumpterbb.net). Strike up conversations with hikers, bicyclers, history buffs, and, during the winter months, snowmobilers and both downhill and cross-country skiers. *Note*: For road conditions on the major mountain passes in the area, call (800) 977-6368 or go to tripcheck.com. Be prepared to carry traction devices into all highway and byway areas of northeastern Oregon during winter months.

To explore the historic Sumpter area on your own, get a copy of the *Elkhorn Drive Scenic Byway* map, which is packed with helpful information and photographs. This self-guided summertime drive will take you along the 106-mile Sumpter Valley loop, where you can see old mines, abandoned mine shafts, and even a ghost town or two. If you're a ghost town buff, visit the remains of several mining towns along the route. You can pick up the Elkhorn Drive Scenic Byway map from the Wallowa-Whitman Ranger District in Baker City (541-523-6391; fs.usda.gov/wallowa-whitman).

Located about 16 miles northwest of Sumpter via the Elkhorn Drive Scenic Byway, *Granite*, population 250, sits at a crisp elevation of 4,800 feet and offers travelers a jumbo-size log-style inn, *The Lodge at Granite* (541-755-5200). At the handsome 6,200-square-foot structure of 8-inch pine, two-sided cut, with the traditional white chinking, folks can choose from eight pleasant guest rooms on the second floor. A continental breakfast is served to guests.

Also while in the hamlet of Granite, snoop into history and see vintage structures such as the ca. 1888 schoolhouse, J. J. O'Dair general store, and the dance hall that was once home to a saloon and boardinghouse.

Oregon Trail Territory

The settlement of **Baker City** grew up around a mill built in the 1860s by J. W. Virtue to process ore brought from those first hard-rock gold mines. By 1890, the town had grown to nearly 6,700, larger than any city in the eastern section of the state, and a fledgling timber industry had been started by David Eccles, who also was founder of the Sumpter Valley Railroad. When mining declined after World War I, loggers, cattle herders, and ranchers replaced those colorful miners and gold prospectors.

The **Baker City Historic District** includes about sixty-four early buildings, some constructed from volcanic tuff and stone. Also worth a visit is the **Historical Cemetery**, located near the high school. For both attractions, pick up the self-guided walking-tour map at the visitor center on Campbell Street. And plan a visit, too, to the **US National Bank**, at 2000 Main Street, where you'll see a whopping, 80.4-ounce gold nugget that was found in the area during the early gold rush days.

To sleep in sumptuous splendor in Baker City, consider the renovated and refurbished 1889 **Geiser Grand Hotel**, located at 1996 Main Street (541-523-1889; geisergrand.com). Guests choose from thirty suites and guest rooms and enjoy the hotel's historic restaurant and lounge, and, perhaps the loveliest space and fine dining location, the splendid oval mahogany Palm Tea Court with skylight. In the more casual hotel eatery, **1889 Cafe**, you could order such tasty entrees as Buffalo burgers and steamed clams.

Located just a few blocks north of the visitor center, at the corner of Campbell and Grove Streets, is the **Baker Heritage Museum**, 2480 Grove Street (541-523-9308; bakerheritagemuseum.com), featuring a collection of pioneer artifacts gathered from the Old Oregon Trail. Often such prized possessions as trunks, furniture, china, silver, and glassware were left along the Oregon Trail to lighten the wagons. The kids will enjoy the historic gold-mining exhibits, an impressive gem and mineral collection, and regional Native American baskets, arrowheads, tools, and clothing. Be sure to look for the vintage freight wagon, the old school bus, the large sleigh, and a number of vintage autos and trucks, all stored in a cavernous space to the rear of the building. Each one has a story to tell. The museum is open daily from 9:00 a.m. to 4:00 p.m. mid-March to October.

For cozy lodgings in Baker City, check with **Blue Door Inn**, 2324 1st Street (541-801-7962; bakercitybluedoorinn.com), and with **Crown Courtyard Inn**, 1784 Broadway (541-519-8523). For fresh roasted coffee and pleasant eateries in the Baker City area, stop at **Sorbenots Coffee**, 1270 Campbell Street (541-523-1678), for fresh baked goods and tasty lattes blended by friendly baristas, or **Sweet Wife Baking**, 2080 Resort Street (541-5403-6028), in the quaint old town area for fare such as warm bread pudding, breakfast pizza, and sweet and savory scones. Other favorites in Baker City include **Lone Pine Café**, 1825 Main Street (541-523-1805), with tasty Reubens and delicious Benedicts along with gourmet soups and fresh breads. Also pop into the much-loved **Barley Brown's Brewpub**, 2190 Main Street (541-523-4266; barleybrowns.com), which offers fish and chips, juicy burgers, pasta dishes, and their exceptional and award-winning brews and ales. Then make room for the large portions of fresh ice cream at **Charlie's Deli & Ice Cream Parlor**, 2101 Main Street (541-524-9307), on your way out of town.

From Baker City detour about 5 miles east on Highway 86 to Flagstaff Summit to visit the impressive **National Historic Oregon Trail Interpretive Center** (22267 Highway 86; 541-523-1843; blm.gov/or/oregontrail). This panoramic site overlooks miles of the original wagon trail ruts that have, over the last century and a half since the 1840s and 1850s, receded into the sagebrush- and bitterbrush-littered landscape. Now the ruts are just dim outlines, reminders of the pioneer past, and eyes squint to follow the old trail across the wide desert toward the Blue Mountains, a low, snow-dusted range that hovers on the far northwestern horizon.

In the main gallery of the 23,000-square-foot center, more than 300 photographs, drawings, paintings, and maps depict the toil, sweat, and hardships of the 2,000-mile journey from Independence, Missouri, to Fort Vancouver, Oregon City, and the lush Willamette Valley located south of the Portland area. The interpretive center is open daily April through October from 9:00 a.m. to 6:00 p.m., November through March from 9:00 a.m. to 4:00 p.m. **Note**: Bring wide-brimmed hats and water if you want to walk the nature trails here—summers are hot and dry, with temperatures often reaching 90 to 100 degrees Fahrenheit.

Hells Canyon and the High Wallowas

While the Oregon Trail left the Snake River at Farewell Bend, southeast of Baker City toward Ontario, and continued northwest into Baker Valley and over the Blue Mountains toward the Dalles, the ancient river headed directly north, chiseling and sculpting **Hells Canyon**—a spectacular 6,000-foot-deep fissure between high craggy mountains. To experience this awesome chunk of geography that separates Oregon and Idaho and is the deepest river gorge in the world, head east to Halfway via Highway 86 from Flagstaff Summit.

Included in this vast region are the 108,000-acre **Hells Canyon Wilderness**, the 662,000-acre **Hells Canyon National Recreation Area**, and the **Wild and Scenic Snake River Corridor**. Visit the canyon during spring or early autumn, when native shrubs, trees, and flowers are at their best; summers are quite hot and dry. If possible, take one of the float or jet-boat trips on the river or, if you're in good shape, a guided backpack or horseback trip into the wilderness areas. For helpful information, contact the USDA Forest Service Wallowa Mountain Visitor Center in Enterprise (541-426-5546; fs.usda.gov/wallowa-whitman) and the Wallowa County Visitor Center (309 S. River Street, Enterprise; 541-426-4622; wallowacountychamber.com), which has an excellent list of resources for adventuring in the Hells Canyon National Recreation area.

Try lovely **Hewitt Park** and the 50-mile **Brownlee Reservoir** for picnicking, fishing, and camping on the waters of the Snake River behind Brownlee Dam, just south of Halfway.

Refill your picnic basket and cooler in Baker City, gas up, and take the narrow route, Hells Canyon Dam Road, that winds to the small community of Halfway and also from Oxbow Dam along a narrow and winding 23-mile scenic stretch of the Snake River down to **Hells Canyon Dam** spillway and one of the jet-boat launch areas. There is a portable restroom here and a visitor information trailer, but no other services. In late spring, you'll see masses of yellow lupine, yellow and gold daisies, and pink wild roses blooming among crevices in the craggy basalt bluffs and outcroppings that hover over the narrow roadway. It's well worth the 46-mile round-trip to experience this primitive but accessible section of the Hells Canyon National Recreation Area (541-426-5546; fs.usda.gov/wallowa-whitman).

Halfway, North Powder, and Union

You could enjoy your picnic at the boat-launch site or return to **Hells Canyon Park**, located about halfway back to Highway 86. The park offers picnic areas, comfortable grassy places to sit, and a boat launch, all next to the river. Overnight campsites are available at **Copperfield Park**, located on this scenic drive about 17 miles from Halfway. If you'd like to linger overnight nearby, check out comfortable bed-and-breakfast inns in the Halfway area. **The Inn at Clear Creek Farm**, 48212 Clear Creek Road (541-742-2238; clearcreekinn.com), is an especially good choice for couples and for nature lovers. **Pine Valley Lodge** offers funky and fun bed-and-breakfast accommodations in downtown

Halfway, 163 N. Main Street (541-742-2027; pvlodge.com). For casual eats in Halfway, pop into *Wild Bill's Café & Bar* on Main Street (541-742-5833).

From Halfway you can head back to Baker City via Highway 86 and then turn north from there toward La Grande. Take old US 30 instead of I-84 and detour at *Haines* to eat at a well-known restaurant and a favorite with locals, the Old West-style *Haines Steak House* (541-856-3639; hainessteakhouse.com). After loading up at the Chuck Wagon salad bar, you'll work your way through a bowl of hearty soup, Western-style baked beans, and a delicious charcoal-grilled steak fresh off the rangelands. The restaurant, open for dinner daily except Tuesday, is on old US 30, Front Street, in Haines, about 10 miles north of Baker City.

If you pass through this region of the Beaver State in mid-spring—say, late May—continue from Haines on Highway 237, bypassing I-84 for a while longer, and drive slowly through the small community of *Union*. Pause here to feast your eyes on a number of enormous lilac trees in full, glorious bloom. Many of the original cuttings were brought across the Oregon Trail in the 1840s. Also look for patches of wild iris that bloom profusely in pastures and fields between North Powder and Union.

During the winter months, you can see some 200 head of Rocky Mountain elk at the winter feeding area; take the North Powder exit 285 off I-84 and go west to the *Elkhorn Wildlife Area* (541-898-2826; myodfw.com). Rocky Mountain elk and mule deer gather at this feeding site December to March. For amazing lumberjack eats in the small community of North Powder, pop into *North Powder Café* on Second Street (541-898-2868), where locals, truckers, and travelers gather. In Union, visit the *Union County Museum* (333 S. Main Street; 541-562-6003; ucmuseumoregon.org), in a structure built in 1881. Besides showing the evolution of the cowboy myth, from nineteenth-century dime novels to 1940s B movies, you'll see boots, spurs, saddles, and hand-braided ropes galore. The exhibit also spotlights early Texas trail drives, railhead towns such as Abilene and Dodge City, and flinty-eyed frontier marshals. The exhibit is open Monday through Saturday from 10:00 a.m. to 4:00 p.m., and Sunday 1:00 p.m. to 4:00 p.m.

Travelers will find pleasant overnight lodgings at the renovated ca. 1921 *Union Hotel*, 326 N. Main Street (541-562-1200; thehistoricunionhotel.com). Guest rooms come with names like Annie Oakley Room, Clark Gable Room, and Mount Emily Room. The seventy-six-room hostelry was completely renovated in the 1990s, including stripping old paint, repainting, carpeting, and decorating the lobby, ladies' parlor, restaurant, and guest rooms. Some forty Main Street properties, including the hotel, have been included in the city's new Historic District.

TOP ANNUAL EVENTS IN NORTHEASTERN OREGON

MAY
Pendleton Underground Comes to Life
Pendleton
(541) 276-0730
pendletonundergroundtours.org

JUNE
Wallowa Valley Festival of the Arts
Joseph
(541) 426-4622
wallowacountychamber.com

AUGUST
Bronze, Blues, and Brews
Joseph City Park

(541) 426-4622
wallowacountychamber.com

SEPTEMBER
Pendleton Round-Up/Happy Canyon Pageant
Pendleton
(800) 547-6336
pendletonroundup.com

Hells Canyon Mule Days
Enterprise
(541) 426-8271
hellscanyonmuledays.com

La Grande, Enterprise, and Joseph

In *La Grande*, just a few miles northwest of Union via Highway 203, you could enjoy eateries such as *Mamacita's Café*, for tasty hamburgers, shrimp pasta, steak sandwiches, and luscious desserts (2003 4th Street; 541-963-6223); and *Ten Depot Street*, for casual fine dining in a historic brick building with an early 1900s bar; try the prime rib and tenderloin or grass-fed lamb (541-963-8766; tendepotstreet.com). For breakfast eats try *Joe & Sugars Café*, 1119 Adams Street (541-975-5282), for loaded omelets, warm bagels with cream cheese, veggie quiche, or awesome breakfast burritos; top this off with tasty cappuccinos or lattes. While out and about La Grande, stop to see a number of vintage fire engines at the *Eastern Oregon Fire Museum & Learning Center* (541-963-8589), located at 102 Elm Street in the historic former fire station.

An Inn with a View Near a Ghost Town

Take Highway 3 north from Enterprise about 35 miles and follow the signs to *Rim-Rock Inn* (83471 Lewiston Highway; 541-828-7769; rimrockinnor.com), open to outside guests for dinner on Friday and Saturday nights with advanced reservations. Guests of the inn enjoy dinner as well as a full breakfast in the morning. Enjoy your meal on the outdoor deck with panoramic high desert views of Joseph Creek Canyon.

Stay in the suite in the inn, ask about camping in one of the cozy tepees overlooking the canyon or, better yet, book the entire inn for a special event.

North on Highway 3 less than a mile is the ghost town of **Flora**, population less than twenty. Park your vehicle, grab the camera, and wander Flora's two streets housing a number of gray and weathered structures preserved by the high desert sun. Vines scramble out windows and doors, the fragrant aroma of sagebrush fills the air, and soft breezes rattle doors hanging by rusted hinges. It's a favorite of both photographers and artists, and a number of folks are working to bring the small hamlet back to life.

The Landing Hotel (1501 Adams Avenue; 541-663-1501; ladgrandelanding hotel.com) is La Grande's boutique hotel and restaurant option, a 1900-era home renovated in 2017 to a chic destination. Before you settle in for the night, refuel at *Side A Brewing* for locally sourced meals and tasty pints of ales and lagers.

Next, drive from La Grande about 65 miles via scenic Highway 82 to *Enterprise*, Joseph, and Wallowa Lake to treat yourself to a ride on the *Wallowa Lake Tramway* (541-432-5331, summer, and 503-781-4321, winter; wallowalaketramway.com). Snug with three other mountain lovers in a small gondola, you'll ascend safely in 15 minutes about 3,800 feet to the top of 8,200-foot *Mount Howard* for some of the most breathtaking views in the entire region. More than a mile below, Wallowa Lake shimmers in the afternoon sun, reaching into the Eagle Cap Wilderness and mirroring eight other snowcapped peaks. To the east lie the rugged canyons of the Imnaha and Snake Rivers. As one soaks in the alpine vastness of it all, it's easy to understand why Chief Joseph and his Nez Percé tribe fought to remain in this beautiful region in the mid-1800s when the first white settlers began to encroach on their territory. At the top of the tramway are short trails for hiking and enjoying more wide-angle views. Also, at the top check out *Summit Grill & Alpine Patio* (541-432-5331) for lunch before you ride the gondola back down the mountain. Call ahead for the current schedule, although the tram is generally open daily from June through August and part-time in May and September.

Rather than hanging in the clouds in a gondola you'd prefer being closer to terra firma? Not to worry—call the *Eagle Cap Excursion Train* and ask about current schedules for scenic train rides departing from Elgin and traveling through the pines from Elgin to Minam or Wallowa along the Minam River (call 800-323-7330 for reservations; see various schedules and events at eaglecap trainrides.com) during spring, summer, and fall.

The **Wallowa Lake** area, 6 miles from Joseph, opens for the summer season on Memorial Day weekend; winter visits offer miles of cross-country ski trails through a snowy wonderland. If the notion of packing your tent and camping beneath tall alpine fir at the edge of a mountain lake during summer and early fall sounds inviting, consider making a reservation at the **Wallowa State Park** campground; call the state reservation number (800-452-5687; oregonstateparks.org) at least six months ahead, because everyone else likes to go off the beaten path here as well.

Or you can make reservations at **Historic Wallowa Lake Lodge** (541-432-9821; wallowalake.com), perched at the south end of the lake since 1923 and totally renovated. In addition to twenty-two rooms in the lodge, the eight cozy cabins with kitchens and fireplaces are also available year-round. In the lodge dining room, you can sit at a table overlooking the lake and enjoy delicious entrees from Northwest farms, fields, and streams. The lodge and restaurant are open from late May until late September.

For a pleasant overnight bed-and-breakfast experience, about as far off the beaten path as you can get in the Beaver State, seek out **Imnaha River Inn Bed & Breakfast** (541-577-6002; imnahariverinn.com) to see about rooms in a 7,000-square-foot log home near the Imnaha River and the hamlet of Imnaha—about 30 miles north of Joseph. Guest rooms come with names like Elk, Fish, Bear, Cowboy, and Indian; baths are shared, but each room has its own sink. Check with the Wallowa County Visitor Center in Enterprise (800-585-4121; wallowacountychamber.com) for information about wilderness cabins, RV parks, and other campgrounds.

Joseph is known for its art scene, including several galleries and the **Valley Bronze Foundry** (541-432-7551; valleybronze.com), which offers tours year-round, although schedules may vary, so call ahead. On the 1-hour tour, you'll see the labor-intensive bronze-casting process, including the "lost wax process," a production method the business has used since it began operation with a handful of workers in 1982. Many elegant bronze sculptures are on display, some of which have been sent as far away as Berlin, Germany. Throughout the small, charming, and scenic downtown, fun retail outlets and galleries await the eager shopper, like **Mad Mary's**, 5 South Main Street (madmarys.com), offering quirky but lovable gift items.

In a Big Country

The Wallowas and Elkhorns are famous for their size. These mountains are big, big, big. Itching to explore but not sure of your own ability to venture into such rugged country, especially knowing that cell phone of yours will be next to useless? To partake in a firsthand experience of the great outdoors in the area in the company of true pros, contact **Go Wild** (541-403-1692; gowildusa.com) to arrange a natural history, birding, backpacking, or fly-fishing tour. They'll take care of the gear, the food, the interpretation, and your safety. From multi-day trips to fun adventures like "Stars and Wine," these pros will get you outside without the worry or planning.

OTHER ATTRACTIONS WORTH SEEING IN NORTHEASTERN OREGON

Eastern Oregon Fire Truck Museum & Learning Center
La Grande
(541) 963-3123

Elgin Opera House (ca. 1912)
Elgin

Union County Museum
Main Street
Union
(541) 562-6003

Pendleton Round-Up & Happy Canyon Pageant
Pendleton
(541) 278-0815

Tamastslikt Cultural Institute Museum
Pendleton
(541) 966-9748

Umatilla County Courthouse and its century-old Seth Thomas clock and clock tower
Pendleton

For maps and information about camping and hiking in the Wallowa Mountains and Eagle Cap Wilderness, contact the USDA Forest Service Wallowa Mountains Visitor Center in Enterprise (201 E. 2nd Street; 541-426-5546; fs.usda.gov/wallowa-whitman). If you'd like to see this spectacular mountain wilderness area by horseback, experienced guides and outfitters to contact include **Wallowa Lake Pack Station**, 59761 Wallowa Lake Highway, Joseph (541-432-7433; wallowalakepackstation.com). Ask about short or long horseback rides, including overnight pack trips. For pack trips into Minam Lodge, located in the heart of the Eagle Cap Wilderness and accessible only by horseback, hiking, or small airplane, check with **Steen's Wilderness Adventures** in Joseph (541-432-6545; steenswildernessadventures.com). During winter months, **Wallowa Alpine Huts/Wing Ridge Ski Tours** (541-348-1980; wallowahuts.com) leads experienced skiers on hut-to-hut overnight ski tours in the snowy Wallowa Mountains.

To explore on your own, during summer months and with a sturdy four-wheel-drive vehicle, ask about the condition of the gravel road up to *Hat Point*, elevation 6,982 feet, with its showstopping views of the Snake River Canyon, which is 1,276 feet deep, and Idaho's Seven Devils Mountains, over 9,000 feet in elevation. The spectacular viewpoint is accessed about 25 miles from *Imnaha* (restaurant, limited groceries, seasonal motel, but no gasoline), which is located about 30 miles northeast of Joseph via Highway 350 and skirting Little Sheep Creek. Gas up before leaving Joseph.

For delicious eats in the Joseph-Enterprise area, check out *Old Town Cafe* (541-432-9898) on Main Street in Joseph and, *Arrowhead Chocolates*, 100 N. Main Street (541-432-2871; arrowheadchocolates.com), which offers Stumptown coffee and awesome chocolate truffles, also located in Joseph. Pop into *Vali's Alpine Restaurant* (541-432-5691) on Wallowa Lake Highway, just outside Joseph; and in nearby Enterprise visit friendly *Terminal Gravity Brewery & Pub*, 803 E. 4th Street (541-426-3000), or pop into *Sugar Time Bakery*, 107 N. River Street (541-426-0362), to enjoy tasty cinnamon rolls, scones, muffins, and cupcakes.

The farthest northeastern corner of the state, in the high Wallowa Mountains and Eagle Cap Wilderness, was once home to Chief Joseph and the Nez Perce Indians. To experience a historic section of the Nez Perce country, ask for directions to Nez Perce National Historic Trail, or *Nee-Me-Poo Trail* (meaning "route to freedom"), located about 15 miles north of Imnaha (the last 10 miles are best negotiated with high-clearance vehicles; no vehicles pulling trailers). Here you can walk in the footsteps of Chief Joseph and his people. Chief Joseph, in 1879, said, "The earth is the mother of all people, and all people should have equal rights upon it . . . let me be a free man . . . free to travel."

Places to Stay in Northeastern Oregon

BAKER CITY

Quality Inn Sunridge Inn
Sunridge Lane
(541) 523-6444
choicehotels.com

Eldorado Inn
695 Campbell Street
(541) 523-6494
eldoradoinn.net

JOHN DAY-MT. VERNON

Best Western John Day Inn
315 W. Main Street
(541) 575-1700
bestwestern.com

JOSEPH

Kokanee Inn
700 S. Main Street
(541) 432-9765
kokaneeinn.com

LA GRANDE

La Grande Inn
2612 Island Avenue
(541) 963-7195
lagrandeinn.com

The Landing Hotel
1501 Adams Avenue
(541) 663-1501
lagrandelandinghotel.com

HELPFUL TELEPHONE NUMBERS AND WEBSITES FOR NORTHEASTERN OREGON

Baker County Visitor and Convention Bureau
(541) 523-5855
visitbaker.com

Grant County Visitor Center
(541) 575-0547
gcoregonlive.com

La Grande/Union County Visitor Center
(541) 963-8588
visitunioncounty.org

Milton-Freewater Visitor Center

(541) 938-5563
mfchamber.com

Oregon Road Conditions
(800) 977-6368
tripcheck.com

Oregon State Parks, Campgrounds
oregonstateparks.org
(541) 555-6949, general information

Pendleton Visitor Center
(541) 276-7411
travelpendleton.com

Wallowa County Chamber of Commerce and Visitor Center
(541) 426-4622
wallowacountychamber.com

Wallowa-Whitman National Forest
Enterprise-Joseph
(541) 426-5546
fs.usda.gov/wallowa-whitman

PENDLETON

Rugged Country Lodge Motel
1807 SE Court Avenue
(541) 966-6800
ruggedcountrylodge.com

PRAIRIE CITY

Riverside School House Bed & Breakfast
28076 N. River Road
(541) 820-4731
riversideschoolhouse.com

SUMPTER

Sumpter Bed & Breakfast
344 N. Columbia Street
(541) 894-0048
sumpterbb.net

Places to Eat in Northeastern Oregon

BAKER CITY

Geiser Grand Hotel
1996 Main Street
(888) 434-7374
geisergrand.com

ENTERPRISE

Heavenly's Burger Cafe
500 W. North Street
(541) 426-4195

Terminal Gravity Brewery & Pub
803 E. 4th Street
(541) 426-3000

JOHN DAY—PRAIRIE CITY

1188 Brewing
141 E. Main Street
(541) 575-1188
1188brewing.com

The Snaffle Bit Dinner House
830 S. Canyon Boulevard
(541) 575-2426

JOSEPH

Arrowhead Chocolates
100 N. Main Street
(541) 432-2871
arrowheadchocolates.com

Cheyenne Café
209 N. Main Street
(541) 432-6300

Red Horse Coffee Traders Café
306 N. Main Street
(541) 398-8331
redhorsecoffeetraders.com

LA GRANDE

Benchwarmers Pub & Grill
210 Depot Street
(541) 963-9597
benchwarmerspubandgrill
.com

Joe & Sugars Café
1119 Adams Avenue
(541) 975-5282
joe-sugars.business.site

MILTON—FREEWATER

Burger Hut
5 South Main Street
(541) 938-6226

NORTH POWDER

North Powder Café

975 2nd Street
(541) 898-2868

PENDLETON

Hamley Steak House & Saloon
830 SE Court Street
(541) 278-1100

Roosters Country Kitchen
1515 Southgate Pl.
(541) 966-1100

Portland and Environs

In the late 1840s, **Portland** was a small clump of log cabins on the banks of the Willamette River, where riverboats laden with people and supplies scuttled back and forth between Fort Vancouver (near present-day Vancouver, Washington) and Oregon City, some 20 miles upriver. Early settlers chopped down stands of tall Douglas fir along the riverbanks to make room for those first small cabins, and the place was called the Clearing. Later the tree stumps were whitewashed to prevent folks from stumbling over them after dark, and the nickname Stumptown emerged.

During the 1850s and 1860s, steamboats appeared, and Stumptown became a full-fledged town with a new name Portland, decided by the toss of a coin. Now, a century and a half later, the greater Portland area is a large region containing three of the most populated counties in the state—Multnomah, Washington, and Clackamas—and offering visitors a variety of gorgeous snowcapped mountains and scenic rivers as well as vineyards and wineries, museums, and historic sites. The greater Portland area also offers contemporary homes, historic neighborhoods, and vintage farms as well as theaters, zoos,

festivals, gardens, unique shops, a popular raft of fabulous eateries, cozy bed-and-breakfast inns, and comfortable hostelries.

The city proper and its far-flung environs are now situated on both sides of the broad **Willamette River**, stretching east toward snowcapped Mount Hood, west into the Tualatin Hills toward the Tualatin Valley and Coast Range, and south toward Lake Oswego, West Linn, and historic Oregon City. The Willamette flows into the mighty Columbia River just a few miles northwest of the downtown area. The whitewashed stumps are long gone, but today's visitor will find broad avenues and fountains, parks and lovely public gardens, and, of course, nearly a dozen bridges spanning the Willamette that connect the east and west sides of town.

Downtown and Old Town

One of the best ways to get acquainted with Oregon's largest city is to take a walking tour of the **Historic Old Town** area, where Stumptown began. First, stop by the Portland Visitor Information Center (877 SW Taylor Street; 503-427-1372; travelportland.com), for helpful brochures and maps. Then slip into your walking shoes and head 6 blocks down to the paved esplanade along the Willamette River.

Incidentally, travelers who like to walk can inquire at the visitor center to get the current schedule of walks with a hale and hearty group, an international group of volksmarchers—walking aficionados—that began in Germany, then came to the United States. For further information visit walkoregon.org.

For a shoreside view of the river, first while away an hour or so at **RiverPlace**, located on the west riverbank near the heart of the downtown area. It contains condominiums and offices, restaurants—one of them floating right on the water—and delis, gift shops and boutiques, the European-style **Kimpton RiverPlace Hotel** (503-228-3233; riverplacehotel.com), and a large boat marina. There are comfortable benches for sitting and watching myriad activities, both on the water and ashore. On blue-sky days, lunching at one of the round tables outdoors is a pleasant option. From here you can also ogle Portland's tram system (gobytram.com) that takes two enclosed gondolas from the waterfront just next to the Ross Island Bridge up the southwest hill to the medical complex that locals call Pill Hill.

To continue your walking tour of the downtown waterside area, head north from RiverPlace and Waterfront Park on the paved esplanade along the seawall. During Portland's annual **Rose Festival**, held the first three weeks in June, the seawall is filled with ships of all sizes and lengths, hailing from US Navy and Coast Guard bases as well as Canadian ports, and some can be toured during the festival. At SW Ankeny and 1st Avenues, stop to see the *Skidmore Fountain*, one of the city's first public fountains. It was donated by a local druggist "for the benefit of the horses, men, and dogs of Portland." *New Market Theatre*, at 50 SW 2nd Avenue, is now an office building but was built in 1872 as both a market and a theater—sopranos sang arias on the second floor while merchants sold cabbages on the first. And at the north end of the *Central Fire Station* is a small museum devoted to firefighting and containing vintage fire engines; find it just across from Ankeny Park and the Skidmore Fountain.

Rowing Clubs Abound on the Willamette River

On almost any day from Portland's downtown waterfront you can see master rowers, members of the *Station L Portland Rowing Club* (stationlrowingclub.com) sculling on the Willamette River in sleek shells that hold from two to four rowers. One of the best times to watch, though, is at 5 a.m., when some of the most devoted rowers scull across the river's early morning, glasslike surface. When the group formed in 1879, it was called the Portland Rowing Association; by 1891 the North Pacific Association of Amateur Oarsmen had been established by active rowing clubs in Portland and as far away as Vancouver, British Columbia, and Coeur d'Alene, Idaho.

World War II brought an end to rowing in Portland for about thirty years, until the early 1970s, when a group of former college oarsmen organized a group called Station L, composed of master oarsmen and college club crews from both Reed College and Lewis and Clark College. Given the former dusty, leaking Station L boathouse and empty racks, the sport in Portland has come far—the spiffy racing shells, and ardent rowers, have found a permanent home at the *Portland Boathouse,* on the east side of the Willamette River located at 403 SW Caruthers Avenue and near the Oregon Museum of Science and Industry (OMSI). You can watch various racing events from the east side of the river near OMSI or from the west side at RiverPlace Marina and the grassy sloping lawn at *Tom McCall Waterfront Park*, just next to the RiverPlace Hotel. For the current calendar of racing events, check stationlrowingclub.com.

You can also visit the *Portland Police Museum*, located in the Justice Center at 1111 SW 2nd Avenue (503-823-0019; portlandpolicemuseum.com); be sure to see the *Portland Police Highland Guard* bag-pipers in their colorful kilts on the website! You and the kids can also visit the *Oregon Maritime Museum*, located in the vintage steam sternwheeler on the Willamette River, downtown at SW Pine and Waterfront Park (503-224-7724; oregonmaritimemuseum.org). For other small museums in the area, browse pdxmonthly.com for a list of traditional and quirky museums open to the public. For the kids, be sure to visit the **Oregon Rail Heritage Center**, 2250 SE Water Avenue on the east side of downtown (503-233-1156; orhf.org), for Trains! Trains! including three vintage steam locomotives. Visit Thursday and Friday, 1:00 p.m. to 5:00 p.m.; Saturday and Sunday 12:00 p.m. to 5:00 p.m. Also nearby, the kids will love the hands-on exhibits, planetarium, and IMAX theater at OMSI, the **Oregon Museum of Science and Industry**, 1945 SE Water Avenue (503-797-4000; omsi.edu/); huge parking area. The **Pioneer Courthouse**, downtown at SW 5th and Yamhill, was built in 1869, making it the oldest public building in the Pacific Northwest. Just across the street from the courthouse, detour through **Pioneer Square**, an enormous, block-wide square almost in the heart of the city; colorful outdoor events are held here throughout the year including the tall Christmas tree lighting. Also snoop into the various food carts in the square area that serve everything from espresso drinks to tasty ethnic foods and pastries such as doughnuts and sugary elephant ears.

The nearby **Park Blocks**, constructed on land set aside in 1852 for a city park, stretch from SW Salmon Street south and slightly uphill to the Oregon Historical Center, the Portland Art Museum, and the campus of Portland State University. Here you'll find shady places to walk, rest, and watch the busy pigeons, and you may well encounter roving musicians or street performers from local theater groups along with the ever-present college students, museumgoers, and people watchers. Enjoy autumn walks with myriad leaf colors on tall trees!

The **Oregon Historical Society** (503-222-1741; ohs.org), at 1200 SW Park Avenue, comprises a fine museum of changing exhibits, a historical research library, a gift shop, and a bookstore. The museum is open Tuesday through Saturday from 10:00 a.m. to 5:00 p.m. and on Sunday from noon to 5:00 p.m. You can also visit the **Architectural Heritage Center** on the east side of the Willamette River at 701 SE Grand Avenue (503-231-7264; visitahc.org), open Wednesday through Saturday at 10:00 a.m., where you can see exhibits related to historic preservation in the region. Also ask about programs, lectures, and walking tours of historic houses offered by the center staff.

Located directly across the downtown Park Blocks from the Oregon Historical Society, the **Portland Art Museum** (1219 SW Park Street; 503-226-2811; portlandartmuseum.org) contains an excellent permanent exhibit of Northwest Coast Indian art and artifacts, visiting and rotating exhibits, a film center, small cafe, and museum gift shop. Museum and gallery lovers can also inquire here about the numerous small galleries sprinkled throughout the downtown area. The art museum is open daily from 10:00 a.m. to 5:00 p.m., Thursday and Friday to 8:00 p.m. While exploring shops in the downtown area, pop into the **Pendleton Home Store**, 210 NW Broadway (503-535-5444), open Monday through Saturday at 10:00 a.m. to 5:30 p.m. You'll find all kinds of historic and modern Pendleton blankets and Pendleton woolens along with cozy displays, accessories, and western wear much loved by cowboys, cowgirls, and others in the region. The original *1909 Pendelton Mill* is located some 3 hours east of Portland via I-84 in Pendleton and is still turning out the famous blankets and woolens as well as offering tours of the manufacturing process (pendleton-usa.com).

Should you walk through the lower downtown area on a weekend, stop by the colorful *Portland Saturday Market* (503-222-6072; portlandsaturday market.com), located at North Waterfront Park and Ankeny Plaza open Saturday and Sunday spring through December. Here you can stroll among dozens of booths and meet friendly folks who offer an array of Oregon and Pacific Northwest goods, from pottery, wood, and leather to jewelry, candles, and handwoven items. From open-air food stands and food carts, you can choose tasty, ready-to-eat meat and veggie items.

TOP HITS IN PORTLAND AND ENVIRONS

Aurora National Historic District
Aurora

Historic Sellwood neighborhood
SE Portland

Lan Su Classical Chinese Garden
Portland, downtown
lansugarden.org

Oregon Zoo
Off Highway 26/SW Canyon Road
oregonzoo.org

Portland Downtown Aerial Tram
gobytram.org

Portland's Food Carts
Downtown, SE, NE, and N
neighborhoods
foodcartsportland.com

Sauvie Island
Off US 30

Waterfront Park & Willamette River Esplanades
Downtown Portland, east and west sides of the river

Willamette Falls & Willamette Falls Locks
Oregon City and West Linn

World Forestry Center & Hoyt Arboretum
Off SW Canyon Road (US 26)
worldforestry.org and
hoytarboretum.org

Portland's Fabulous Gardens

There is nothing quite like a beautiful garden to bring everyone out-of-doors, especially in the spring, summer, and fall. Folks of all ages including the kids, grandkids, and grandparents can enjoy the wonderful scents of old and new roses as well as a plethora of other colorful annuals and perennials, ornamental shrubbery, and dozens of tree species along with the musical sounds of bubbling streams, ponds, lakes, or small waterfalls cascading down rocky inclines. Pull on your sturdy walking shoes, add some water bottles and healthy snacks, and enjoy these favorite gardens in the city during all four seasons of the year:

PORTLAND'S EAST SIDE

Crystal Springs Rhododendron Garden

Located at SE 28th Avenue off Bybee Boulevard near Reed College; open daily dawn to dusk. Stroll paths among azaleas, huge rhododendrons, and tree species; see visiting ducks, waterfalls, and stream plantings; and then walk alongside Crystal Springs Lake and across the lake's boardwalk for wide views of the water and Eastmoreland Golf Course in the distance (503-267-7509; rhodies.org).

Leach Botanical Garden

Head farther east on Foster Road to SE 122nd Avenue and turn south to the garden's parking area; open Tuesday through Sunday dawn to dusk. The 9-acre garden glen and house, once home to John and Lilla Leach, offers paths in the native woodland garden, bog garden, riparian zone, shaded rock garden, sunny rock garden, and Lilla Leach's discoveries section. See hardy fuchsias on the upper terrace, a test garden for the Oregon Fuchsia Society (503-823-1671; leachgarden.org).

The Grotto Gardens

Entrance on NE Sandy Boulevard just east of 82nd Avenue; open daily year-round. Stroll the peaceful woodland sanctuary of garden rooms, statuary, shrines, and reflection ponds atop a basalt cliff on the city's northeast side. The gardens and gift shop are open daily; those interested can inquire about the daily Mass schedule held outdoors or in the Chapel of Mary. The gardens sparkle with lights and offer concerts during the Christmas holiday season (503-254-7371; thegrotto.org).

Ladd Circle Park & Rose Gardens

Located at SE 16th Avenue and Harrison Street and just south of Hawthorne Boulevard, this splendid garden features old rose varieties planted in large diamond-shaped formal beds that fill four blocks surrounding Ladd's Circle (portlandoregon.gov/parks, click on Rose Garden). This is one of Portland's oldest neighborhoods. You won't find crowds of people here. Find cheerful coffeeshops on Hawthorne Boulevard after your visit to this lovely neighborhood.

Peninsula Park Rose Garden

Located in northeast Portland at 700 N. Rosa Parks Way just west of I-5. The sunken Rose Garden is lovely and well cared for by the Portland Parks staff (portlandoregon. gov/parks, click on Rose Garden). The grounds offer play structures for the kids and picnic areas near tall Douglas fir.

PORTLAND'S WEST SIDE

Elk Rock Garden at the Bishop's Close

Located at 11800 SW Military Ln., open daily 8:00 a.m. to 5:00 p.m. The 11-acre former estate, ca. 1916, of Scotsman Peter Kerr offers a lush 6-acre garden he developed with generous lawns, trees, and shrubs, including pink dogwood, elegant magnolias, Japanese cherry, rhododendrons, and azaleas. In mid-May, you can see a magnificent old wisteria vine with drapes of pale lavender blossoms that grows across a rocky ledge in the upper parking area. Other pathways lead across a wood bridge, around a stream and pond area planted with irises and ferns, and on to upper views of the Willamette River at the south section of the grounds, where native wildflowers grow. Some sections of the garden are wheelchair accessible. *Note*: The estate and grounds now house the offices of the Episcopal Diocese of Oregon. Parking is limited, and there are no public facilities available here (503-636-5613; elkrockgarden.org).

Portland Japanese Garden

Located at 611 SW Kingston, just above Washington Park International Rose Test Gardens, immerse yourself in five traditional garden styles of ancient Japan in this 5.5-acre garden gem, including *Shukeiyen*, the natural garden; *Rijiniwa*, the tea garden; *Chisen-Kaiyui-Shiki,* the strolling pond garden; *Seki-Tei,* the sand and stone garden; and *Hiraniwa*, the flat garden. Enjoy wide views of the city and Cascade Mountains, including snowcapped Mt. Hood, from the bluff area near the garden pavilion. Park below, near the tennis courts at the Washington Park Rose Gardens, and walk the winding path up to the Oriental-style wood entry gate or take the free trolley up to the entrance. Visit early or late in the day and midweek for the most solitary strolls (503-223-1321; japanesegarden.com).

International Rose Test Gardens and Shakespeare Garden at Washington Park

Located at 400 SW Kingston Avenue, off West Burnside at Tichenor Street (503-823-3636; portlandoregon.gov/parks), click on Rose Garden. Visitors can park by the tennis courts and walk a set of steps down to the gardens, which also offer grand views of the city and Mount Hood to the east. Morning sunrises here are spectacular! Tucked in the southeast corner and behind a high brick wall, don't miss the intimate Shakespeare garden, which offers a colorful assortment of poppies, lavender, and rosemary combined with clusters of other lush annuals and perennials mentioned in the Bard's writings. Several flowering tree species here offer grand bloom displays in early spring. Enjoy snooping among the beds of test roses, seeing their colors and their individual numbers and names. Also enjoy the miniature rose collection and the lovely espaliered roses cascading from tall archways throughout the garden. For fewer crowds, visit early in the morning or in the early evening and early in the week. Stop also to browse the gift shop near the entry steps (503-227-7033; portlandoregon.gov/parks). *Note*: From November 15 each year, the roses are cut back and won't bloom again until spring and summer.

Portland Institutions—Time-Tested Favorites

Here is a selected list of those places—locales, shops, eateries—that have been around the Portland area a long time and generally do not fit the description of "here today, gone tomorrow":

Chown Hardware
333 NW 16th Avenue
(503) 243-6500
chown.com
Open since 1879, this family-owned hardware store is still going strong.

Dan & Louis Oyster Bar
208 SW Ankeny, downtown in Old Town
(503) 227-5906
danandlouis.com
Serving great oysters, fish and chips, clam chowder, and other seafood since 1907.

Kelly's Olympian
426 SW Washington, downtown in Old Town
(503) 228-3669
kellysolympian.com
Open since 1902, Portland's third continuously operated bar and restaurant was originally called the Olympia Saloon, mostly due to the Olympia Brewing Company's involvement in the inaugural opening.

Pittock Mansion, ca. 1914
3229 NW Pittock Drive, uptown off West Burnside above Washington Park
(503) 823-3623
pittockmansion.org
French-style heritage mansion built by newspaper publisher Henry Pittock and his wife, Georgiana Burton Pittock; wide views east to the Cascade Mountains; wonderful tour any time of year, but especially in spring and in December when decorated for the holidays.

Rich's Cigar Store, Magazines, and Newspapers
820 SW Alder Street, downtown
(503) 228-1700
richscigarstore.com
Since 1894, offering periodicals and tobacco, imported steins and flasks, and the best selection of domestic and foreign newspapers and magazines in the state.

Ringside Steakhouse Restaurant
2165 W. Burnside Street, downtown
(503) 223-1513
ringsidesteakhouse.com
Steaks and onion rings since the 1940s.

If you're ready to leave the bustle of downtown and enjoy a lazy afternoon in the outdoors, visit cool, shady **Forest Park** (portlandoregon.gov/parks/ 35300), one of the largest urban parks in the United States. The 4,700-acre park begins just a few blocks from downtown, off West Burnside Street and adjacent to Washington Park International Rose Test Gardens. The easy **Wildwood Trail** can be accessed from the **World Forestry Center** (worldforestry .org), near the **Oregon Zoo** (oregonzoo.org), just west of **Washington Park**; a scenic winding road links Washington Park with the Forestry Center and the Oregon Zoo.

Portland's mild and moist weather offers an extraordinary haven for wonderful year-round gardens. The city offers gardens and natural areas for strolling, for romantics, for families, and for serious botanic buffs. Gardens and natural areas especially suited for families include nearby **Hoyt Arboretum** (hoytarboretum.org), **Tryon Creek State Park** (tryonfriends.org), and also **Washington Park International Rose Test Gardens**, 400 SW Kingston Avenue (503-823-3636 for the garden and 503-227-7033 for the garden gift shop; portlandoregon.gov/parks, click on rose garden). At the perimeter of this splendid garden above the downtown area, accessed from West Burnside Street, you will find shady lawn spaces to picnic with views of the city and the Cascade Mountains, including snowcapped Mt. Hood, to the east. Also enjoy strolling the International Rose Test, the Miniature Rose Collection, the intimate Shakespeare Garden, and the Gold Medal Award Roses sections of the gardens. The 8,000 roses—500 varieties—bloom all summer, with peak bloom time in June and July. The park and gardens encompass 4 acres and are open daily until dusk; it is most crowded on warm summer weekends. Park near the tennis courts and also enjoy browsing in the rose garden gift shop.

Located just below Washington Park off West Burnside Street is the historic **Nob Hill** neighborhood, an assortment of interesting shops, boutiques, good eateries, and coffee shops that range along NW 21st and 23rd Avenues. A number of Portland's splendid Victorian mansions line the winding streets off Westover Road above 23rd Avenue.

Along 10 miles of trails in nearby **Hoyt Arboretum** (503-865-8733; hoy tarboretum.org), you and the kids can try your hand at identifying Douglas fir, Jeffrey pine, big-leaf maple, hemlock, Western red cedar, and grand fir, as well as cherry, ash, madrone, and Indian plum. Spectacular in the spring are native wildflowers, including trilliums and buttercups. More than 110 different species of birds and over 50 species of mammals have been identified in Forest Park and the arboretum. Pick up arboretum trail maps and informational literature at Hoyt Visitor Center, 4000 SW Fairview Boulevard (503-865-8733). Access the arboretum from the Oregon Zoo and World Forestry Center just off Canyon Road/US

26 as you head west from downtown Portland toward Beaverton. Ask about guided tours through the 175-acre arboretum, which contains some 600 species of trees from all over the world. Information about other guided tours, nature walks, and interesting day trips in the area can also be obtained from the staff at the Portland Parks & Recreation office (503-823-7529; portlandoregon.gov/parks), and from the Metro Regional Parks and Greenspaces Department (503-797-1700; metro-region.org).

To experience another nearby city forest especially suited for families (this one in southwest Portland near Lewis and Clark College, in a splendid forest of second-growth Douglas fir), call the friendly park staff and volunteers at **Tryon Creek State Park** (503-636-4398; tryonfriends.org). Ask about hiking, equestrian, and bicycle trails and about the array of educational and interpretive programs for all ages on science topics, the regional environment, local history, and ecology as well as cultural activities. The park's annual **Trillium Festival** is celebrated the first weekend in April.

Returning to the downtown area, visit the splendid **Lan Su Classical Chinese Garden** (503-228-8131; lansugarden.org), located at NW 3rd and Everett Streets, just north of East Burnside, in Portland's Chinatown area. Behind thick, white walls encompassing the entire city block, stroll decorative pebble and rock paths, walk across small bridges, gaze at reflections on the central pond, and peek into meditative courtyards and wooden teahouses. Lovely and reflective views unfold with every step and reveal an aesthetic fusion of the five elements of a Chinese garden: plants (mature trees, flowering ornamentals), water, outdoor architecture, poetic inscriptions, and ancient rocks. In the Tea House you can enjoy tea and treats. This contemplative garden is open daily, April through October, from 9:00 a.m. to 6:00 p.m., and November through March from 10:00 a.m. to 5:00 p.m.

One of the vintage hostelries in the downtown area, just up Broadway from Pioneer Square and the Visitors Information Center (503-275-8355), is the **Heathman Hotel** at 1110 SW Broadway at Salmon Street (503-241-4100; heathmanhotel.com). Enjoy afternoon tea in the grand Tea Court, looking just as it did in 1927, including its paneling of polished eucalyptus, or try a cold beverage, along with late-afternoon hors d'oeuvres, in the nearby marble and mirrored bar or in the intimate mezzanine lounge. For another downtown option don't miss the ca. 1912 boutique **Hotel deLuxe**, 729 SW 15th Avenue (503-219-2094; hoteldeluxeportland.com),

oregontrivia

In 1887, when the first Morrison Street Bridge opened across the river in the heart of the downtown area, the toll was 5 cents per human pedestrian, pig, or sheep and 10 cents for a cow or horse.

renovated in the Art Deco and Hollywood glamour style of days gone by. *Gracie's* offers classic fare and a comfortable ambience, and the hotel's Driftwood Cocktail Lounge is also reminiscent of Hollywood.

Portland: For the Outdoor Lover

Living in a great outdoor city, most Portlanders enjoy walking, jogging, in-line skating, or biking, in all sections of the city. You'll see business folks doing lunchtime or after-work runs. Families with children, teens and their friends, and older folks thoroughly enjoy the out-of-doors on weekdays and weekends, rain or shine. Paved walkways extend along the Willamette River seawall esplanades on both sides of the river adjacent to the downtown area. More walkways range south of nearby RiverPlace along the river, heading toward the John's Landing area. And you can also see and ride the Portland Aerial Tram, which links RiverPlace and the South Waterfront area to Marquam Hill and offers spectacular views of the city and mountains to the east and north (gobytram.org).

Outdoor aficionados can get helpful information, walking maps, and biking maps from Travel Portland Visitor Information Center at Pioneer Courthouse Square (503-275-8355; travelportland.com). The Portland Bicycle Transportation Alliance (503-226-0676; btaoregon.org) also provides helpful information and links to other websites around the state.

The ***Portland Center for the Performing Arts***, 1111 SW Broadway (503-248-4335; portland5.com), is also downtown and close to the South Park Blocks and Portland State University. The center includes three theater spaces including the large ***Schnitzer Concert Hall***, the intimate Edwardian-style ***Newmark Theatre***, and the black box-style ***Winningstad Theatre***. Located a few blocks from this complex, theatergoers also find the ca. 1917 ***Keller Auditorium***, 222 SW Clay Street, which was completely renovated in 1968. Explore a variety of offerings in all these theater spaces including traveling Broadway shows, traveling performers, and lecturers, as well as local plays and performances by the Portland Ballet Company, Portland Symphony, and Portland Opera. The newest theater space is ***Brunish Theatre*** located inside ***Antoinette Hatfield Hall***, 1111 SW Broadway. Browse the center's website for current offerings and ticket information (portland5.com).

Music and theater lovers can also check out summertime offerings, some outdoors; for example, bring-your-own-picnic summer concerts on the lawn, ***Summer Concerts at the Zoo***, in July and August (503-226-1561; oregonzoo.org).

And don't miss taking the kids to visit the nearby **World Forestry Center**, 4033 SW Canyon Road/US 26 (503-228-1367; worldforestry.org), located next to the zoo where you can see forest exhibits from around the world, learn how smokejumpers fight forest fires, learn how to go river rafting, see animals that live in and under the forest, learn how timberjacks harvest the forests, and ride a lift up into the canopy of a really tall Douglas fir tree. Then take the kids' pictures with *Peggy*, a 42-ton steam locomotive built in 1909 that once carried logs to mills in Oregon and Washington. When you get to town, pick up a copy of *Willamette Week*, a free weekly newspaper at news boxes and retail outlets all over town, for current listings of stage, theater, gallery, and film offerings, as well as bistro and restaurant listings and free concerts at Pioneer Square. For more information about lodging and eateries in the area, check with Travel Portland Visitors Information Center (503-427-1372; travelportland.com) located downtown in Director Park.

Where the Rivers Merge

For another pleasant excursion head north and west of downtown via 23rd Avenue to access US 30, and then drive about 10 miles, passing the graceful St. John's Bridge, to **Sauvie Island**, a pastoral area lying along the confluence of the Willamette River from the south and the Columbia River from the east. The small island was settled in the late 1840s, and at one time some forty dairy farms were scattered about it. The southern half now contains strawberry and raspberry fields, fruit orchards, and vegetable farms; many Sauvie Island farmers offer their homegrown fruit and produce in open-air stands and U-Pick fields all summer and into early autumn. October is particularly bustling with pumpkin patches and harvest fairs.

After crossing the Sauvie Island Bridge onto this flat, oblong island that is loved by weekend bicyclers, enjoy meandering along the quiet roads that nearly encircle the terrain. Take in some serious bird-watching, canoe on tiny Sturgeon Lake or quiet Multnomah Channel, or bring your bicycle and pedal around the island's quiet byways. The northern half of the island—where Oak Island and Sturgeon Lake are located—remains a native wetlands area, the **Sauvie Island Wildlife Refuge**, 18330 NW Sauvie Island Road (503-621-3488; dfw.state.or.us and click on Visitors Guide); the refuge office is open Monday through Friday from 8:00 a.m. to 5:00 p.m., except for noon to 1:00 p.m. Stop here to purchase the refuge parking permit. Hundreds of birds migrating along the busy Pacific Flyway make pit stops here twice each year to rest and refuel.

Tour Time

The best way to see a city can be by following someone else who knows it better than you. Maybe you don't have friends or family in Portland, but you can still find a great tour guide. Portland is home to some terrific guided tour options. Consider a stroll with *Portland Walking Tours* (portlandwalkingtours.com), which offers a variety of tours daily including Best of Portland and Underground Portland. A step-up from walking, without actually getting in a car, is possible with *Portland Segway Tours* (portlandbysegway.com), which tour Portland downtown and westside for a taste of the Rose City's history and present-day delights. Take the Portland Brewery Bike Tour with *Pedal Bike Tours* (pedalbiketours.com) to sip your way around the city and its wonderful craft brew institutions.

With the aid of binoculars, you'll probably spot Canada geese, snow geese, white-fronted geese, assorted ducks, and smaller birds and wildlife. Without binoculars, however, you'll often see many larger birds, such as marsh and red-tailed hawks, vultures, tundra swans, sandhill cranes, and blue herons. During winter a population of about thirty bald eagles roosts in an old-growth forest some miles away, leisurely commuting to Sauvie Island at sunrise to spend the day.

Because something like 500,000 acres of US "wetlands"—a composite description for ponds, lakes, and sloughs

oregontrivia

Meriwether Lewis and William Clark also passed near this area on their trek to the Northwest during the early 1800s. On November 3, 1805, Clark, while camped along the Columbia River and feeling somewhat disgruntled, wrote in his journal that the party couldn't sleep, "for the noise kept up during the whole of the night by the swans, Geese, white & Grey Brant, Ducks, &c on a small Sand Island . . . They were imensely numerous, and their noise horid."

and their adjacent grasslands and meadows loved by waterfowl, other birds, and wildlife—are being drained and filled each year, the number of birds using the Pacific Flyway has changed dramatically since the days of the Lewis and Clark expedition. For helpful information about efforts to conserve wetlands in the Portland area, including a schedule of bird-watching treks to Sauvie Island and other nearby wildlife habitats, contact the *Portland Audubon Society*, located at 5151 NW Cornell Road (503-292-6855; audubonportland.org). Better yet, stop by the society's visitor center on your way from downtown Portland via Lovejoy Street (head west), for maps and bird-watching lists before continuing out to Sauvie Island.

While exploring Sauvie Island, especially if you can bring a hearty picnic, stop at the ca. 1850 *James Bybee House* at *Howell Territorial Park* and enjoy your repast at one of the picnic tables near the orchard. In the pioneer orchard, you can see some 115 varieties of apple trees. The restored farmhouse is currently not open for tours, but you can walk around the grounds, inspect the vintage rose garden, and see the enormous barn where pioneer farm equipment and old-time wagons are stored.

Portland: Food Cart City!

Looking for breakfast, lunch, snacks, dinner, late night, and weekend eats? Portland's food carts have it covered. From food cart pods in the downtown area to pods in many outlying neighborhoods, food lovers can find a staggering and eclectic selection of foods and beverages at bargain prices. You'll find baked potatoes, barbecue, bowls, crepes, coffee and espresso, fish and chips, hot dogs, panini, pizza, sausages, soups, and wraps as well as Cajun, German, Greek, Hawaiian, Japanese, Jewish, Mediterranean, Middle Eastern, Mexican, and Thai entrees, plus snacks and treats! A number of pods have also added large tents with windows and picnic tables for folks to sit, munch, sip, and also to meet, greet, and chat. Try these eclectic pods for great eats and drinks:

Killingsworth Station Food Carts offers a variety of carts in northeast Portland.
BGs Food Cartel in Beaverton has a little bit of everything with over thirty food carts to choose from.
A la Carts, located at SE Stark and 102nd Streets, is a pod attracting more food lovers near Mall 205.
Mississippi Marketplace, located at North Mississippi Avenue at Skidmore Street, also offers covered seating. This is a great spot for breakfast.
Happy Valley Station Carts, SE 145th Avenue and Sunnyside Road (541-419-7253) east of I-205 and Clackamas Towne Center; large pavilion tent with seating, coffee, gelato, and a brews purveyor with some forty taps.

Find several food cart pods in the downtown area: SW Alder Street at 9th; Portland State University area at SW Hall and 3rd Avenue; and SW 5th Avenue between Stark and Oak Streets.

Browse foodcartsportland.com or call (503-896-2771) for a comprehensive list of food carts in specific neighborhoods, along with their current food offerings. It's updated often. Enjoy!

Reaching the farmstead is simple: After crossing narrow Multnomah Channel on the Sauvie Island Bridge from US 30, follow the signs to 13801 NW Howell Park Road and turn down the lane to the large parking area. The Bybee House grounds are open daily, and there are outdoor restroom facilities here. The house and grounds are maintained by Metro Parks and Green

Spaces (sauvieisland.org and oregonmetro.gov). Collect picnic goodies before heading out US 30 at the well-stocked grocery store on NW Lovejoy Street and 13th Avenue. It offers a variety of deli sandwiches, salads, cheeses, and rustic breads as well as bottled water and Starbucks coffee drinks. Farm stands on Sauvie Island also may offer seasonal berries, fruits, and vegetables for sale.

Also while visiting the pastoral island, stop by **Blue Heron Herbary** and lavender farm, 27731 NW Reeder Road (503-621-1457; blueheronherbary.com), where you'll find a large variety of culinary herbs to grow as well as lavender plants and products. Visit **Sauvie Island Farms**, 19818 NW Sauvie Island Road (503-621-3988; sauvieislandfarms.com), which opens in June for pick your own fruits and vegetables and continues through December for Christmas trees. At **The Pumpkin Patch Farm**, 16511 NW Gillihan Road (503-621-3874; thepumpkinpatch.com), open seven days a week in summer and fall, you can choose from fresh berries, fruits, and veggies in season; pet animal babies in the big red barn (built in the 1920s as a dairy barn); take the kids on a hayride; snoop for gifts in the Pumpkin Cottage Gift Shop; and find a comfy seat at the Patio Cafe for casual lunch fare.

You could also stay the night on Sauvie Island by arranging pleasant camping quarters at **Island Cove RV Park**, 31421 NW Reeder Road (503-601-9872), with RV sites with hookups. There are on-site restrooms and showers at the park.

If time allows, leave Sauvie Island and continue west out US 30 about 12 miles farther, to **St. Helens**, to enjoy a panoramic view from the historic waterfront area of this ca. 1844 city. Follow Columbia Boulevard through downtown and find **Columbia View Park** just next door to the courthouse, then walk down a few steps to watch the powerboats, sailboats, and barges on the Columbia River. For tasty bistro fare stop at **Dockside Steak & Pasta**, 343 S. 1st Street (503-366-0877), with good views of the river. Pop into **Kozy Korner Restaurant & Lounge**, 371 Columbia Boulevard, for homey diner eats. You can also arrange pleasant overnight sleeps and yummy breakfasts in the St. Helens area at **Nob Hill Riverview Bed & Breakfast**, 285 S. 2nd Street (503-396-5555; nobhillbb.com). From the inn's location in the historic waterfront area, guests enjoy fine views of the Columbia River and on clear days, Mount St. Helens rising to the north. From here travelers find easy access via US 30 to Astoria on the north coast and the nearby Long Beach Peninsula on the Washington coast.

Best Historic Neighborhoods for Browsing and Shopping in Portland & Environs

Portland has rediscovered its wonderful old neighborhoods, and they're being transformed to vibrant avenues for browsing, shopping, walking, jogging, bicycling, in-line skating, and generally hanging out. You can pop into old and new shops and find cozy places to hole up with friends over tasty espresso drinks, great hamburgers, or healthy pastas, delicious salads, and tasty desserts. These shops include every sort of enthusiastic local entrepreneur and every sort of business—from antiques, collectibles, and vintage or new clothing to trendy kitchen boutiques, flower and garden shops, havens for books and magazines and cigars, and shops for backyard bird lovers and for pet lovers. Check these out and enjoy:

Multnomah Village: Located between Capitol Highway and Multnomah Boulevard from SW 31st to SW 40th Avenues. This neighborhood is eclectic, funky, and has a number of coffee shops and several good eateries.

Nob Hill District: Located uptown between NW 21st and NW 23rd Avenues and extending north from West Burnside Street to Vaughn Street. This is a trendy, busy, and fun neighborhood with great eateries and good coffeehouses.

Pearl District: Located downtown between NW 10th and NW 13th Streets and extending north from West Burnside to NW Hoyt Street. This vibrant, renovated historic area is hopping with new stores, cafes, restaurants, coffee shops, and condominiums.

EAST SIDE

Hawthorne Boulevard: The heart of the area extends from about SE 20th to SE 50th Avenues. This neighborhood is very laid-back, funky, and fun and has many good eateries.

Historic Sellwood: Located across the Willamette River via the Sellwood Bridge to SE 13th Avenue, this area is much loved by antiques buffs, and it also offers excellent bakeries, coffee shops, restaurants, and food carts.

Northeast Broadway: From the Broadway Bridge, the area extends from NE 12th Avenue east to about NE 20th Avenue. There is an unusual variety of shops, good eateries, and friendly coffee shops.

OUTER EAST SIDE

North Main Avenue in Gresham: From downtown take the MAX train out to the end of the line in Gresham, or drive the scenic route heading east across the Ross Island Bridge and onto Powell Boulevard, continuing about 10 miles east to Gresham. Park near the City Park on Powell Boulevard and walk across to Main Avenue; the area ranges several blocks and extends to 2nd, 3rd, and 4th Streets. This neighborhood features great shops and excellent restaurants.

Historic East Side Neighborhoods

Enjoy visiting a bevy of secondhand stores and antiques shops in the *Historic Sellwood* neighborhood, via Macadam Avenue and Sellwood Bridge, located just south of the downtown and Old Town areas. This old neighborhood, with its small homes and tidy lawns, skirts the Willamette River's east bank near the Sellwood Bridge and Oaks Park. Amble along SE 13th Avenue, stopping for lunch or tea and dessert at one of the many delis or small restaurants in the area, or take a picnic down to the park along the river, just north of the Sellwood Bridge. You can also visit nearby Oaks Park to see and ride the refurbished *Oaks Park Carousel*, which survived four Willamette River floods—in 1948, 1964, 1974, and 1996. Then, at nearby *Westmoreland Park* you and the kids can watch youngsters and oldsters sail their small boats on the large pond. You'll find comfortable benches for sitting and enjoying the view all along the west side of the pond. Access Westmoreland Park just off Bybee Boulevard near 20th Avenue.

From Westmoreland Park continue east on Bybee Boulevard, where you'll pass *Eastmoreland Golf Course* (503-775-2900), and circle around to SE Woodward Street and 28th Avenue (along the way notice the vintage homes of Eastmoreland shaded by enormous old deciduous trees). Detour onto 28th Avenue for a block or so to find the entrance to lovely *Crystal Springs Rhododendron Garden* (rhodies.org).

Wish you had brought a picnic lunch to eat at one of the benches along Crystal Springs Lake? It's easy, stop first at *Otto's Sausage Kitchen and Meat Market*, just up the hill past Reed College, at 4138 SE Woodstock Boulevard (503-771-6714; ottossausage.com), to collect sandwiches, salads, chips, imported cheeses, imported and domestic ales, muffins, cookies, coffee, and lattes. Otto's has been making great sausages such as bockwurt, hunter sausage, smoked pork links, Cajun sausage, and more since 1929 and is open Monday through Saturday from 9:30 a.m. to 6:00 p.m. and Sunday 10:00 a.m. to 5:00 p.m. On weekends the barbecue is fired up just outside the entry offering tasty treats.

Then wend your way over to the *Hawthorne* neighborhood by turning north onto 39th Avenue at Woodstock Boulevard. On Hawthorne Boulevard, between 20th and 50th Avenues, you'll find a restored area of interesting shops, delis, restaurants, and boutiques. Stop by *Grand Central Bakery*, 2230 SE Hawthorne Boulevard (503-445-1600; grandcentralbakery.com), for homemade soups, yummy cinnamon rolls, scones, and espresso as well as the rustic Italian breads for which the bakery has become famous: thick, crusty, free form, and very chewy, made by slow-rise and long-fermentation processes.

Detour next to Belmont Street and 34th Avenue, just a few blocks north, to visit another renovated neighborhood. *Stumptown Coffee Café* is nearby at 3356 SE Belmont Street (503-232-8889) and offers delicious coffee drinks from freshly roasted beans. Visit a video rental store that is also a museum, displaying original costumes and props from classic films, at *Movie Madness* (4320 SE Belmont; 503-234-4363; moviemadness.org). *Horse Brass Pub* (4534 SE Belmont; 503-232-2202; horsebrass.com) is another Belmont classic destination. This traditional English-style pub has served proper pints since 1976. At Southeast Belmont and 43rd, visit the pod of food carts called *Good Food Here* for an eclectic selection of coffees, pizzas, sandwiches, and other good lunch items. Also at this pod of carts you'll find a cozy covered seating area in case of inclement weather.

Continue east on Hawthorne Boulevard and drive up 600-foot *Mount Tabor* for a view of the city from atop one of Portland's extinct volcanic cinder cones. You could take a picnic and find picnic tables in shaded or sunny places under towering Douglas firs, their long branches swaying in the gentle breezes. Drive or hike around the park for views of snowcapped Mount Hood, to the east.

You can also discover comfortable places to spend the night on the east side of town. Among the coziest are *Portland's White House* at 1914 NE 22nd Avenue (503-287-7131; portlandswhitehouse.com) and *The Lion & the Rose Victorian B&B* at 1810 NE 15th Avenue (503-287-9245; lionrose.com)—fine bed-and-breakfast inns. For hip lodging closer to the Willamette River, try *Hotel Eastlund* at 1021 NE Grand Avenue (503-235-2100), a luxury boutique hotel with views of downtown.

Park on any side street near 15th Avenue and enjoy walking and browsing the trendy *Northeast Broadway neighborhood*—dozens of great shops, delis, coffeehouses, cafes, and galleries range from NE 10th to NE 20th Avenues. Also nearby are Memorial Coliseum, the Rose Quarter, and the *Oregon Convention Center*, 777 NE Martin Luther King Jr Boulevard (503-235-7575; oregoncc.org), where sports and other public events, such as Winter Chocolate Fest, Winter Seafood & Wine Fest, Spring Beer & Wine Fest, Portland Golf Show, and Garden & Patio Show are held throughout the year.

Oregon Trail's End

Those blue-sky afternoons often beckon young and old alike to the *Willamette River*, just as they did when the first pioneers arrived and settled near the base of the falls at Oregon City. In the late 1800s, the Willamette River was the "main street" for life in the Willamette Valley: People traveled by riverboats and stern-wheelers, produce and supplies were shipped in and out by steamboats, and Oregon's principal cities started as river towns and steamboat landings. No fewer than seven major cities are located along the river, and more than half the people in Oregon live within 10 miles of the Willamette River; in fact, more than 60 percent of all Oregonians live within the Willamette River Basin.

Historic ca. 1872 Willamette Falls Locks

The giant wooden doors open wide, and recreation boats or barges move into the first of four enormous watery chambers. The lock master waves from the small station, keeping track of the gates and traffic on a television monitor while relaying instructions to a second lock tender in the upper station. It takes about 30 minutes to reach the upper Willamette River channel above the falls with the help of the historic locks. Constructed in 1872 by Chinese laborers, these locks have operated since 1873. In 1974 Willamette Falls Locks were placed on the National Register of Historic Places, and in 1991 the American Society of Civil Engineers, Oregon Section, designated the locks a national civil engineering landmark.

To see the historic locks, from downtown Portland drive about 10 miles south via Macadam Avenue and Highway 43 through Lake Oswego to West Linn. Continue under the I-205 bridge to the redbrick building housing West Linn City Hall and Police Department, and look for the sign—just before the old Oregon City Bridge—that says Willamette Falls Locks and Army Corps of Engineers. Don't give up—it's well worth the effort to find this out-of-the-way gem. Park nearby and walk the paved lane and series of concrete stairs that lead down to the viewing area. *Note*: At this writing the grounds are closed to visitors and the locks are closed to tugboats, barges, and pleasure boats. The National Trust for Historic Preservation, the Willamette River Coalition, the Willamette Falls Heritage Foundation, and also a number of government and city groups are working to undertake the repair and reopening of the historic locks. For current information call (503) 656-3381 or (541) 374-8307.

One of the best ways to cool off and see this historic area from a different perspective is to take a boat ride upriver about 18 miles, south toward Lake Oswego, West Linn, Milwaukie, Gladstone, and Oregon City. The boat proceeds south from downtown Portland, first maneuvering under the Ross Island Bridge, and then continues upriver past tiny Ross Island toward the Sellwood area. Sunlight sparkles from the moving water, and the city skyline recedes in midafternoon's golden light. The air smells fresh and clean.

Cruising upriver at a comfortable speed, the boat may pass a flotilla of small sailboats engaged in a race. White sails catch the wind, and sunlight turns them brightly translucent. Tinkly music from the Oaks Park Carousel wafts across the water as the boat passes under the Sellwood Bridge, continuing south toward the small communities along both banks of the river and to Willamette Falls at Oregon City.

A profusion of greenery passes by—cool canopies of trees, shrubbery, and mosses clinging to basaltic ledges and rocky walls here and there on both the east and west banks of the river. The boat cruises past waterside homes; a small pontoon plane crouches at its dockside resting place; water-skiers glide past on wide skis; and great blue herons—Portland's official bird—catch the wind overhead, often in the company of seagulls who have flown in from the coast some 80 miles west.

At **Clackamette Park**, near Gladstone and Oregon City, peer over the railing to see where the smaller Clackamas River quietly enters the Willamette. The boat passes beneath the I-205 and old Oregon City bridges, toward the falls.

Sternwheelers and large cruisers can be seen cruising up both the Willamette and Columbia Rivers. To join one of the cruises on either river, check with the staff at **Portland Spirit** (503-224-3900; portlandspirit.com). The *Portland Spirit*, a modern and spacious cruise vessel, offers dinner cruises on the Willamette River from downtown Portland until mid-October. A large sternwheeler vessel also cruises during summer and early fall from the Port of Cascade Locks located about 40 miles east of Portland via I-84 into the western Columbia Gorge area; browse the website listed above for current information.

Willamette and Oregon City

To visit the small community of **Willamette**, the most historic part of West Linn, head west on the frontage road, Willamette Falls Drive, winding above the Willamette Falls Locks and the Willamette River for a couple of miles. Here you'll find a couple of antiques shops, several good eateries and coffee shops, and a large city park along the river (great spot for a picnic).

Back track along Willamette Falls Drive and cross the Willamette River from West Linn via the old Highway 99 Oregon City Bridge. Here you'll find historic **Oregon City**, which boasts the distinction of being the first incorporated city west of the Rocky Mountains. In the winter of 1829–1830, however, there were just three log houses here, and the following spring, the first vegetables—potatoes—were planted. Apparently, the local Native Americans resented this infringement on their territory and reportedly burned the houses. A flour mill and a sawmill, constructed near Willamette Falls in 1832 by the British Hudson's Bay Company, made use of the first waterpower in the territory.

The emigration over the Oregon Trail in 1844 added several hundred folks to Oregon City's population. The provisional government body, formed in 1843 at Champoeg, on the banks of the Willamette River south and west a few miles, chose Oregon City as its seat; the first provisional legislature assembled here in June 1844, at the Rose Farm.

By 1846 Oregon City contained some 70 houses and about 500 white settlers fresh from the Oregon Trail. In January 1848, Joe Meek carried the request of the provisional legislature for territorial status to President James K. Polk in Washington, DC. Meek returned in March 1849 with the newly appointed territorial governor, Joseph Lane. Oregon City was made the territorial capital and remained so until 1852, when the seat of government was moved to Salem, some 50 miles south, in the heart of the Willamette Valley.

To begin your tour of the Oregon City area, stop first at the *End of the Oregon Trail Interpretive & Visitor Center* (503-657-9336; historicoregon city.org), located at 1726 Washington Street, at Abernethy Street—you can't miss the three gigantic pioneer wagon sculptures fashioned of metal. The center offers visitor information and changing displays on the Oregon Trail and Clackamas County history as well as the Abernethy Green, a Heritage Kitchen Garden, and a Country Store with gifts and handmade pioneer goods, books on the Oregon Trail, pioneer games, bonnets, and more. The kids can enjoy activities such as pioneer puzzles and pioneer dress-up, and interpretive guides in period dress often share stories about the Oregon Trail and early life in the area. Crafts such as butter-making, candle-dipping, and quilting are also offered. A covered picnic shelter offers space for a picnic lunch.

Next, pick up the Historic Walking Tour brochure and map, park on Main Street near the Clackamas County courthouse, and walk a few blocks to the *Oregon City Municipal Elevator*, accessing it via the lower entrance, on Railroad Avenue at 7th Street. You'll take a 30-second vertical ride up the face of the 90-foot basalt cliff—the city is built on two levels. The elevator—one of only four municipal elevators in the world—replaced the old Indian trails and pioneer paths that originally led from the river's edge to the top of the basalt bluff.

The first elevator, which took 3 minutes to travel up and down, was powered by water. It was constructed in 1915—much to the chagrin of citizen Sara Chase, who objected to its location in front of her Victorian mansion. Not only did Sara never use the municipal elevator, but she had a heavy wrought-iron fence erected so that "none of those elevator people" could trespass on her property. On the interior wall of the observation area atop the elevator, you can see an artist's painting of the Chase mansion.

Walk south a few blocks along the upper paved *Promenade* (it's also wheelchair accessible) for a spectacular view of the Willamette River and Willamette Falls. Imagine what the area must have been like before the settlers arrived, before power lines and buildings, before bridges and freeways and automobiles. Actually, the first long-distance transmission of electricity in the United States happened here—from Oregon City to Portland—in 1888.

The early Native American families fished for salmon along the forested riverbanks amid stands of Douglas fir, the roar of the falls ever present. The falls cascade some 42 feet over several basaltic ledges in the middle of the wide Willamette River. You can sit at any of the public benches along the Promenade, basking in the late afternoon sun while imagining a bit of Oregon history.

Sneak Across the Columbia River to Visit Vancouver, Washington, and the Evergreen State

A quick guide to great places not to be missed on your travels through Washington State:

Vancouver USA: In downtown Vancouver, Washington (visitvancouverusa.com) amble about lovely *Esther Short Park*, see the splendid *Salmon Run Bell Tower* and take in the rose garden and the fantastic renovated waterfront district, which boasts upscale restaurants with river views and tasty food. Then visit the ca. 1845 *Fort Vancouver National Historic Site*, with its British Gardens and living history programs (nps.gov/fova); *Pearson Air Museum* and *The Jack Murdock Aviation Center* (360-816-6232; nps.gov/fova); and nearby *Officer's Row* located near the National Park visitors center (360-816-6230) on Reserve Street. Access the park from E. Evergreen Boulevard from downtown Vancouver. Don't miss it! *Note*: Go north on I-5 from Portland early in the day and early in the week for less congested traffic and plan to stay overnight in downtown Vancouver at the Hilton Hotel Vancouver near the Columbia River and across from *Esther Short Park*, 301 W. 6th Street (360-993-4500).

Mount St. Helens: Head north via I-5, take the Castle Rock exit 49, and then go east on Highway 504 for about 40 miles to *Johnston Ridge Observatory* (360-274-2140; fs.usda.gov/giffordpinchot), open daily at 10:00 a.m. mid-May to October 31, for great views of Mount Saint Helens, the volcanic mountain that blew its top on a sunny morning in May 1980. Also check out the scenic *Mount Rainier National Park* area (visitrainier.com and nps.gov/mora) and plan to stay a couple of nights at cozy *National Park Inn* (360-569-2475; mtrainierguestservices.com), located in Longmire, several miles below *Paradise Lodge* and the 14,000-foot snowy peak. The National Park Inn sports a wide covered porch with rocking chairs (with mountain views on clear days), a lovely restaurant, and cozy guest rooms.

Tacoma: Continue north via I-5 north of Olympia to Tacoma (253-284-3254; traveltacoma.com) and visit the splendid *Museum of Glass* (museumofglass.org), walk across the Chihuly Bridge to the *Washington History Museum* (252-272-3500; washingtonhistory.org), and see the *Tacoma Art Museum*, all located in the revitalized Thea Foss Waterway area west of the freeway. Find cozy lodgings and also eateries galore in the area with awesome views of 14,000-foot Mount Rainier to the east on clear days.

Gig Harbor and Whidbey & Camano Islands: Pop over to *Gig Harbor* (gigharborguide.com) and then friendly *Whidbey Island* (whidbeycamanoislands.com). Spend a couple of fun days in each location to enjoy great shops, scenic gardens, comfortable lodgings, and pleasant eateries.

Port Townsend and Olympic Peninsula: This corner of the Evergreen State is filled with wide tidal waters and mountain views, scenic drives along *Hood Canal*, and hikes in the *Olympic National Park* (360-565-3130; nps.gov/olym) along with a plethora of great sleeps and eats in Port Townsend (360-385-2722; enjoypt.com), Sequim, and Port Angeles (360-452-8552; olympicpeninsula.org).

San Juan Islands: Board a large Washington State ferry (206-464-6400; wsdot.wa .gov/ferries) at *Anacortes* (360-293-3832; anacortes.org) and sail to Shaw, Lopez, Orcas, and San Juan islands (888-468-3701; visitsanjuans.com); stay as long as you're able; find good eats and cozy sleeps on *San Juan Islands*, the largest and most populated island.

Bellingham & North Coast: More awesome water views, *Historic Fairhaven District*, and fabulous eats and sleeps; stay overnight at *Fairhaven Village Inn* (360-733-1311; fairhavenvillageinn.com, bellingham.org) with views of Bellingham Bay. From here overnight ferries depart for destinations in southeastern Alaska.

Vancouver and Victoria, British Columbia: With passports and identification papers in hand, stop at the international border crossing at Blaine, Washington, and enjoy visiting scenic *Vancouver, BC* (tourismvancouver.com) as well as ferrying to the lovely and very British city of *Victoria* on Vancouver Island (bcferries.com and tourismvictoria .com).

Continuing a few blocks north and east, visit the ca. 1846 *McLoughlin House National Historic Site* (503-656-5151; mcloughlinhouse.org), at 713 Center Street, Oregon City, which is generally open Wed through Sat from 10:00 a.m. to 4:00 p.m. This was the home of Dr. John McLoughlin, a dominant figure in not only the Hudson's Bay Company but also the early development of the region. Appointed chief factor, or superintendent of trade, of the British company in 1824, the tall, white-haired, cane-carrying man ruled over the entire Columbia country before the Oregon Trail migration began in 1843.

Under orders from the Hudson's Bay Company, McLoughlin established the first settlement at Oregon City, and he later moved here from Fort Vancouver, across the Columbia River, when he resigned from the company in 1845. Incidentally, reconstructed Fort Vancouver, nearby in Vancouver, Washington, and its splendid reclaimed British-style vegetable, herb, and flower gardens are well worth a visit. Inside the large reconstructed stockade, you can visit living-history programs in the kitchen quarters, baking quarters, general store, blacksmith shop, and main house, which are provided by National Park Service staff and community volunteers. **Fort Vancouver National Historic Site**, open daily, is located just across the Columbia River from Portland, at 612 E. Reserve Street, Vancouver, Washington (360-816-6230; nps.gov/fova). Browse the website for special living history programs throughout the year, which include the Soldiers Bivouac, the Brigade Encampment, and the Holiday Candlelight Tours.

Born in the Canadian province of Quebec, McLoughlin became a US citizen in 1851 and spent his later years operating his store, gristmill, and sawmills near the base of Willamette Falls at Oregon City. His house, a large clapboard-style building with simple, dignified lines, was saved from demolition and moved from its original location along the Willamette River near the falls up to the top of the bluff and placed in what is now **McLoughlin Park** at 7th and Center Streets. On the lovely grounds are large rhododendrons, clumps of azaleas, and old roses, and to the rear of the house sits a moss-covered fountain, shaded by tall Douglas firs and trailing ivy.

Also stop to see splendid exhibits of pioneer quilts, early fashions, and river and steamboat memorabilia at the Clackamas County Historical Society's **Museum of the Oregon Territory**, located on a bluff just above the Willamette River and Willamette Falls, at 211 Tumwater Drive (503-655-5574; clackamashistory.org). Call ahead for current hours.

Another rural loop from Oregon City offers a ramble into the eastern section of Clackamas County, reaching into the foothills of the Cascade Mountains. Take the Park Place exit from I-205 and turn left at the first light, toward Park Place. Settle into the slow lane and wind along Clackamas River Drive toward Carver. Rather than crossing the river here just yet, continue east on Springwater Road; then just beyond the boat-ramp entrance, turn right, and proceed for about a quarter mile to the **German Methodist Church** and the **Baker Cabin**, located at the corner of Hattan and Gronlund Roads.

The small church, built around 1895, sits like a tidy dowager under tall firs surrounded by well-kept grounds. Walk the gravel drive to the far end of the grassy area to inspect the Baker Cabin, which dates from 1856. Notice the old grapevine, with its enormous main trunk, which must have been planted around the same time as the cabin was built. The logs were hand-hewn into square-shaped timbers that deftly interlock at the four corners. Tiny ferns and wildflowers grow from crevices in the old rock fireplace chimney at the west end of the cabin.

Pacific Northwest Live Steamers

Take a ride with the kids in one of the small open--air rail cars behind your "Sunday engineer" at *Molalla Train Park at Shady Dell* (pnls.org). Two long toots signal "start" or "release brakes"; a long and a short mean "warning"; three shorts when a train is stopped designate "back up"; and one long whistle indicates the train is approaching a station. The miniature engine huffs and puffs steam from a tiny smokestack, just like its full-size original counterpart—the sleek steam locomotive that replaced both horse-drawn wagons as well as Pony Express riders and helped to settle the West. At Shady Dell Park volunteer engineers run miniature trains on some 6,000 feet of track from noon to 5:00 p.m. on Sun May through October. In recent decades, these mechanical marvels have all but disappeared, especially the steam locomotives, although many full-size models are also being restored and put back into service for nostalgic week-end trips and dinner excursions; examples are the *Mount Hood Railroad* in Hood River (800-872-4661; mthoodrr.com); the *Sumpter Valley Railroad* in Sumpter, near Baker City (541-894-2310; sumptervalleyrailroad.org); the *Oregon Coast Scenic Railroad* in Tillamook (503-842-7972; oregoncoastscenic.org). Also check out the days and hours for the splendid *Medford Railroad Park* in southern Oregon (541-890-8145) and the *Portland and Columbia Gorge Model Railroad Club* (503-28-TRAIN; columbiagorgemodelrailroadclub.com). Also be sure to take the kids and grandkids to visit the *Oregon Rail Heritage Center* located near the Willamette River and OMSI (Oregon Museum of Science and Industry), 2250 SE Water Avenue in southeast Portland (503-233-1156; orhf.org). Browse the website to determine current hours to view several renovated steam engines used for hauling logs and other goods on Oregon and Washington rails years ago.

Now backtrack to the Carver bridge, cross the Clackamas River, and go farther off the beaten path by taking Highway 224 east about 15 miles toward Estacada. For history buffs, your next stop is the *Philip Foster National Historic Farm* (503-637-6324; philipfosterfarm.com), located just off Highway 224 at 29912 SE Highway. 211, Eagle Creek. Offering a number of excellent living history programs from May through October, this site provides a nostalgic look at the 1840s, when Philip and Mary Foster ran a general store, restaurant, and resting place for Oregon Trail pioneers on the final leg of their trek to the West. You'll see Mary's lilac tree blooming in the front yard; it was planted in 1843, having survived the arduous journey "around the horn" from Calais, Maine. Mary, bless her heart, cooked meals for some 10,000 emigrants during those early trail years. And she raised nine children and tended the orchards and gardens as well. On the last Saturday in October, stop by the farm to take in the annual Cider Squeeze and Harvest Festival.

In the small community of Estacada look for **Harmony Bakery** (971-400-7987), tucked away at 221 SW Wade Street. Here you can join a diverse group of local folks who meet to drink coffee, eat freshly made bagels and yummy pastries, and, of course, have a good morning or afternoon chat about the weather and the state of the world's affairs. Try the omelet with spicy hash-brown potatoes, vegetarian fare, or more traditional sandwiches and burgers. The restaurant is open seven days a week from 8:00 a.m. to 3:00 p.m.

From Estacada continue south another 15 miles or so via Highway 211 to Molalla to discover **Prairie House Inn Bed & Breakfast** at 524 E. Main Street (503-829-8245; theprairiehouseinn.com). The large prairie-style farmhouse with its deep wraparound porch has been restored as a comfortable bed-and-breakfast inn with four guest rooms on the second floor. Breakfast is served in the cozy dining area with such treats as freshly made muffins, gourmet frit-tatas, and seasonal fruits served along with steaming hot coffees and teas. From Molalla it's an easy trek to Mount Angel, Silverton, and the Salem area farther south into the heart of the Willamette Valley.

Farm and Flower Country

Aurora and Canby

From Molalla you can complete your rural loop back to the Portland area by heading west on Highway 211 to Woodburn and turning north on old Highway 99E through Hubbard to Aurora, Canby, and back to Oregon City. Old **Highway 99**, which divides into two sections, 99E and 99W, as it winds through Willamette Valley towns, was the first paved north–south route (it followed sections of the early stagecoach route) linking all cities and towns along the Willamette River and south into the Umpqua and Rogue River valleys. In those early days, trips on Highway 99 took seven "long" hours of driving from Medford and Grants Pass in southern Oregon to Portland.

Although travelers can now whiz up and down sleek I-5, covering the same distance in about four and a half hours, once in a while it's nice to get off the freeway and ramble along sections of old Highway 99 and its rural tributaries. It's a nostalgic trek into yesterday for Oregonians, one generously shared with visitors.

Pull off Highway 99E in Aurora to visit the **Aurora National Historic District** and the **Old Aurora Colony Museum** at 15018 2nd Street Northeast (503-678-5754; auroracolony.org), which inhabits a large, refurbished ox barn. The colony's history began in the Harmony Colony in Pennsylvania, from which William Keil, a German tailor, physician, and preacher, and his followers first emigrated to found the town of Bethel, Missouri, near the start of the Oregon Trail.

Some of the historic landmarks at the Aurora Museum have vanished over the years, but many of the buildings remain, including the ox barn that houses the museum, a small log cabin, a washhouse, and a machine shed; there's also an assortment of farm machinery, and a lovely miniature garden, the **Emma Wakefield Herb Garden**. The colony was well known for its fine cooking and music; its brass band entertained at community festivities and events. In the museum you'll see many of the brass instruments, including the schellenbaum, a rare bell tree.

TOP ANNUAL EVENTS IN PORTLAND AND ENVIRONS

JANUARY

Oregon Truffle Festival
Willamette Valley
oregontrufflefestival.org

MARCH

Portland Seafood and Wine Festival
Portland
pdxseafoodandwinefestival.com
(360) 258-0746

APRIL

Spring Beer & Wine Fest
Oregon Convention Center, Portland
springbeerandwinefest.com

MAY

Fiesta Cinco de Mayo
Portland
cincodemayo.org

JUNE

Chamber Music Northwest Summer Festival
Portland
(503) 223-3202
cmnw.org

Lake Oswego Festival of the Arts
(503) 636-1060
lakewood-center.org

Portland Rose Festival
Portland
(503) 227-2681
rosefestival.org

JULY

Oregon Brewers Festival
Tom McCall Waterfront Park, downtown Portland
oregonbrewfest.com

SEPTEMBER

Feast Portland
feastportland.com

DECEMBER

Christmas Ship Parades
Columbia River & Willamette River
christmasships.org

OTHER ATTRACTIONS WORTH SEEING IN PORTLAND AND ENVIRONS

Canby Farm Loop
canbyfarmloop.com

Oregon Museum of Science and Industry (OMSI)
Portland's eastside on the Willamette River
omsi.edu

Pearson Air Museum, Fort Vancouver National Historic Site, and 1840s British Gardens
Vancouver, Washington
(360-816-6232)

pearsonairmuseum.org
nps.gov/fova
(360-816-6230)

Salmon Run Bell Tower and Historic Slocum House
Esther Short Park
Downtown Vancouver, Washington
visitvancouverusa.com

The museum also has an excellent collection of historic quilts made by various women of the Aurora community, and many of these quilts are displayed throughout the year. In early March, take in the popular **Spinning Wheel Showcase** (503-678-5754; auroracolony.org), held at the ox barn museum. The museum complex is open Friday and Saturday from 11:00 a.m. to 4:00 p.m.; Sunday noon to 4:00 p.m.; closed during January.

Antiques buffs can browse more than two dozen shops in Aurora. Try **Main Street Mercantile**, 21610 Main Street (503-678-1044; mainstmerc.com), for antiques and collectibles in more than 15,000 square feet of space; **Home Again Antiques**, 21631 Main Street (503-678-0227), open Tuesday through Sunday 11:00 a.m. to 5:00 p.m., for Americana and primitives; **Scatter Creek Junction**, 21641 Main Street in the historic 1865 Jacob Miley House (503-678-1068; scattercreekjunction.com), offers early country Americana, folk art, and a cafe in the cozy log room of the original house; and **Time After Time Antiques, Teas & Gifts** in the 1872 William Fry House at 21611 Main Street (503-678-5463; timeaftertimeoregon.com), open Tuesday through Sunday at 11:00 a.m. The **Colony Pub** at 21568 Highway 99E, Aurora (503-678-9994; auroracolonypub.com) is famous locally for its burgers and other tasty pub fare; it is open daily for lunch and dinner and weekends for breakfast.

Head north from Aurora about 3 miles to the small town of Canby to find **Puddin' River Chocolates**, 1438 S. Ivy Street (503-263-2626; puddinriver chocolates.com), open daily. Locals also rave about **Backstop Bar & Grill**,

211 N. Grant Street, Canby (503-263-6606; backstopbarandgrill.com). *Wild Hare Saloon* at 1190 SW 1st. Grand Street (503-651-4273; thewildharesaloon.com) serves lunch and dinner daily plus tasty breakfasts and brunches on weekends.

From Canby you can take another side ramble by turning east onto Barlow Road and proceeding about 4 miles to *St. Josef's Winery* at 28836 S. Barlow Road (503-651-3190; stjosefswinery.com). The Fleischmann family produced its first vintage in 1978. The tasting room is open from noon to 5:00 p.m. on weekends; phone ahead on weekdays.

As you head back toward Canby on Barlow Road to Highway 99E, notice the large fields of tulips and other bulbs that bloom during mid-April. In these far southern reaches of Clackamas County, the rich alluvial soils from ancient rivers support more than a hundred nurseries, where growers raise everything from annuals and perennials to ornamentals and fruit stock, and acres of lush green turf grass.

Most of the nurseries are the wholesale variety, shipping to destinations throughout the United States, but a few are open to the public. Near Canby, just a few miles west of the downtown area at 995 NW 22nd Avenue, visit *Swan Island Dahlias* (503-266-7711; dahlias.com) and wander through some 43 acres of the gorgeous perennials that bloom in late summer, beginning in August and lasting until the first frost, sometime in mid to late October. This large nursery has been operated by the Gitts family since the 1950s, and dahlias have been part of the Canby area since the late 1940s. The farm features more than 250 dahlia varieties, with blooms ranging from 12 or more inches in diameter to those of tiny pompons, at less than 2 inches across.

From Canby you can get to Swan Island Dahlias via Ivy Street to 2nd Street, then Holly Street to 22nd Street. During the farm's annual *Dahlia Festival*, usually held the first or second weekend of September, you can watch professional designers fashion the vibrant blooms into creative arrangements. If you miss that event, you can still stroll through the blooming fields daily beginning in August, from 8:00 a.m. to 8:00 p.m.

If the kids or the grandkids are along, stop at the nearby *Flower Farmer and Phoenix & Holly Railroad*, located at 2512 N. Holly Street (503-266-3581; flowerfarmer.com). The railroad runs Saturday and Sunday from 11:00 a.m. to 6:00 p.m. Daily train rides to the farm's Pumpkin Patch in October are a special treat. The open market stand is loaded with the freshest seasonal varieties of corn, beans, tomatoes, peaches, and the like; the indoor gift shop offers a fine selection of dried flowers and fresh flowers from the fields. It's open June through October from 10:00 a.m. to 6:00 p.m. Ask if the nearby *Canby Ferry* is running (it carries less than a dozen cars); if so, take the 5-minute ride across this section of the Willamette River. From here you can drive west toward **Sandelie Golf Course**, 28333 SW Mountain Road (503-655-1461), and access I-5 at nearby Wilsonville.

To delve into more history of the area, stop at the **Canby Depot Museum** (503-266-6712) at the north edge of town. The museum, maintained by the Canby Area Historical Society, is housed in the oldest railroad station owned by the C&C Railroad. The restored building is just off Highway 99E at the Fairgrounds exit and is open Thursday through Sunday from 1:00 to 4:00 p.m., March through December. Also, be sure to poke into the charming restored caboose located a few steps from the museum's entry door. To inquire about the old-fashioned **Clackamas County Fair**, one of the best late summertime events in the area, contact the Canby Visitor Center at 191 SE 2nd Street (503-266-4600; visitcanby.com). You and the kids can also enjoy trekking around the **Canby Farm Loop** (canbyfarmloop.com), which offers a self-guided loop to farm stands, gift shops, U-Picks, wineries, eateries, and lodgings in the farm region.

Places to Stay in Portland and Environs

PORTLAND—VANCOUVER

Best Western Rivershore Inn
1900 Clackamette Drive
Oregon City
(503) 644-7141

Hotel Eastlund
1021 NE Grand Avenue
Portland
(503) 235-2100
hoteleastlund.com

Hilton Hotel Vancouver
301 W. 6th and Columbia
Street
(360) 993-4500

Hotel deLuxe
729 SW 15th Avenue
Portland
(503) 219-2094

Portland's White House Bed & Breakfast
1914 NE 22nd Avenue
Portland
(503) 287-7131
portlandswhitehouse.com

ST. HELENS

Best Western Oak Meadows Inn
585 S. Columbia River Highway 30
(503) 397-3000
bestwestern.com

Nob Hill Riverview Bed & Breakfast
285 S. 2nd Street
(503) 396-5555
nobhillbb.com

TROUTDALE

Best Western Troutdale
23525 NE Halsey Street,
(503) 491-9700
bestwestern.com

McMenamins Edgefield
2126 SW Halsey Street
Troutdale
(503) 669-8610
mcmenamins.com

Places to Eat in Portland & Environs

AURORA

Scatter Creek Junction
21641 Main Street
(503) 678-1068
scattercreekjunction.com

White Rabbit Bakery & Deli
21368 Main Street
(503) 267-9044
whiterabbitbakery.com

CANBY

Backstop Bar & Grill
211 N. Grant Street
(503) 263-6606
backstopbarandgrill.com

Puddin' River Chocolates
1438 S. Ivy Street
(503) 263-2626
puddinriverchocolates.com

GRESHAM

Boccelli's Italian Ristorante
246 N. Main Avenue
(503) 492-9534

Sugar Cubed Cakes
101 N. Main Avenue
(503) 512-7871
sugarcubedcakes.com

Sunny Han's Wok & Grill
305 N. Main Avenue
(503) 666-3663

HELPFUL TELEPHONE NUMBERS AND WEBSITES FOR PORTLAND AND ENVIRONS

Aurora Colony Visitors Association
Aurora
(503) 678-5754
auroracolony.com

Canby Visitor Information Center
Canby
(503) 266-4600
visitcanby.com

End of the Oregon Trail Historic Site and Mt. Hood Territory Visitors Center
Oregon City
(503) 657-9336
historicoregoncity.org

Metro Parks and Natural Areas
(503) 797-1700
oregonmetro.gov

Oregon Historical Society
(503) 222-1741
ohs.org

Portland Parks & Recreation
(503) 823-7529
portlandoregon.gov
/parks

South Columbia County Visitor Center
St. Helens and
Scappoose

(503) 397-0685
sccchamber.org

Travel Portland Visitors Information Center
(503) 427-1372
travelportland.com

West Columbia Gorge Visitor Center
Troutdale
(503) 669-7473
westcolumbiagor
gechamber.com

OREGON CITY

The Highland Stillhouse
201 S. Second Street
(503) 723-6789
highlandstillhouse.com

Mia Famiglia Pizza
701 Main Street
(503) 594-0601
mia-famiglia.com

Ranee's Café & Bar on Main
1003 Main Street
(503) 305-7827
raneesonmain.com

Singer Hill Café
623 Seventh Street
(503) 656-5252
singerhill.com

PORTLAND

Al la Cart Food Carts pod
SE 50th and Division
Streets
foodcartsportland.com

Cadillac Cafe
1801 NE Broadway
(503) 287-4750
cadillaccafepdx.com

Cup & Saucer Café
3566 SE Hawthorne
Boulevard
(503) 236-6001
cupandsaucercafe.com

Dan & Louis Oyster Bar
208 SW Ankeny Street
(503) 227-5906
danandlouis.com

**Deschutes Brewery
Portland Pub**
210 NW 11th Avenue
(503) 296-4906
deschutesbrewery.com

**Island Cafe on the
River**
250 NE Tomahawk
Island Drive
(503) 283-0362

**Moonstruck Chocolate
Cafe**
608 SW Alder Street
(503) 241-0955
moonstruckchocolate.com

Old Town Pizza
226 NW Davis Street
(503) 222-9999
oldtownpizza.com

Papa Haydn Cafe
701 NW 23rd Avenue
(503) 228-7317
papahaydn.com

**Petite Provence Bou-
langerie & Patisserie**
4834 SE Division Street
(503) 233-1121
provence-portland.com

Pine State Biscuits Cafe
1717 NW 23rd Street

(971) 407-3621
pinestatebiscuits.com

The Pearl Coffeehouse
1235 NW Marshall Street
(971) 279-2957
sisterscoffee.com/pearl.html

Voodoo Doughnut
1501 NE Davis Street
(503) 235-2666
voodoodoughnut.com

ST. HELENS

Dockside Steak & Pasta
343 S. 1st Street
(503) 366-0877

**Kozy Korner Restaurant &
Lounge**
371 Columbia Boulevard
(503) 397-9754

Columbia River Gorge and High Cascades

The Columbia River Gorge extends east from Troutdale for more than 80 miles alongside the wide Columbia River. Those early Oregon Trail pioneers in the 1840s found this mighty river filled with dangerous rushing rapids, and equally dangerous strong currents, when they floated their belongings downriver on flatboats from The Dalles. Bound for the then-established Fort Vancouver located on the river near present-day Vancouver, Washington, many lives and belongings were lost during those arduous voyages.

Today, driving along streamlined I-84, you'll see a still-wide but much calmer river due to a number of dams which have tamed the rapids and currents. This allows commercial barge traffic, as well as pleasure boats, to safely navigate the Columbia upriver and downriver. At the Tri-Cities area of Washington State, the Snake River empties from the east into the Columbia and joins the journey west to the Pacific Ocean. Along this scenic drive, you'll also see geological formations on both sides of the Columbia Gorge, where eons ago streams of molten lava and enormous mud flows left their marks high on the rocky outcrops. Approaching Hood River from the west, you'll see Mt. Hood looming more than 11,000 feet on

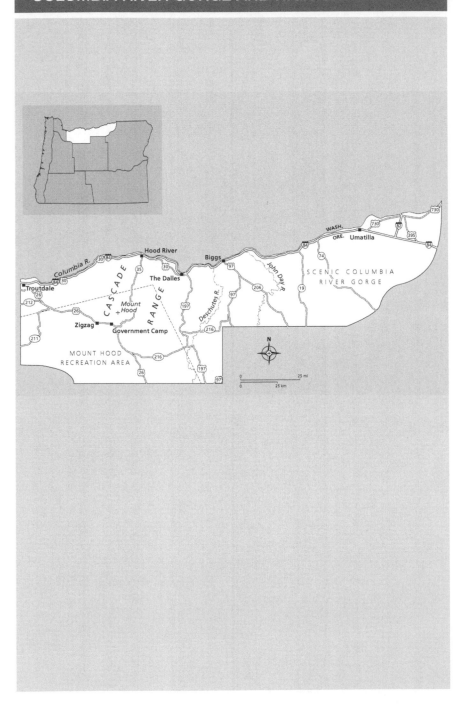

the Oregon side and Mt. Adams rising some 9,000 feet on the Washington side of the Columbia River. You will be treated to the sight of dozens of waterfalls along the way, including one that falls more than 600 feet from its stream at the cliff-top. Continuing east from Hood River to The Dalles, you'll find dozens of vineyards and wineries, along with lush apple, pear, and cherry orchards.

In 1845, an alternate road for the Oregon Trail pioneers was organized by Samuel K. Barlow. It was hacked out of the dense alpine forest and lower elevation Douglas fir forest on the western side of Mount Hood, toward what are now the communities of Government Camp, Rhododendron, Welches, and Sandy. Pacific Northwesterners have trooped up to Mount Hood since the early 1900s, long before a paved road was constructed. In those days, it took folks up to two days to reach the mountain, whereas today you can easily drive there in about an hour. At the mountain, you can alpine or cross-county ski during winter months, and camp and picnic in summer months. There are dozens of shady campgrounds, scenic lakes, and fine ski areas just outside the Portland area.

Scenic Columbia River Gorge

Although much of the original winding highway, clinging alongside the Columbia River Gorge since 1915, has deteriorated or become part of streamlined I-84, visitors can enjoy two good-size segments of the historic *Columbia River Scenic Highway* east of Portland between Troutdale and The Dalles.

Troutdale and Multnomah Falls

Before heading east into the Columbia River Gorge, particularly if you've not eaten, consider stopping in *Troutdale* to find the *Power Station Pub* (503-492-4686) and the *Black Rabbit Restaurant* (503-492-3086), two eateries at *McMenamins Edgefield* (mcmenamins.com). It is located at 2126 SW Halsey Street, just south of I-84 at the Wood Village exit. The pub's juicy hamburgers are legendary, and during warm weather you can eat outside at *The Loading Dock*, where the outdoor grill is fired up. In the Black Rabbit, the more formal restaurant, you might order such Northwest fare as salmon with hazelnut butter or clams steamed in ale. If time allows, tour the 25-acre complex that, in the early 1900s, housed the fully self-contained Multnomah County Poor Farm. Now completely restored, including a perennial and herb garden and small vineyard, the complex includes lodging, meeting rooms, a winery and wine cellar pub, an outdoor barbecue and picnic area, a movie theater, a concert venue and a small nine-hole golf course.

The small community of Troutdale is a pleasant destination for antiques buffs, with fun shops such as ***Troutdale Antique Mall*** (503-674-6820). After shopping for antiques, you can also browse in several gift shops such as The ***Troutdale General Store & Cafe*** (503-492-7912); and ***Celebrate Me Home*** (503-618-9394; celebratemehomeonline.com), which offers home furnishings, gifts, and the Espresso Bar with specialty drinks, sandwiches, and pastries. Visit the artists' collective, studio and gallery the ***Troutdale Art Center*** (503-386-7006) for a glimpse of artists at work and a variety of art for sale. These establishments, and more, are located on Troutdale's main street, the Historic Columbia River Highway. Park by the Troutdale Rail Depot Museum at the east end of the downtown area and enjoy browsing along Troutdale's main street.

If time allows, however, ease into ***Ristorante di Pompello*** at 177 E. Historic Columbia River Highway (503-667-2480; dipompello.com), an eatery also on Troutdale's main street, and enjoy breakfast, lunch, or dinner with a tasty Italian flair.

History buffs visiting Troutdale can call ahead to arrange a visit to the ca. 1900 ***Harlow House Museum***, at 726 E. Historic Columbia River Highway (503-661-2164; troutdalehistory.org). The farmhouse was built in 1900 by the Harlow family; Capt. John Harlow founded the town. The house is cared for by the Troutdale Historical Society. Period furnishings fill the nooks and crannies of the old house, its cupboards spill over with dry goods and period wallpapers, and there may be exhibits of teapots and accessories, early fashions, and quilts. Railroad buffs can plan to stop and browse a collection of memorabilia at the ***Troutdale Rail Depot Museum***, located in downtown Troutdale at 473 E. Columbia River Highway (503-661-2164; troutdalehistory.org). Originally built in 1882, the depot was one of the earliest train stations along the Columbia River route.

TOP HITS IN COLUMBIA RIVER GORGE AND HIGH CASCADES

Baldwin Saloon, ca. 1876
The Dalles

Historic Clackamas Lake Ranger Station
off US 26, east of Government Camp

Historic Columbia River Highway
starting at Troutdale and heading east

Historic Columbia River Highway State Trail
Mosier–Hood River

Timberline Lodge, Mount Hood
Government Camp

The Vista House Visitor and Interpretive Center at Crown Point
Historic Columbia River Highway

A Most Elegant Visitor Center

Located just a few miles beyond Corbett, the ca. 1918 **Vista House Visitor and Interpretive Center** (40700 E. Columbia River Highway; 503-695-2240; vistahouse. com) sits high above the Columbia River on Crown Point, a promontory above busy I-84. Vista House affords grand views both east and west, as well as north across the Columbia River into Washington State. The distinguished-looking stone structure has undergone a complete restoration and refurbishing helped by funds from Oregon Parks and Recreation Department, Oregon State Parks Trust, and the Friends of Vista House. Construction was started on the octagonal structure in 1916 as a memorial to Oregon pioneers and a comfort station for those traveling the Historic Columbia River Highway 30. Don't miss a stop here!

For additional information about the area, contact the staff at the West Columbia Gorge Visitor Center (503-669-7473; westcolumbiagorgechamber.com) on Troutdale's main street, open daily.

Punctuated with a dozen or more cascading waterfalls and enough hiking trails to keep outdoor buffs busy for weeks, the **Historic Columbia River Highway** offers a relaxed alternative to busy I-84. To access the first section of the old highway, detour from the freeway at the Lewis and Clark State Park exit east of Troutdale, just across the Sandy River.

Or, from Troutdale, you can continue east and south on the Historic Columbia River Highway and follow it as it parallels the bank of the Sandy River and loops several miles south, then angles east through a sun-filtered canopy of big-leaf maples and Douglas fir, climbing gradually to the small community of Corbett. Just east of Corbett, pull into **Portland Women's Forum State Scenic Viewpoint**, at Chanticleer Point, for one of the best panoramas of the Columbia River Gorge and the wide Columbia River, which separates Oregon from Washington. The view is almost too vast to absorb. You'll see the massive stone Vista House perched atop Crown Point just a couple of miles distant; the silver ribbon of river shimmering some 750 feet below; the 800-foot **Beacon Rock**, a volcanic monolith about 25 miles upstream on the Washington side of the river; and the Union Pacific railroad tracks and I-84, narrow ribbons paralleling the mighty river.

You could bring a picnic and beverages and travel the **Larch Mountain Road** about 10 miles up to the top of the mountain, where you'll find picnic tables set in cozy wooded glens and short trails out to wide vistas of the gorge.

(**Note**: The road to the top usually opens by June and closes with the first snows.) Take sweaters and warm windbreakers, as temperatures can be brisk at this 1,500-foot elevation. From here backtrack down Larch Mountain Road to return to the Historic Columbia River Highway.

Samuel Hill, a Washingtonian and a lover of roads, inspired the building of the Columbia River Highway. Combining forces with Samuel Lancaster, the consulting engineer, and Portland businessmen Simon Benson and John Yeon, Hill not only envisioned the economic and tourist potential of such a road but appreciated the aesthetic and natural beauty of the gorge as well. The highway was dedicated and opened in 1915 to lure the state's early twentieth-century motorists as well as travelers en route to the 1915 Panama Pacific Exposition in California.

In the design of this first major highway in the Northwest, Lancaster incorporated graceful stone bridges, viaducts, stone walls, tunnels, and stone benches. He had been inspired by a trip to Europe with Sam Hill for the purpose of studying the historic Roman roads there. Alongside the Columbia River the ancient trail of deer, Native peoples, and those first fur trappers was replaced with the functional yet beautiful highway that clung so closely to the gorge's lush moss-and-fern-covered and tree-laden outcroppings.

Stop at the parking area at **Vista House** (503-695-2240) at Crown Point for more camera clicking and history recollecting. Passing Shepperd's Dell Falls, continue on to **Wahkeena Falls** (*wahkeena* is a Native American word for "most beautiful"), where you'll find more parking and a large picnic area. Wahkeena tumbles and cascades in a series of frothy falls; dainty wildflowers bloom around rocks and in mossy crevices.

Multnomah Falls, just east of Latourell and Wahkeena Falls, is the most spectacular in the Columbia River Gorge, cascading in a long drop of 620 feet from the basaltic gorge rim. It's one of the highest waterfalls in the United States. If time allows, walk the easy trail to the upper bridge for a close encounter with the cascading water, accompanied by its swishing roar and cool mist.

An easy, though somewhat steep, trail continues from the bridge up to the rim for a top-of-the-falls, panoramic view of the world below. It's well worth the 2.4-mile round-trip trek, especially midweek, when you'll encounter fewer tourists. Take along some water or another beverage, and keep an eye out for poison oak, which lurks here and there along the trail's edge; the leaves look like a miniature oak leaf, and almost everyone is allergic to every part of the plant.

Waterfall-Watching Along Historic Columbia River Highway 30

The more than seventy-five waterfalls on the Oregon side of the Columbia River Gorge come in all shapes, sizes, widths, and lengths. They cascade down rocky inclines, fall across basalt ledges, separate and fan over other large rocks, spray over rocky terraces, and plunge straight down in lacy drapes. Waterfall-watchers can learn to classify the eight main forms: block, cascade, fan, horsetail, plunge, punchbowl, segmented, and tiered.

Along the winding route are numerous places to pull off and park; some falls are reached by short trails, while others are close to the highway. There are parks, campgrounds, and good places to picnic. Keep an alert eye on young children in your party and be wary of automobile and bicycle traffic along the busy and narrow ca. 1915 **Historic Columbia River Highway 30**, which does not offer the wide shoulders that modern highways usually have. Summer weekends are busiest; try to visit midweek for a more peaceful sojourn.

For helpful information and trail maps, stop at the Forest Service information counter at Multnomah Falls Lodge (503-695-2372; fs.usda.gov/crgnsa), which provides information about the Columbia River Gorge National Scenic Area as well as trails to the waterfalls, directions, and more. Also see Friends of the Historic Columbia River Highway (culturaltrust.org) for current information about the fine efforts to reclaim sections of the historic highway between Troutdale, Vista House at Crown Point, Hood River, Mosier, and The Dalles for walking, hiking, biking, and driving.

At the base of the falls, linger to visit rustic **Multnomah Falls Lodge**, also constructed in 1914–1915, where breakfast, lunch, and dinner are served in the fireplace dining room and also in a lovely atrium dining area; there is also a snack bar, a gift shop, and a Forest Service Visitor Center (503-695-2372; fs.usda .gov/crgnsa). Call the lodge restaurant (503-695-2376) for dinner or Sunday brunch reservations. **Note**: Although there are no overnight accommodations at the lodge, you can find lodgings to the east at nearby Cascade Locks and also at Hood River and also to the west at Troutdale and Portland.

East of Multnomah Falls, and still on the Historic Columbia River Highway, is **Oneonta Gorge**. Oneonta Creek bubbles through the narrowest of high, mossy chasms here, and those who don't mind getting their feet wet can walk up the shallow creek to the cascading falls. Hikers are asked to be cautious of large boulders, however, which can dislodge and cause injury. Just east, a trail at **Horsetail Falls** leads behind the upper falls, crossing Oneonta Creek right before the water plunges over the rim in a frothy ribbon.

For helpful trail maps and hiking information, go to the Forest Service visitor centers located at Multnomah Falls Lodge (503-695-2372) and at Skamania Lodge in Stevenson (509-427-2528), just east on WA 14 on the Washington side of the river (access via Bridge of the Gods at Cascade Locks).

If your visit coincides with the busy summer crush of traffic on the narrow Historic Columbia River Highway 30 and you want to get away from the crowds, continue east toward **Ainsworth State Park**. Instead of pulling onto I-84 at this point, stay to the right on the frontage road that parallels the freeway and continue just a half mile or so to a large parking area and the **Elowah Falls–McCord Creek trailhead.** Bask in the sun on large rounded rocks at the lower falls—take a left at the trail's first fork—or relax in sun-filtered shade on large rocks at the upper falls. Both hikes are easy—less than 2 miles in length—and the views of the falls and gorge are spectacular, particularly on the upper falls route. These quiet, peaceful walks are far removed from the crowds and allow a focused interlude with the incredibly beautiful gorge habitat. **Note**: Be sure to take water and snacks for everyone in your group.

If time permits, don't miss this trek into history, geology, and plant life that numerous wildlife and conservation groups are working to protect. From such organizations as the Native Plant Societies of Oregon and Washington (npsoregon.org and wnps.org) and local chapters of the Audubon Society (audubonportland.org), Friends of the Columbia River Gorge (gorgefriends .org), the Forest Service (fs.usda.gov/crgnsa), the Mazamas (mazamas.org), the Trails Club of Oregon (trailsclub.org), Oregon Wild (oregonwild.org), and Friends of the Historic Columbia River Highway (culturaltrust.org), thousands of folks are dedicated to the task of preserving the fragile and irreplaceable as well as historic habitats and the historic Columbia River Highway within the Columbia River Gorge.

Lewis and Clark Territory

The Corps of Discovery, thirty-three folks plus Clark's Newfoundland dog, Seaman, paused and camped in the eastern section of the Columbia River Gorge and Snake River areas during 1805, on their way to the Pacific Ocean, and in spring 1806, returning home. To learn more about the expedition, and to see some sites where Lewis and Clark were, visit:

Lewis and Clark Timeline, etched in pavement in Clarkston, Washington
Snake River, from the Clarkston-Lewiston area to Pasco, Washington
Columbia River, from Pasco 300 miles to the Pacific Ocean
Sacajawea State Park, campground and interpretive center, near Kennewick, Washington
Maryhill Museum, with native crafts and carvings, near The Dalles, Oregon, and Goldendale, Washington (maryhillmuseum.org)
Hat Rock State Park, near Umatilla, Oregon
Horsethief Lake State Park, east of Bingen, Washington
US 12 east through Dayton, Washington, to Clarkston, Washington, and nearby Lewiston, Idaho, roughly parallels Lewis & Clark's return journey to the East Coast in spring 1806

Backcountry Hiking in the Scenic Columbia River Gorge

Travelers will find more than 200 hiking trails in the Columbia River Gorge, and these are especially suited for spring, summer, and fall treks. Do not hike during the winter months. Forest Service rangers suggest the following preparation for everyone, regardless of how experienced they are with backcountry hiking into the forest:

Always inform someone not traveling with you of your complete route.

Carry these essentials: whistle, map, compass, a flashlight with extra batteries and bulb, waterproof matches, fire starter, first-aid kit, pocket knife, hat and sunburn protection, extra water for every member of the group, snacks and trail food, and adequate clothing.

Carry a cell phone with fully charged battery in case you need assistance. If possible, learn the basic skills of backcountry orienteering with map and compass.

Respect your environment. The gorge receives thousands of visitors a year. Practice leave no trace principles, park in designated spaces only, respect fire, camping and trail restrictions, do not interfere with wildlife, and respect other visitors.

Beginning hikers should choose short trails near established areas or, an even better option, join a guided trek. Check with local ranger stations for trail maps and for information about guided nature hikes. To research current information, start with the Forest Service Information Center at *Multnomah Falls Lodge* (503-695-2372; fs .usda.gov/crgnsa), and check gorgefriends.org for current lists and information about guided hikes, treks, and wildflower walks.

Try an easy day hike, the *McCord Creek Trail* at Elowah Falls. The trailhead is located east of Multnomah Falls near Ainsworth State Park. Take a small picnic and beverages and enjoy munching while sitting on the large flat rocks at the upper falls. It's about a 2-mile hike to the upper falls with showstopping views of the Columbia River Gorge along the way.

Other folks are learning about the many edible wild plants in the region from John Kallas, a guru of edible wild food with a doctorate in nutrition from Michigan State University. He says Oregon is the nirvana of edible vegetation. But he also cautions folks about what not to eat; one such no-no is the wild iris. How about making pudding out of acorns, muffins from cattail flour and blackberries, even vinaigrette from Oregon grape berries? For information on current field trips, contact Kallas at *Wild Food Adventures* or contact Friends of the Gorge (wildfoodadventures.com) or Portland Parks & Recreation (503-823-2223; portlandoregon.gov/parks).

Or, you could just enjoy identifying and photographing the gorge's wildflowers and native plants while walking the trails. For native plant lists and helpful information on best times to view blooming wildflowers, check in July and August with the Forest Service Information Center at Multnomah Falls Lodge (503-695-2372; fs.usda.gov/crgnsa and gorgefriends.org) and for current information and guided hikes. Fall colors in the gorge are supreme during late October and early November, with big-leaf maple, cottonwood, Oregon ash, and leafy shrubs all changing to brilliant hues.

Columbia Gorge Hiking Weekend

Go to the Friends of Columbia River Gorge's website (gorgefriends.org) for information about the annual *Gorge Hiking Weekend*, which offers group hikes of various lengths and terrain in the western section of the gorge in mid-June. Contact the Forest Service Visitor Center at Multnomah Falls Lodge (503-695-2372; fs.usda.gov/crgnsa) to ask about day hikes into old-growth Douglas fir forests in the Mount Hood National Forest, such as Multnomah Creek, Upper Multnomah Loop, Bell Creek, Herman Camp Loop, Herman Creek, North Lake Loop, Indian Springs Loop, Lost Lake Loop, Lost Lake Old-Growth Trail, Lost Lake Butte, and Jones Creek. *Note*: On all hikes in the gorge, be sure to wear sturdy shoes; practice leave no trace principles; stay on the established trails; and pack along water, an emergency trail kit, camera, and binoculars. *Note*: There is poison oak in the gorge, so be wary of the small oak-shaped leaves. Nearly everyone is allergic to all parts of this plant.

Cascade Locks and Stevenson

Connect with I-84 near McCord Creek, continuing east toward Bonneville Dam and Cascade Locks. First detour to see **Bonneville Dam**, the first hydroelectric dam constructed on the Columbia River. Built in the mid-1930s and dedicated by President Franklin Roosevelt in 1937, the dam offers underwater views of salmon and steelhead as they swim up the fish ladders to reach the upper section of the river. There are locks for use by riverboats, a children's playground, and large shallow pools for ogling the enormous Columbia River sturgeon. These light gray, leathery-looking fish reach lengths of 5 feet and longer.

Just east of Bonneville Dam, exit at Cascade Locks to visit a cottonwood-shaded park along the river, 299 SW Portage Rd, just a few blocks east of the main street. At the **Port of Cascade Locks Marine Park**, visit the small historical museum, situated in one of the original lockmasters' houses, that offers an extensive photo and artifact collection. It's open seasonally. On the grounds you can also view the region's first rail steam engine, the Oregon Pony, which was used on a 4-mile stretch of track, Oregon's first railroad, constructed in 1858. During summer and early fall, May through Oct, the 145-foot sternwheeler *Columbia Gorge* takes visitors on 2-hour tours up and down the

Columbia River, boarding from the Marine Park dock. For current information, reservations, and lunch or dinner options during the sternwheeler tour, call Port of Cascade Locks Visitor Center at (541) 374-8427 or (503) 224-3900; portlandspirit.com. Also check out the cozy Locks Waterfront Grill at the Visitor Center, which offers a fine view of the Columbia River. The park also offers RV spaces and tent sites.

In 1875, army engineers recommended building a canal to circumvent the dangerous rapids at both Cascade City and The Dalles; the work was completed in 1896. Before that time passengers and cargo were unloaded and moved overland on the 4-mile rail track to a safer point on the river, where they were reloaded on a different steamboat for the continuing journey. Later, Bridge of the Gods connected the two sides of the Columbia River at Cascade Locks and then other bridges were constructed farther east at Hood River, The Dalles, Biggs, and Umatilla.

A Gorge-ous Chauffeured Tour

Sometimes it's nice to venture out with a personal driver and local pro. *Martin's Gorge Tours* offers wine, wildflower, and waterfall tours of the Columbia River Gorge, and will even pick you up at a handful of Portland and Gorge hotels. Afternoon wine tours of the Gorge and Hood River Valley are offered daily, year-round; Morning Wildflower Tours are offered weekends from Mar through June; and morning waterfall tours are offered mid-week year-round and weekends July through February. Tours run from $49 to $99 per person. For more information contact Martin's Gorge Tours at (503) 349-1323 or see martinsgorgetours.com.

If time allows, cross the historic ca. 1926 **Bridge of the Gods** from Cascade Locks to the Washington side of the river, turning west on WA 14 for a few miles to **Beacon Rock**. A steep, safe trail with sections of steps here and there leads to the top of this volcanic remnant. On a bright sunny day, you can sit rather comfortably on large flat rocks atop the monolith to enjoy great views of the gorge upriver to the east and downriver to the west. You've also got the golf clubs in the trunk? If so, plan a round of nine holes at scenic **Beacon Rock Golf Course** (509-427-5730; beaconrockgolf.com), open daily year-round. The golf course is located just a couple of miles west of Beacon Rock and is a favorite of locals as well as those who drive out from the Portland area.

Then, when you return east on WA 14, continue a couple of miles beyond Bridge of the Gods toward the small community of Stevenson, turning north in just a quarter mile or so to visit the splendid **Skamania Lodge** (509-427-7700; skamania.com). The lodge and grounds overlook the gorge to the east, on the Washington side of the Columbia River. The elegant Cascadian-style lodge (which has an enormous lobby/lounge with a gigantic rock fireplace) offers overnight accommodations, an eighteen-hole golf course, tennis courts, walking and horseback-riding trails, a gift shop, an indoor swimming pool, and a natural rock outdoor whirlpool spa. A restaurant and lounge both take advantage of all that marvelous scenery. Try the lounge menu for good hamburgers and tasty salmon chowder.

And don't miss a visit to the **Columbia Gorge Interpretive Center** (509-427-8211; columbiagorge.org), located just below the lodge at 990 SW Rock Creek Drive. The interpretive center also commands a grand view of the river and gorge toward the east. Inside you'll see the replica of an enormous fish wheel, used by early tribal members, and a gigantic vintage Corliss steam engine, once used in logging, that still actually works. The interpretive center with its splendid collection of artifacts and reference materials is open daily.

Vineyards, Wineries and Tasting Rooms in the Western Columbia River Gorge

The cultivation and growing of grapes, the science of viticulture, and the making of a variety of luscious wines in the western section of the Columbia River Gorge highlights two fertile and sunny areas ranging on both sides of the wide river—in both Oregon and Washington. Toss a corkscrew into the picnic basket, join an eager group of wine aficionados, and plan your trek to some twenty tasting rooms in the region. Enjoy toasting family, friends, and friendly vintners over glasses of tasty wines such as chardonnay, cabernet sauvignon, and pinot noir, as well as grenache, cabernet franc, merlot, and zinfandel.

OREGON SIDE OF THE COLUMBIA RIVER (WESTERN SECTION)

Cathedral Ridge Winery, 4200 Post Canyon Drive, Hood River (800-516-8710; cathedralridgewinery.com). The lovely grounds here offer scenic spots for impromptu summer picnics along with the delicious wines that have garnered many awards over the years.

Gorge White House, 2265 Highway 35, Hood River (541-386-2828; thegorgewhite house.com). There are splendid gardens, a lovely gift shop, and wine bar on-site, featuring local wines and tasty ciders. If time allows be sure to visit the scenic tasting room at *Mt. Hood Winery*, located at 2882 Van Horn Drive (541-386-8333; mthood winery.com). Enjoy scenic views of Mt. Hood and Mt. Adams.

Naked Winery Tasting Room, 606 Oak Street, Hood River (541-386-3700; naked-winery.com). In the pleasant tasting room, you'll notice a playful attitude, reflecting the friendly winemakers and passionate and loyal fan base. They encourage folks to join fellow oenophiles and turn on the romance of Northwest wines as they meet, greet, and sip.

The Pines 1852 Winery and Tasting Room, 202 Cascade Avenue, Hood River (541-993-8301; thepinesvineyard.com). This winery sits on a century-old vineyard, revitalized to grow grapes for delicious wines in the varietals of old vine zinfandel, merlot and syrah. See their tasting room in downtown Hood River, too.

Mt. Hood Winery, 2882 Van Horn Drive, Hood River (541-386-8333; mthoodwinery.com). This tasting room is a great spot to kick up your heels along the Fruit Loop route, while you sip on a pinot gris or chardonnay with a terrific view.

WASHINGTON SIDE OF THE COLUMBIA RIVER (WESTERN SECTION)
AniChe Cellars & Tasting Room, 71 Little Buck Creek Road, Underwood (360-624-6531; anichecellars.com). AniChe offers fine wines crafted by members of the family, a friendly tasting room experience, and a panoramic view of the Columbia Gorge and the river. Call for current hours.

Le Doubblé Troubblé Wine Co., 111 E Jewett Boulevard, White Salmon 509-281-3240; ldtwines.com). Founded by two longtime friends, LDT Winery produces grenache, gewürztraminer, and chardonnay as well as pinot noir. The tasting room in downtown White Salmon offers pours accompanied by cheese and charcuterie plates.

Hood River

Return to the Oregon side of the Columbia River and I-84 via Bridge of the Gods, heading east again. Detour at Hood River, about 18 miles east of Cascade Locks, and wind down to the ***Hood River Boat Basin and Marina Park*** to watch dozens of sports lovers, both men and women, ply the Columbia's rough waters on sailboards with tall sails of bright rainbow colors. This particularly windy stretch of the river from Cascade Locks and east through Hood River and The Dalles to Rufus is a mecca for lovers of wind sports, including windsurfing and kiteboarding. With their oblong boards firmly attached atop cars and vans, these enthusiasts return like flocks of migrating birds, beginning in April and remaining through September.

In mid-July the ***Gorge Games*** feature adrenaline-pumping competition in numerous lively outdoor events—from sailboarding, paragliding, kayaking, and kite-skiing to snowboarding, mountain biking, and rock climbing. For entry information, spectator information, or dates and a schedule of events, check with the Hood River Visitor Center, located near the marina at 720 E. Port Marina Drive (541-386-2000; hoodriver.org).

For a glimpse into Hood River's interesting past, plan to visit the ***Hood River County Historical Museum***, located at 300 E. Port Marina Drive (541-386-6772) near Port Marina Park, where exhibits of Native American culture, pioneer history, lumbering, and fruit-growing memorabilia are displayed. The museum is open Monday through Friday from 9:00 a.m. to 5:00 p.m.

Speaking of fruit, if travels bring you to the Hood River area in early spring, plan to take in the annual *Hood River Valley Blossom Festival* during the third weekend of April. At this time thousands of pear, apple, and cherry trees are in glorious bloom in the scenic Hood River Valley. Local tours through the orchards—along with arts and crafts fairs, quilt sales, antiques sales, and open houses at fruit stands, fruit-packing establishments, wineries, and fire departments—are among the eclectic round of activities that take place throughout the weekend. For the current Fruit Loop map and brochure, contact the Hood River Visitor Center (541-386-2000; hoodriver.org).

Nostalgic Cottages and Historic Hot Springs

Linger overnight at *Sandhill Cottages*, located at 932 Hot Springs Avenue in the small community of Carson (509-427-3464; sandhillcottages.com), just east of Stevenson on the Washington side of the Columbia River. The vintage auto court originally served travelers motoring the Columbia River Gorge in the early 1930s and 1940s, and seeking the healing waters of Carson Hot Springs, across the street. Falling into disrepair in the 1950s, the renovated and refurbished vintage cottages now feature charming retro furnishings, retro decor, and retro appliances. Relax in a simple cabin with front porches overlooking the garden. Alternately, visit *Carson Hot Springs Resort* nearby on St. Martin's Springs Road (carsonhotspringsresort.com) for a healing soak and a selection of accommodations to choose from.

Hood River Fruit and Flower Loop

At these and other open-air markets, fruit stands and farms are open from June through September or October. You'll find a variety of Hood River Valley fruits, berries, nuts (including colossal chestnuts), lavender and lavender products, tasty baked goods, flowers, and even wines and ciders. For maps and current info, browse hoodriverfruitloop.com and hoodriver.org.

Draper Girls Country Farm
6200 Highway 35, Mt Hood-Parkdale
(541) 490-8113
drapergirlscountryfarm.com

Gorge White House
2265 Highway 35, south of Hood River
(near Odell)
(541) 386-2828
thegorgewhitehouse.com

Gorge Fruit & Craft Fair
(mid-April and mid-October)
Hood River County Fairgrounds, Odell
(541) 354-2865
gorgegrown.com

Hood River Lavender Farms
3823 Fletcher Drive, Odell
(541) 490-5657
hoodriverlavender.com

Hood River Saturday Market
5th and Columbia Streets, Hood River
(541) 490-6420
gorgegrown.com

Packer Orchards
3020 Thomson Road
(541) 234-4006
packerorchards.com

Smiley's Red Barn and Fox Tail Cider
Highway 35 at 2965 Enrck Hill Drive,
Hood River
(541) 386-5989
smileysredbarn.com; foxtailcider.com

One of the best offerings is a nostalgic train ride on the *Mount Hood Railroad's Fruit Blossom Express*, which winds through the flowering orchards for some 22 miles to the small communities of Mt. Hood, Parkdale, and Odell. Venerable snowcapped Mount Hood looms more than 11,000 feet high in the near distance. The old railroad, which began in 1906 as a passenger and freight line, was resurrected in 1987, when a group of enterprising Hood River–area citizens purchased it from the Union Pacific Railroad. Several 1910–1926 Pullman coaches have been restored and are pulled by two General Motors/EMD GP-9 locomotives built in the 1950s. Be sure to ask about the brunch and dinner trains along with the *Oregon Murder Mystery Train Ride*. The *Polar Express* train is available during the holidays. For current information contact the staff at Mount Hood Railroad, 110 Railroad Avenue, Hood River (800-872-4661; mthoodrr.com).

Another outdoor adventure will take you and the older kids to nearby *Double Mountain Horse Ranch*, 3995 Portland Drive, Hood River (541-513-1152; ridinginhoodriver.com). The professional cowgirl staff will take beginners on short rides on gentle horses through the orchards or along short sections of the *Pacific Crest National Scenic Trail* with scenic views of Mt. Hood and Mt. Adams. Experienced riders can choose longer and more adventurous rides along the Pacific Crest National Scenic Trail to foaming waterfalls, to those awesome mountain views and, for another outdoor adventure, a Sunset on the Mountain ride. Call ahead for reservations and information about age restrictions.

For overnight accommodations check with the staff at the classic **Hood River Hotel**, at 102 Oak Street (800-386-1859; hoodriverhotel.com) in the uptown area and near the railroad depot. Renovated in the early 1990s, the four-story redbrick structure offers twenty-six guest rooms with historical decor and comfortable furnishings. The restaurant Broder Ost serves Nordic brunch on the hotel's street level. Consider **Oak Street Hotel**, 610 Oak Street (541-386-3845; oakstreethotel.com), which offers delicious breakfasts and lovely guest rooms. At **Westcliff Lodge** you'll find bright clean rooms set on 5 acres with scenic views of the Columbia River (877-386-2992; westclifflodge.com). Nearby is the **Columbia Gorge Hotel** (4000 Westcliff Drive; 541-386-5566; columbiagorgehotel.com), a historic gem built in 1921 and boasting Victorian charm with an Art Deco twist, and perched on a cliff over the river. **Bigfoot Lodge Bed & Breakfast**, at Mt Hood-Parkdale (541-399-4222; bigfoot-lodge.com), has panoramic views of Mount Hood and breakfasts that might include seasonal fruits, warm pastries such as muffins and scones, frittatas, baked eggs with smoked salmon, and maple sausage. For current information about other comfortable lodgings in the area, contact the Hood River Visitor Center (541-386-2000; hoodriver.org), Columbia River Gorge Visitors Association (crgva.org), or the Hood River Bed & Breakfast Association (541-386-6767; gorgelodging.com).

If you decide to detour from Hood River driving south toward Odell, Parkdale, and the Mount Hood Recreation Area, pop into **Packer Orchards**, 3900 Highway 35 (541-234-4481) to sample and purchase pear butter, apple pumpkin butter, ginger pear jam, tart cherry jam, and cowboy cookies. Closer to town **pFriem Family Brewers**, 707 Portway Avenue Ste. 101; (541-321-0490; pfriembeer.com), is a good place to sample excellent craft brews and dine with the whole family with views of the waterfront. Be sure to pop into **Bette's Place Diner**, 416 Oak Street (541-386-1880; bettesplace.com), for yummy Grandma's Cinnamon Rolls, large breakfast and lunch portions plus small-town diner friendliness.

Also welcoming travelers to Hood River is **3 Rivers Grill** at 601 Oak Street (541-386-8883; threeriversgrill.com), offering Northwest cuisine with French flair, and **Solstice Wood Fire Pizza, Bar & Catering** at 501 Portway Avenue (541-436-0800; solsticewoodfirecafe.com), offering heated patio seating and river views with delicious pizzas topped with Northwest ingredients.

Antique Aeroplanes Galore, Hood River

The **Western Antique Aeroplane & Automobile Museum**, located at 1600 Air Museum Road in Hood River (541-308-1600; waaamuseum.org), offers close-up views of more than twenty-five vintage airplanes from the early twentieth century. Most of them have been restored and are functional, including several biplanes. The collection also includes some thirty vintage automobiles, early models made by Ford, Studebaker, Packard, and Dodge. You can also see various airplanes, military vehicles, and autos that are in the process of being restored. Notable aeroplane models you can ogle include a restored and rare 1917 Curtiss JN4D Jenny, built to train pilots in World War I, and a 1943 Cessna UC78 Bobcat. Don't miss the yearly Fly-In the weekend after Labor Day when guest antique planes and pilots also fly in for two days. Fun activities include the Lion's Club Pancake Breakfast, the Full Sail Brewery afternoon Beer Garden, and the opportunity to arrange a flight in a 1930s biplane or other vintage plane from days gone by. Also nearby you can pop into the nearby vintage 1950s-style **Twin Peaks Drive-In Café** for fabulous burgers!

On Two Wheels

How about a scenic bike tour of the gorgeous Hood River and Columbia Gorge landscape? Try **MountNBarreL Wine Country Bike Tours** (1850 Country Club Road; 541-490-8687; mountnbarrel.com). This company offers a variety of guided wine country bike tours on both the west side and east side of Hood River. All you have to do is show up—the team will set you up with what you need for a leisurely, incredibly scenic bicycle tour with wine tasting to boot. New is an e-bike option so people of all ability levels can participate. Hit the road, in style!

Mosier

You might now head into the eastern section of the Columbia River Gorge, taking I-84 for about 20 miles to The Dalles. On the way, stop to walk or bike a scenic section of the old Columbia Gorge Highway for about 4.5 miles between Hood River and Mosier on the **Historic Columbia River Highway State Trail**, now open only to hikers and bicyclers. En route, twin open-air tunnels, closed since 1946, stretch 400 feet along a cliff that overlooks the river—the view is awesome. Access the western section of the trail at the Mark O. Hatfield West Trailhead, just east of Hood River on Old Columbia River Drive. Access the eastern section of the trailhead by driving east on I-84 from Hood River for 5 miles, taking exit 69 to the small community of Mosier. Proceed a few blocks from here to US 30, and as you enter Mosier immediately turn left onto Rock Creek Road and climb 0.5 mile up to the Mark O. Hatfield East Trailhead parking area. From here walk back down the road for about 2 blocks to access the paved trail, formerly part of Historic Highway 30; there is handicap parking here if needed. Because of the 5 percent gradual but consistent grade on the route, take along plenty of water when you hike this trail. Maps and additional information can be obtained at the Mark O. Hatfield West Visitor Center at the west trailhead (541-387-4010; oregonstateparks.org). You can also obtain more information about the efforts for restoring other sections of the historic Highway 30 by browsing the Friends of the Historic Columbia River Highway, US 30, hcrh.com.

For additional refreshments before or after your hike on the state trail, slow down on your way through the community of *Mosier* and pop into *The Rack and Cloth Tasting Room*, 1104 First Avenue (541-965-1457), open daily March through December for a farm to table menu and their craft apple hard ciders (pressed once a year from local fall apples). If an overnight stay in the area beckons, pop across the river to Bingen and book a cabin, lodge room or bunk at *The Society Hotel Bingen* (210 N Cedar Street, Bingen; 509-774-4437; thesocietyhotel.com). This old schoolhouse turned retreat, spa and event center is a great getaway in its own right, but proximity to so much recreation and scenery only makes it better. Soak in the hot saline pools, try the spacious sauna, visit the unique sanctuary carved into the hillside, or kick back in a hammock with a view of the Columbia.

From Mosier wind east on another section of the Historic Columbia River Highway 30 and stop at scenic *Rowena Plateau* and at *Tom McCall Preserve* to see carpets of wildflowers during spring and summer along with more panoramic views of the Columbia River. This 15-mile stretch of the old scenic highway joins I-84 at The Dalles.

Once Upon a Time, 40 Million Years Ago . . .

The story of the **Columbia River Gorge** starts with the volcanic peaks strung along the crest of the Cascade Mountain Range like a long snowy necklace. Eons ago their fires erupted, leaving lava and mudflows up to 2 miles thick. Although moss, lichen, wildflowers, and trees now obliterate much of the ancient volcanic activity, most everyone can identify the solidified flows stacked one on top of another along the cliffs when driving through the gorge.

The next chapter in the formation of the gorge started about 15,000 years ago, near the end of the last ice age. A warming trend melted thick ice fields in the Montana region, causing gigantic floods up to 1,200-feet deep in the Inland Northwest region, and these carved the river corridor, scoured steep cliffs, and left many streams hanging high above the bed of the river. These bubbling creeks and streams cascade down the basalt cliffs, creating a large concentration of splendid waterfalls, particularly in the western section of the gorge.

Be sure to gather a picnic and beverages, sturdy shoes, and warm layers and take the kids, the grandkids, and the grandparents to explore the scenic and historic **Columbia River Gorge National Scenic Area** (fs.usda.gov/crgnsa). The website contains links to cultural history, geology, recreation reports, mountain bike trails and roads, established hiking trails, hiking trail of the month and trail conditions, backcountry preparation, campgrounds, fall colors, endemic wildflowers, waterfalls, education and interpretive programs, gorge views and maps, special-use permits, and volunteer opportunities. There are also links to nearby Mount Hood National Forest and to Gifford Pinchot National Forest on the Washington side of the gorge. Travelers are also invited to pick up information at the Columbia River Gorge National Scenic Area/USDA Forest Service Visitor Center, 902 Wasco Avenue, Ste. 200, Hood River (541-308-1700; fs.usda.gov/crgnsa), open Monday through Friday from 8:00 a.m. to 4:30 p.m. There is also a Forest Service Visitor Center at Multnomah Falls Lodge (503-695-2372).

For guided hikes and wildflower walks, check with Friends of the Columbia Gorge (gorgefriends.org); Oregon Wild (oregonwild.org); and Native Plant Society of Oregon (npsoregon.org).

Vineyards, Wineries, and Tasting Rooms in the Eastern Columbia River Gorge

Within the two grape-growing regions—Columbia River Gorge and Columbia Valley—in the Columbia Gorge National Scenic Area, travelers find dozens of vineyards, wineries, and tasting rooms all within a 40-mile driving route between Hood River, The Dalles, and Arlington on the Oregon side (via I-84) and Goldendale, Maryhill, Wishram, Dallesport, Lyle, Bingen, and Husum on the Washington side (via WA 14). Check out these possibilities for meeting a host of vintners and tasting their handcrafted wines in the eastern section of the Columbia Gorge:

OREGON SIDE OF THE COLUMBIA RIVER
Sunshine Mill Artisan Plaza, Winery and Tasting Room at the ca. 1911 Sunshine Mill, 901 E. 2nd Street, The Dalles; (541) 298-8900; sunshinemill.com. Seated inside the cavernous renovated vintage mill, oenophiles can enjoy tasty appetizers and local wines.

WASHINGTON SIDE OF THE COLUMBIA RIVER
Cascade Cliffs Vineyard & Winery, Mile Marker 88.6 on WA 14, Wishram, (509) 767-1100; cascadecliffs.com. A family-owned winery specializing in red wines that capture the Piedmont varietals Barbera, Dolcetto, and Nebbiolo. The wide windows in the tasting room offer visitors panoramic views of the vineyard, towering basalt cliffs, and Mt.

Hood in the distance. Outdoor seating offers a pleasant place to relax, sip, and enjoy an impromptu picnic.

Klickitat Canyon & Columbia Gorge Winery, 6 Lyle-Snowden Road, Lyle; (541) 400-8147; klickitatcanyonwinery.com. A small family-run organic winery where the natural wines are perfected in a more old-world tradition—processed by hand.

Maryhill Winery, 9744 WA 14, Goldendale; (509) 773-1976; maryhillwinery.com. Maryhill offers a magnificent 3,000 square-foot tasting room, scenic picnic grounds with a patio and arbor, an adjacent 4,000-seat outdoor amphitheater that features summer concerts, plus all that stunning scenery in the eastern Columbia Gorge. The focus here is on premium red wines such as Syrah and Sangiovese, along with Zinfandel, Merlot, Cabernet Franc, and Grenache.

Syncline Wine Cellars, 111 Balch Road, Lyle; (509) 365-4361; synclinewine.com. Syncline is an estate vineyard, Steep Creek Ranch, which is situated near a series of 300-foot cliffs close to the Columbia River, where the moist western part of the gorge transitions to the semi-arid eastern region from The Dalles. The winemaker crafts unusual and interesting wines, such as lively red blends with great personality, in addition to lemon/lime, honeydew, and green apple flavors; and a Pinot Noir, rosé, and Roussanne.

For other wineries and tasting rooms in the region, browse gorgewine.com (541-965-1528) and wineyakimavalley.org (800-258-7270). In The Dalles, you can stop at *Petite Provence Boulangerie & Patisserie* at 408 E. 2nd Street (541-506-0037) for French-style baked goods, excellent coffee, and delicious breakfast and lunch fare, open daily at 8:30 a.m. The ca. 1876 *Baldwin Saloon*, 205 Court Street (541-296-5666; baldwinsaloon.com), open Monday through Saturday at 11:00 a.m. offers an early 1850s western-style decor with large vintage paintings, a 1900s mahogany bar, good service, splendid entrees, and Northwest wines and spirits that get raves from locals. You and the kids could also pop into *Cousins' Restaurant*, 2116 W. 6th Street (541-298-2771; cousinscountryinn.com), which features "down-home cookin." Diners are greeted with a friendly "Hi, cousin," from waiters dressed in black slacks, white shirts, and black vests. The bar stools in the cafe section are fashioned of stainless-steel milk cans with round seats covered in black vinyl; the Formica table tops are of whimsical black and white cowhide patterns. When seated the coffee appears at your table along with a complimentary large cinnamon roll. Lodgings are also available here at *Cousins Country Inn* (541-298-5161).

The Dalles and Dufur

Over the years, the power-generating dams built on the Columbia River gradually obliterated both the historic rapids and the ancient fishing grounds of Native peoples. An example is the famous *Celilo Falls*, which was near the site of *The Dalles Dam*. For information about visiting the dam, stop at The Dalles Area Visitor Center at 404 W. 2nd Street (541-296-2231; thedalleschamber.com). On Saturday from mid-May to October, you can take in the weekly farmers' market from 8:00 a.m. to 1:00 p.m. at 5th and Union in the city park.

Also inquire about the area's festivals, such as the *Celilo Wyam Salmon Feast* in early April, the *Cherry Festival* in mid-April, the *Tygh Valley All-Indian Rodeo* in mid-May, the *Fort Dalles Rodeo* in mid-July, the historic *Dufur Threshing Bee* in early August, and the *Wasco County Fair* in mid-August.

To better understand the historical significance of this area, visit the *Fort Dalles Historical Museum* (541-296-4547; fortdallesmuseum.org) at 500 W. 15th Street, located in the only remaining building, the Surgeons Quarters, at the 1857 Fort Dalles. The charming carpenter Gothic structure is listed on the National Register of Historic Places, and the museum is open daily March through October.

Ask, too, about the self-guided walking or driving tour of historic homes and buildings and for directions to *Sorosis Park*, located above the city and offering a magnificent viewing spot and a rose garden at the top of the bluff. From the viewing area notice the large bend in the Columbia River. By the point where the river reaches The Dalles, the Douglas fir-clothed western section of the gorge has changed to another elevation, above 2,000 feet, to the sunny eastern high desert. Now the rounded, hunched hills are sparsely clad, and in nearby canyons, sagebrush and bitterbrush bloom splashes of yellow in the spring and early summer. Rolling wheat country extends east and north of The Dalles up into Wasco, Moro, and Grass Valley, and thousands of cherry trees blossom each spring in nearby orchards as well.

To learn more about the history of the gorge and its settlement, visit the *Columbia Gorge Discovery Center* and the *Wasco County Historical Museum*, 5000 Discovery Drive in The Dalles (541-296-8600; gorgediscovery. org); access the museum complex via exit 82 from I-84, just west of The Dalles city center. You and the kids travel back in time to an early-nineteenth-century town and can board a side-wheeler, make your own canning label, or dress up in vintage clothing. The museum complex and *Basalt Rock Cafe* are open daily from 10:00 a.m. to 5:00 p.m. except for major holidays.

Short excursions on the near Washington side of the Columbia River include the impressive European-style ca. 1914 *Maryhill Museum of Art* built by Sam Hill, an early entrepreneur and road-builder in the region, 35 Maryhill Museum Drive, Goldendale WA (509-773-3733; maryhillmuseum.org); cross the river via the Biggs Rapids-Sam Hill Bridge about 20 miles east of The Dalles and go east a few miles on WA 14. You and the kids can see an extensive collection of vintage chess sets, a sampling of Rodin sketches and large sculptures, and a splendid restored collection of French designer mannequins (miniatures) dating back to postwar 1945. The museum's *Cafe Maryhill* offers deli-style lunches and outdoor seating overlooking the Columbia River. The museum closes in November for the winter and reopens in mid-March. Located nearby *Maryhill*

Winery (877-627-9445; maryhillwinery.com), located at 9774 Highway 14, Goldendale, just west of the museum, offers samples of its wines, such as pinot noir, merlot, zinfandel, and chardonnay. The handsome mahogany bar in the tasting room was salvaged from the Fort Spokane Brewery. Maryhill Winery is open daily at 10:00 a.m., and it has an arbor-shaded patio that invites picnics and overlooks the scenic gorge and the river. The winery's 4,000-seat outdoor amphitheater offers music events by well-known artists and musicians during the summer; bring a picnic and your folding chairs and blankets.

From The Dalles, take another pleasant side trip from I-84 into the rural past, by heading south on US 197 just 13 miles to the small farming community of *Dufur*. You're definitely in the slow lane now. Gently rolling wheat fields, the color of golden honey, extend for miles in all directions, and several tall grain elevators punctuate the wide blue skyline. You see Mount Hood's snowy peak rising to the west. There is no freeway noise, just quantities of fresh, clean air, and friendly smiles from local residents. You ease into the rhythm of the farmland.

Ultimate Room with a View!

If you're more than a bit adventurous, consider camping a couple of days at *Five Mile Butte Fire Lookout Cabin*, located west of Dufur at the 4,600-foot elevation level in the Mount Hood National Forest. In a 14-foot-square rustic cabin-shelter atop a 30-foot wood tower, campers have the ultimate room with a view—a stunning 360-degree panorama of snowcapped Cascade Mountains peaks, alpine and Douglas fir forests, and the rolling wheat fields of central and eastern Oregon. Lots of stairs? Yes, but the view is worth it! The lookout is available year-round; campers need to bring in their own water, food, and gear and be prepared for snow and very cold weather. For current information and regulations, contact the Barlow Ranger Station in Dufur (541-467-2291; fs.usda.gov/mthood). Many other lookouts are available for overnight lodging around Oregon. See firelookout.org. And keep in mind reservations go quickly so plan ahead!

Pause in the small farm community of Dufur and hunker down at the *Dufur Pastime Cafe & Saloon*, 25 S. Main Street (541-467-9248), for breakfast, lunch, or dinner. The cafe, with a homey hunting style decor, is open daily except Monday. Stop at Kramer's Market & Deli to pick up snacks and beverages and see if the large stuffed cougar is still on display there. If you're seriously into hunting wild turkeys, deer, or elk and able to get a hunting tag during the fall hunting season, Kramer's can grind your meat either burger style or sausage style. The *WE3 Coffee & Deli* on NE 5th Street offers tasty salads, wraps, and, sandwiches plus milkshakes and ice cream. Also linger at the nearby *Dufur Living History Museum* (541-467-2205) to stroll the grounds and see the vintage Schreiber Log Cabin with its original chinking along with a collection of weavings and vintage photos plus farm and ranch tools and vintage farm machinery. If possible, plan to linger overnight in Dufur at the historic ca. 1907 *Balch Hotel*, 40 S. Heimrich Street (541-476-2277; balchhotel.com), which offers cozy rooms on the second and third floors. The friendly innkeepers offer afternoon cookies along with a sumptuous and hearty breakfast in the morning.

From Dufur continue about 30 miles south on US 197 through Tygh Valley to Maupin and the *Deschutes River Recreation Area*. In addition to many campgrounds and places to fish, including fly fishing, you could bed down in rustic comfort at *Imperial River Company Lodge* located at 304 Bakeoven Road (541-395-2404; deschutesriver.com), on the banks of the Deschutes River near the small community of Maupin. The owners offer comfortable guest rooms and specialize in one- to three-day rafting trips (with gourmet meals) on this popular stretch of the Deschutes River. The nearby *Oasis Cabin Resort*, 609 US Highway 97 South in Maupin (541-395-2611; oasiscabinresort.com), offers a number of cozy cabins, and a classic diner. Additional information about the area can be obtained from the Maupin Visitor Center (541-993-1708; maupinoregon.com), located in a small log structure at the edge of town. From here you can also continue on toward Tygh Valley, Madras, Redmond, and Bend located on central Oregon's high desert region. On the way along this route, you could stop for tasty breakfast fare at *Molly B's Diner* on Main Street (541-483-2400) in the small community of Tygh Valley; call ahead for current hours.

Mount Hood Recreation Area

Mount Hood, an imposing, snow-covered, andesite volcano rising some 11,237 feet from the forested Cascade Mountains, easily dominates the skyline to the south of Hood River and is always seen on clear days from Portland, 50 miles to the west. The iconic peak identifies home territory to many Pacific Northwesterners.

Mount Hood East Side

One of the most scenic routes to the mountain is accessed from Hood River at the exit near Port Marina Park. Along Highway 35 you'll encounter the venerable, snowcapped peak around many bends while winding south up through the Hood River Valley's lush orchards. When driving through the area in the fall, detour at **Apple Valley Country Store** to sample fresh apple cider and purchase homemade applesauce and gift packages of delicious apples and pears. The store is situated west of Highway 35; travel to Odell, then north on Odell Highway to Tucker Road. A popular nosh-and-shop, the organic farm is located at 2363 Tucker Road (541-386-1971; applevalleystore.com). It's open daily June through Oct, with seasonal hours the rest of the year. You'll feel that you've stepped back in time as you browse the store's wares, from corn relish and spiced peaches to huckleberry preserves and apple cider.

The Legend of Wy'East Mountain

Legend passed down by Native peoples says that 11,237-foot-high **Mount Hood** was at one time a mighty volcano known as **Wy'East**, a great chief turned into a mountain, spouting flame and hurling boulders skyward in anger. The first recorded non-Native people to visit the area, members of the British Royal Navy, saw the mountain in 1792 from their vessel while sailing up the Columbia River. A British naval officer named it Hood, after his admiral. The earliest non-Native folks to trek over the slopes of Mount Hood were most likely French fur trappers, in about 1818; botanist David Douglas, in 1833; and a few other hardy souls who followed the main deer and Indian trails connecting the east and west sides of the mountain. For a good bit of history and a helpful map of the first emigrant road across the Cascades along those ancient Indian trails, visit the Mt. Hood Cultural Center and Museum in Government Camp (mthood museum.org).

A good choice for dinner along Highway 35 is to detour at **Cooper Spur Mountain Resort**, located at 10755 Cooper Spur Road (541-352-6692; cooper-spur.com) about 23 miles south of Hood River. Located snugly on the eastern flank of Mount Hood, the log cabin-style dinner house, **Crooked Tree Tavern & Grill**, is noted for serving generous portions of food in its rustic mountain atmosphere. It's open seven days a week for lunch and dinner. You'll also enjoy a choice of six cozy rooms in the lodge, five log cabins, three lodge-style condos, a homestead cabin, and a large log home for overnight stays. Call ahead for reservations.

During snowy winter months, **Cooper Spur Ski Area**, at 11000 Cloud Cap Road (541-352-6692; cooperspur.com), just up the road from the inn, is a great place for families and beginners to enjoy skiing on easy terrain. Here you'll encounter just 350 vertical feet of terrain, 4,350-foot top elevation, with one rope tow and one T-bar. For cross-country buffs there are 6.5 kilometers of groomed Nordic trails. Another excellent area for beginning skiers and for the kids is **Summit Ski Area** (503-272-0256; summitskiarea.com) in Government

Camp, on the southwest flank of the mountain. The top elevation at Summit Ski Area is 4,306 feet, with a 306-foot vertical drop. There is a good inner-tubing hill here, as well as a 10K Nordic track for cross-country skiing.

The **Barlow Road**, opened in 1845, completed the Oregon Trail as a land route from Independence, Missouri, to the Willamette Valley. This alternate land route to Oregon City on the Willamette River became a major entry into western Oregon for those who wanted to avoid the dangers or costs of floating their families and wagons on flat barges down the Columbia River from The Dalles to Fort Vancouver.

Samuel K. Barlow, his family, and others literally chopped the crude wagon trail through the thick evergreen forest on the southeast and southwest flanks of Mount Hood to a location between Government Camp and Rhododendron. Following roughly the same route, Highway 35 winds past Cooper Spur Ski Area and intersects with US 26 just south of the busy **Mount Hood Meadows Ski Area** (503-337-2222; skihood.com). Historic Government Camp is about 6 miles west. (You can also head southeast at this point, toward Warm Springs, and the central Oregon high desert.)

As you travel to Government Camp via US 26, stop at **Trillium Lake** and take a look at the remnants of the Barlow Trail and Summit Meadows, one of the places where the emigrants camped. The Forest Service access road, from US 26, is just opposite the **Snow Bunny Ski Area**—a great place for families with small children—a few miles west of the Highway 35 junction. Near the large meadow you can find a small pioneer cemetery and the site of one of the early tollhouses.

At this site once stood early pioneer Perry Vicker's log cabin, barn, lodge, and shingled tepee. Vicker also built, across the north edge of the meadows, a corduroy road—a type of early road constructed by laying small tree trunks side by side. Such roads became familiar surfaces for horse-drawn wagons and, later, for the first automobiles. Needless to say, traveling in those early days was a distinct challenge and more often than not included moving branches, or even fallen trees, off the roadway to continue the journey.

Continue down to Trillium Lake for a picnic and stay in one of the nearby campgrounds: one right on the lake and the other, **Still Creek Campground**, along the creek just north of the pioneer graves and Summit Meadows. During July and August, you'll probably find delicious huckleberries along Still Creek; during winter folks step into cross-country skis and trek across the snowy meadow and onto the same roads all the way around the picturesque frozen lake. This is a lovely, and easy, trek not to be missed, especially on a crisp blue-sky day.

Then, too, you can enjoy this forested area in the warm spring, summer, and fall months, finding a cluster of small lakes in which to swim, canoe, row, and fish. These small lakes are also great places to camp away from the crowds: Timothy Lake, Little Crater Lake, Clackamas Lake, Summit Lake, Clear Lake, Trillium Lake, and Frog Lake. For information on the lakes and campgrounds, call or stop by the Zigzag Ranger Station (503-622-3191; fs.usda.gov/mthood) in Zigzag about 10 miles below Government Camp.

Mount Hood's Early Climbers

According to records at the Oregon Historical Society research library in Portland, the earliest settlers to climb *Mount Hood*, on July 11, 1857, were members of a party from Portland led by Henry L. Pittock, who published *The Oregonian* newspaper. Pittock later assisted in forming the long-standing mountain lovers' club, Mazamas, based in Portland. In 1867, two women, Frances Case and Mary Robinson, climbed the mountain wearing traditional Victorian long skirts! Another notable mountaineer, Elijah Coalman, first climbed Mount Hood at age 15, in 1897. He later became the first fire lookout on top of the mountain in 1914, and in 1915 he built the first shelter at the 11,237-foot summit. Elijah must have thrived on deep snow, chilling winds, and icy crevasses, for he climbed Mount Hood nearly 600 times and stayed on as lookout until 1930.

In 1964, the US Congress passed the Wilderness Act, and there are now five wilderness areas in the Mount Hood National Forest (fs.usda.gov/mthood). Elijah, it is certain, would be pleased to know that the region's wilderness areas that he loved have been preserved for generations to come.

Mount Hood West Side

In historic *Government Camp*, just off US 26 at the base of Mount Hood, you could stop for breakfast, lunch, or dinner and legendary huckleberry pie at *Huckleberry Inn Restaurant*, 88611 Government Camp Loop (503-272-3325; huckleberry-inn.com), open 24 hours. At *Mt. Hood Brewing Co.*, 87304 E. Government Camp Loop (503-272-3172; mthoodbrewing.com), mountain travelers enjoy sampling the tasty brews brewed here since 1992. Also plan to visit the *Mt. Hood Cultural Center & Museum*, 88900 Government Camp Loop (503-272-3301; mthoodmuseum.org), where you can learn more about the historic communities in the Mount Hood Recreation Area. For current lodging information on the mountain, including motels and hotels, bed-and-breakfasts, cabins, resorts, and RV and tent campgrounds, browse mthood.info and mthoodterritory.com.

In the early 1900s, pioneer guide Oliver Yocum built a hotel at Government Camp, and it survived until 1933, when a fire destroyed it. Within ten years after Sam Barlows' pioneering route over the shoulder of Mount Hood, the mountain became a much sought-after landmark, instead of a formidable nuisance, and for more than a century and a half, it has drawn city dwellers to its slopes year-round.

As early as 1890, skiers and climbers flocked to the snowy slopes of **Mount Hood**. And in those days, it took folks at least two days' travel to get from Portland to the mountain. Until a graded road was constructed to Government Camp in the 1920s, the last day's trek during winter months was via snowshoes from Rhododendron. In 1924, the first hotel at timberline was built by the Forest Service, near the present Timberline Lodge. Serving as emergency shelter during summer and winter, the original lodge was about 8 by 16 feet, with several additional tents nearby. Mountain lovers brought their own blankets, rented a mattress, and got a meal.

Today, however, you can sleep in more luxurious comfort at this 6,000-foot level by checking in at one of the state's oldest mountain inns, **Timberline Lodge** (503-272-3311; timberlinelodge.com), located just 6 miles up the mountain from Government Camp.

Construction of Timberline Lodge was approved in 1935 by President Franklin Roosevelt as a project of the Works Progress Administration during the Great Depression. A contingent of more than 250 Northwest artisans—carpenters, stonemasons, woodcarvers, metalworkers, painters, weavers, and furniture makers—created in two years a magnificent lodge that looks like the rough-hewn castle of a legendary Norse mountain king.

Most of the fifty-nine guest rooms at venerable Timberline Lodge are one of a kind, with carved headboards, patchwork quilts, and hooked rugs. Everything was made by hand—some of the original curtains were made from dyeing old army uniforms and blankets. The original fabrics and weavings, along with the Native American, pioneer, native wildflower, and animal motifs, have all been restored and repaired through the painstaking efforts of the Friends of Timberline. The person who initiated the fine restoration of Timberline Lodge in the 1950s was longtime mountain lover Richard Kohnstamm. Above the second-floor common area and restaurant is a quaint, hexagonal balcony housing the **Ram's Head Bar**, with tables and couches for dining or casual happy hour drinks. From some places, guests can see straight up or down the mountainside. To the north, floor-to-ceiling windows frame spectacular Mount Hood.

If time allows, plan to have breakfast, lunch, or dinner with a view in the **Cascade Dining Room**, located on the second floor in Timberline Lodge; reservations are required for dinner (503-272-3104; timberlinelodge.com). Breakfast is served from 8:00 to 10:00 a.m., lunch is served from 11:30 a.m. to 2:00 p.m., and dinner is served from 6:00 to 8:00 p.m. Other places to eat inside the lodge include the informal **Blue Ox Bar**, tucked away in the lower level of the lodge.

In the early 1940s, the state highway commission decided upon a great experiment: to keep the section of narrow road between Welches and Government Camp open throughout the entire winter. Winter sports enthusiasts were exhilarated. They flocked to the mountain, and the pilgrimage to Mount Hood has never ceased. For information about Alpine and Nordic skiing areas, as well as the names of expert instructors and mountain climbing guides, contact the staff at Timberline Lodge (503-272-3311; timberlinelodge.com). **Note**: Do not entertain the notion of climbing Mount Hood—or any other mountain in the high Cascades—without expert guidance, preparation, and assistance.

TOP ANNUAL EVENTS IN COLUMBIA RIVER GORGE AND HIGH CASCADES

APRIL
Hood River Valley Blossom Festival
Hood River
(541) 386-2000
visithoodriver.com

Northwest Cherry Festival
The Dalles
(541) 296-2231
thedalleschamber.com

MAY
All Indian Rodeo
Tygh Ridge
(541) 296-2231

JUNE
Annual Gorge Hiking Weekend
Columbia River Gorge
gorgefriends.org

JULY
Fort Dalles Junior Rodeo
The Dalles Rodeo Grounds
(541) 296-2231
thedalleschamber.com

AUGUST
Hood-to-Coast Relay
Timberline Lodge to Seaside
(503) 292-4626
hoodtocoastrelay.com

SEPTEMBER
Hood River Hops Fest
Downtown Hood River
(541) 386-2000
visithoodriver.com

OCTOBER
Hood River Valley Harvest Fest
Hood River
(541) 386-2000
visithoodriver.com

If you visit the Mount Hood Recreation Area from July through September—summer on the mountain—obtain maps for hiking and exploring at the Zigzag Ranger Station, just below Toll Gate Campground and Rhododendron, 70220 E. US 26 (503-622-3191; fs.usda.gov/mthood and wilderness.net), open Monday through Friday from 8:00 a.m. to 4:30 p.m. In the nearby **Salmon Huckleberry Wilderness** is the easily accessed **Salmon River National Recreation Trail**. The Salmon River Gorge, with its many waterfalls, is a picturesque area of volcanic plugs, pinnacles, and forested cliffs. The trail lies several hundred feet above the river, except for the lower 2.5-mile section. Also ask for directions to the **Hidden Lake Trail**, located just 6 miles east of the Zigzag Ranger Station. In early to mid-June, you'll find the lakeside section of the trail punctuated with masses of pale pink blooms from the stately native rhododendrons.

In addition, the 2-mile **Mountaineer Trail**, located higher on the mountain, is an especially good hike for families. Passable from August through October, this trail is on the east side of Timberline Lodge and climbs through gnarled alpine fir beyond the timberline to **Silcox Hut**, at the 7,000-foot level. Silcox Hut offers dormitory-style lodging for small groups. For information and reservations call Timberline Lodge staff at (503) 272-3311. On the hike up to Silcox Hut you'll have splendid panoramic views of Mount Jefferson, Three Sisters, and Broken Top to the south and east and, on a clear day, of the Coast Range some 95 miles to the west. The trail, though quite steep in some places, is easy to navigate during summer months and takes about 2 hours round-trip. **Note**: Should you arrange to stay overnight at Silcox Hut during the winter months, you and your party will be transported by snowcat up the snowy slopes.

Rhododendron, Zigzag, and Welches

If you decide to take a snack or a picnic along on your mountain hikes, pause for lunch or dinner at **Zigzag Inn Restaurant**, 70162 E. US 26 (503-622-4779; zigzaginn.com), for juicy hamburgers and homemade pizza as well as pasta and steaks. You're eating in a warm ski-lodge atmosphere that dates back to the 1950s, a bit rustic and well-worn but well-loved by locals and visitors. For more gourmet eats try **The Rendezvous Grill & Tap Room**, 67129 E. US 26 in Welches (503-622-6837; thevousgrill.com), at milepost 40. And, to order a tasty latte or espresso, pastries, and casual food fare, stop at **Coffee Brewsters**, 68224 E. Highway 26 (503-622-3396; coffeebrewsters.com); turn at the light onto Welches Road and into the small Thriftway Hoodland Plaza shops, open daily at 7:00 a.m. for bagels, freshly baked scones and pastries, as well as lunch fare and coffee. You can also gas up here. If an overnight stay is in order, consider *Sandy Salmon Bed & Breakfast Lodge*, an elegant log lodge located on the Sandy River near Brightwood and Welches at 61661 E. Highway 26 (503-622-6699; sandysalmon.com).

Summer visitors can take in *Sandy Mountain Festival* (503-668-5900; sandymountainfestival.org), held in the community of Sandy, just down the mountain from Welches and Brightwood, toward Gresham and Portland. Highlighting the mid-July festival are, in addition to a carnival and parade, the international Bed Race finals, a wine fair and feast, the annual Black Powder Shoot, and a gathering of about 150 Northwest artists and craftspersons who display, demonstrate, and sell their wares in shady *Meinig Memorial Park*. While visiting Meinig Memorial Park, stroll through the lovely garden designed for the blind; it contains a variety of scented herbs and an assortment of perennials and annuals of different textures.

Historic Clackamas Lake Ranger Station, ca. 1933

The *Historic Clackamas Lake Ranger Station* complex, now listed on the National Register of Historic Places, dates from 1933, when it was constructed by members of the Depression-era Civilian Conservation Corps. Walking through the complex you'll see two wood-frame houses built for the district ranger and his assistant, a gas station, a road and trails warehouse, a mess hall, a blacksmith shop, a pump house, a barn, and a fire warehouse. The buildings are beautifully crafted and enhanced with fine stonework. One cabin is available for seasonal recreational overnight lodging rental. The complex is open, depending on snow conditions, from Memorial Day weekend to mid-September, Thursday through Monday from 9:00 a.m. to 5:00 p.m. There's also a scenic 2-mile hike that starts at the ranger station. At an elevation of 3,400 feet, there are about 45 campsites here, drinking water, and vault toilets. Most of the narrow roads traveling to the lakes from US 26 are paved and can accommodate small RVs. For current information and directions, contact the Zigzag Ranger Station (503-622-3191; fs.usda.gov/mthood), located off US 26 about 10 miles down the mountain from Government Camp, near the small communities of Rhododendron, Zigzag, and Welches.

While in Sandy, for breakfast, lunch, or dinner, you could stop at the much-loved *Tollgate Inn Restaurant*, located at 38100 US 26 (503-668-8456; visittollgate.com). The food is tasty and the portions generous. Also, pop into the adjacent *Tollgate Inn Bakery* (503-826-1009) for outrageous pastries baked fresh every morning and steaming espresso and coffee drinks using Tully's coffee beans. The bakery also offers box lunches to go.

Places to Stay in Columbia River Gorge and High Cascades

CASCADE LOCKS— STEVENSON, WA

Best Western Columbia River Inn
735 Wanapa Street
Cascade Locks
(541) 374-8777
bestwestern.com/columbi-ariverinn

Columbia Gorge Riverside Lodge
200 SW Cascade Avenue
Stevenson
(509) 427-5650
cgriversidelodge.com

THE DALLES

Cousins Country Inn
2114 W. 6th Street
(541) 298-5161
cousinscountryinn.com

The Dalles Inn
112 W. 2nd Street
(541) 296-9107
thedallesinn.com

HOOD RIVER— PARKDALE—WHITE SALMON—BINGEN— TROUT LAKE

Best Western Hood River Inn
1108 E. Marina Way
Hood River
(541) 386-2200
bestwestern.com/hoodriver inn

Bigfoot Lodge Bed & Breakfast
3747 Pinemont Drive
Mt Hood-Parkdale
(541) 399-4222
bigfoot-lodge.com

Inn of the White Salmon
172 W. Jewett Boulevard
White Salmon, WA
(509) 293-2335
innofthewhitesalmon.com

Kelly's Trout Creek Inn B&B
25 Mt. Adams Road
Trout Lake, WA
(509) 395-2769
kellysbnb.com

Old Parkdale Inn Bed & Breakfast
4932 Baseline Road
Parkdale
(541) 352-5551
hoodriverlodging.com

The Society Hotel Bingen
210 N. Cedar Street
Bingen, WA
(509) 774-4437
thesocietyhotel.com

MOSIER

Three Sleeps Vineyard Bed & Breakfast
1600 Carroll Road
(541) 478-0143
threesleepsvineyardbandb. com

OTHER ATTRACTIONS WORTH SEEING IN COLUMBIA RIVER GORGE AND HIGH CASCADES

Columbia Gorge Interpretive Center
Stevenson, WA
columbiagorge.org

Goldendale Observatory
Goldendale, WA
goldendaleobservatory .com

Maryhill Stonehenge
Maryhill
maryhillmuseum.org

Mt. Hood Cultural Center & Museum
Government Camp
mthoodmuseum.org

Mt. Hood Winery
Hood River
mthoodwinery.com

MOUNT HOOD SKI AREA INFORMATION

For current information about snowshoeing, mushing/skijoring, sledding, and snowmobiling as well as alpine, snowboarding, and cross-country ski areas on both the west and east sides of Mount Hood, check these resources:

ALPINE, SNOW-BOARDING, AND CROSS-COUNTRY SKIING

Cooper Spur Ski Area
north of Hood River via
Highway 35
(541) 352-6692
cooperspur.com

Mount Hood Meadows Ski Area
north of US 26 via Highway. 35
(503) 337-2222
skihood.com

Mount Hood Ski Bowl
at Government Camp off
US 26
(503) 272-3206
skibowl.com

Summit Ski Area & Kids Tubing Hill
at Government Camp off
US 26
(503) 272-0256
summitskiarea.com

Timberline Lodge Ski Area
6 miles above Government Camp off US 26
(503) 272-3311
timberlinelodge.com

MUSHING/SKIJOR-ING, SLEDDING, SNOWMOBILING & SNOWSHOEING

Barlow Ranger District/ Dufur Ranger Station
(541) 467-2291
fs.usda.gov/mthood
Click on Recreation,
Winter Sports

Hood River Ranger Station
6780 Highway 35, south
of Hood River
(541) 352-6002
fs.usda.com/mthood

Zigzag Ranger Station
on US 26 at Zigzag,
between Welches and
Rhododendron
(503) 622-3191
fs.usda.gov/mthood
Click on Recreation,
Winter Sports

OUTDOOR RECRE-ATION CLASSES & DAY TRIPS

Portland Park & Recreation

Department
(503) 823-5132
portlandoregon.gov/parks

HELPFUL TELEPHONE NUMBERS AND WEBSITES FOR COLUMBIA RIVER GORGE AND HIGH CASCADES

Columbia Gorge Wind-surfing Association
(541) 386-9225
cgw2.org

Columbia River Gorge—Hood River Bed & Breakfast Association
(541) 386-6767
gorgelodging.com

Columbia River Gorge National Scenic Area Visitor Center
(541) 308-1700
fs.usda.gov/crgnsa

The Dalles Area Visitor Center
(541) 296-2231
thedalleschamber.com

Friends of the Historic Columbia River Highway
hcrh.org

Gorge Winds Aviation, Troutdale Airport
(scenic flights)
(503) 665-2823
gorgewindsinc.com

Hood River County Visitor Center
720 E. Port Marina Drive
(541) 386-2000
visithoodriver.com

Mount Adams Visitor Center
1 Heritage Plaza
White Salmon, WA
(509) 493-3630
mtadamschamber.com

Mount Hood Recre-ation Area, ZigZag Ranger Station
(503) 622-3191

fs.usda.gov/mthood
mthoodterritory.com

Multnomah Falls, Forest Service Visitor Center
(503) 695-2372
fs.usda.gov/crgnsa

National Forest Campgrounds
(877) 444-6777
recreation.gov

Oregon Department of Fish and Wildlife
Columbia River information
(971) 673-6000
dfw.state.or.us

Oregon Road Conditions and Weather Reports
(800) 977-6368
tripcheck.com

Oregon State Parks and Campgrounds
(800) 551-6949 (general information)
(800) 452-5687 (reservations)
oregonstateparks.org

Sandy Area Visitor Center
(503) 668-4006
sandyoregonchamber.org

Skamania County Visitor Center
(509) 427-8911, (800) 989-9178
skamania.org

West Columbia Gorge Visitor Center
Troutdale
(503) 669-7473
westcolumbiagor
gechamber.com

MOUNT HOOD AREA/ GOVERNMENT CAMP— WELCHES—BRIGHTWOOD

Best Western Mt. Hood Inn
87450 E. Government Camp Loop
Government Camp
(503) 272-3205
bestwestern.com

Hidden Woods Bed & Breakfast
19380 E. Summertime Drive
Brightwood
(503) 622-5754
thehiddenwoods.com

Mt. Hood Oregon Resort
68010 E. Fairway Avenue
Welches
(503) 622-3101
mthood-resort.com

Mount Hood Village RV Resort
65000 US 26
Welches
(503) 622-4011
mthoodvillagerv.com

SANDY

Best Western Sandy Inn
37465 US 26
(503) 668-7100
bestwestern.com/sandyinn

Places to Eat in Columbia River Gorge & High Cascades

CASCADE LOCKS— STEVENSON, WA

Big T's Diner
73 First Street
Stevenson, WA
(509) 427-0333

The Locks Waterfront Cafe
Marine Park
Port of Cascade Locks
(541) 645-0372
locksgrill.com

Multnomah Falls Lodge
I-84 at Multnomah Falls east of Troutdale
(503) 695-2376
multnomahfallslodge.com

THE DALLES

Baldwin Saloon
1st and Court Streets
(541) 296-5666

Cousins' Restaurant
2114 W. 6th Street
(541) 298-2771
cousinsthedalles.com

Petite Provence Boulangerie & Patisserie
408 E. 2nd Street
(541) 506-0037
provencepdx.com

HOOD RIVER–MOSIER— WHITE SALMON, WA

Everybody's Brewing
177 E. Jewett Boulevard
White Salmon
(509) 637-2774
everybodysbrewing.com

Full Sail Tasting Room & Pub
506 Columbia Street
Hood River
(541) 386-2247
fullsailbrewing.com

pFriem Family Brewers
707 Portway Avenue #101
Hood River
(541) 321-0490
pfriembeer.com

The Pines 1852 Winery & Tasting Room
202 Cascade Avenue
Hood River
(541) 993-8301
thepinesvineyard.com

Solstice Wood Fire Pizza, Bar & Catering
501 Portway Avenue
Hood River
(541) 436-0800
solsticewoodfirecafe.com

MT. HOOD AREA/ GOVERNMENT CAMP— ZIGZAG—WELCHES

Coffee Brewsters
68224 E. Highway 26 at
Hoodland Plaza

Welches
(503) 622-3396
coffeebrewsters.com

Crooked Tree Tavern & Grill
Cooper Spur Ski Area
(541) 352-6692
cooperspur.com

Huckleberry Inn Restaurant
88661 E. Government
Camp Loop
(503) 272-3325
huckleberry-inn.com

Mt. Hood Brewing Co.
87304 Government Camp
Loop
(503) 272-3172
Mthoodbrewing.com

The Rendezvous Grill & Tap Room
67149 E. Highway 26
Welches
(503) 622-6837
vousgrill.com

Zigzag Inn Restaurant
70162 E. Highway 26 at
Lolo Pass Road

Zigzag
(503) 622-4779
zigzaginn.com

SANDY

Toll Gate Inn Restaurant & Bakery
38100 US 26
(503) 668-8456
visittollgate.com

TROUTDALE

Power Station Pub
2126 SW Halsey Street
(503) 492-4686
mcmenamins.com

Ristorante di Pompello
Main Street/Historic
Columbia River Highway
(503) 667-2480
dipompello.com

The Willamette Valley

Eons old, with rivers meandering through and bisecting its green hills and rich alluvial soils, the **Willamette Valley** was surely a welcome sight to the weary pioneers fresh off the Oregon Trail. Out of those abundant soils grew many farms in the 1840s and 1850s and, much later, the hundreds of orchards, nurseries, gardens, and vineyards that continue to thrive in this moist and mild zone between the high Cascade and lower Coast Range mountains and the Pacific Ocean.

This gentle region, now scattered with cities, towns, hamlets, and inviting side roads that skirt I-5 and old Highways 99E and 99W, was also home to the Calapooya Indians. For thousands of years, they roamed throughout the broad valley, digging tiny bulbs of the purple camas in early spring, picking juicy blackberries in late summer, and hunting deer and fishing its rivers and streams nearly year-round. If you visit in mid-May, you'll see waves of purple camas blooming along roadsides in meadows throughout the valley.

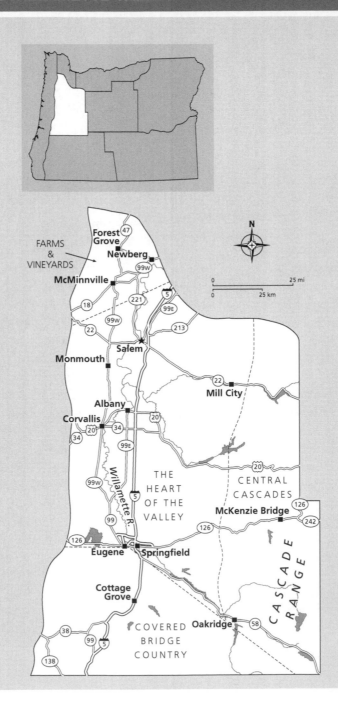

Farms and Vineyards

To get acquainted with this large region, which lies like an enormous green carpet between the Cascades and the Coast mountain ranges, first head south from Portland on I-5 past Wilsonville to exit 278 and head west to ***Champoeg State Park and State Heritage Area*** (503-678-1251 for information or 800-452-5687 for campground reservations; oregonstateparks.org).

This 567-acre park preserves the historic site of the May 2, 1843, meeting at which valley settlers, by a narrow vote, established the first organized territorial government in the Northwest. George Abernethy was elected the territory's first governor. Champoeg was later an important stagecoach stop, trading post, and river landing for steamboats.

The Champoeg Interpretive Center is open year-round, with exhibits that bring alive the ways of the Kalapuya Indians, fur trappers, explorers, and settlers. Living history events take place during the summer, celebrating the lives of early settlers with demonstrations of plowing, blacksmithing, harnessing, shoeing, and wheelwrighting. From May through October, visit the ***Butteville Store***, the oldest continuously operating retail store in Oregon, which sits here on the banks of the Willamette River at the end of the Champoeg walking path. Dine on delicious homemade soups, sandwiches, salads, and desserts, including Tillamook ice cream and fresh fruit pie. You can linger overnight in this scenic spot, in the state park campground section, which offers tent camping and RV sites along with six comfy yurts and six cozy log cabins (800-452-5787 for reservations; oregonstateparks.org).

When the Willamette River Was the Valley's Highway

From 1850 to 1916, more than fifty steamboats took on passengers, mail, and produce and traversed both the lower and upper sections of the *Willamette River* south from Portland and Oregon City. To skirt the wide cascading *Willamette Falls* at Oregon City, the boats, after 1873, navigated around the falls by entering the four chambers of Willamette Falls Locks, on the West Linn side of the river, reaching the upper stream. Regular stops upriver included landings at Champoeg, Salem, Albany, Corvallis, and finally, Eugene, some 100 miles south. The river was the region's "main street" in those days. In Oregon City, visit *Willamette Falls Scenic Viewpoint* to view the falls, and from a distance, the locks, which are long closed. For scenic cruises on the lower Willamette River and on the Columbia River, contact the **Portland Spirit** (portlandspirit.com, 503-224-3900).

TOP HITS IN THE WILLAMETTE VALLEY

Champoeg State Park and State Heritage Area
Wilsonville

Covered bridges in Linn and Lane Counties

Deepwood Museum & Gardens and Bush House Museum
Salem

Enchanted Forest
Turner

Hendricks Park Rhododendron Garden
Eugene

Historic Carousel & Museum
Albany

Mary's Peak to Pacific Scenic Byway
Corvallis

McKenzie Pass Scenic Byway and Dee Wright Observatory
McKenzie Bridge

Mount Angel Abbey
Silverton

Mount Pisgah Arboretum
Eugene-Springfield

The Oregon Garden
Silverton

Schreiner's Iris Gardens
Salem

Newberg, McMinnville, and Forest Grove

Before continuing south toward Salem, the state capital, meander west from the Portland area to Newberg, McMinnville, and Forest Grove to see where many of the old orchards were planted, where many fields of wine grapes now are rooted, and where fine old homes are living new lives as tasting rooms or inns. Hundreds of acres are planted with premium wine grapes, and scores of small wineries process the fruit into more than 100,000 gallons of vinifera wines and into 1,000 of gallons of premium fruit and berry wines. With helpful maps, strike out on your own to visit many wineries and tasting rooms.

To plan a self-guided tour, pick up handy maps and directions at the **Washington County Visitors' Association** in Beaverton, 12725 SW Millikan Way (503-644-5555; tualatinvalley.org). The locations of these wineries and vineyards range from Beaverton and Newberg west toward the Coast Range to Hillsboro, McMinnville, and Forest Grove. **Note**: The gentle back roads in this area are fine for bicycling as well; ask about bike maps at the Washington County Visitors' Association (tualatinvalley.org).

If you head out toward the Hillsboro area from Portland or Beaverton via US 26 (the Sunset Highway), plan to detour and stop at the **Helvetia Tavern** located at 10275 NW Helvetia Road (503-647-5286), just beyond where the road dips under the railroad trestle, about 2 miles north of US 26. Your reward for finding this local gem will be hamburgers the size of dinner plates and fresh-cooked fries—with skins left on—piled all around. Watch the folks play pool and notice the interesting collection of hats hanging from the walls and rafters. The tavern is open for lunch and dinner every day.

If the notion of gargantuan burgers sounds too much for lunch, backtrack on the Sunset Highway a couple of miles, exit at Cornelius Pass, and head south for a lunch or dinner stop at the **McMenamins Cornelius Pass Roadhouse**, located at 4045 NW Cornelius Pass Road (503-640-6174; mcmenamins.com). The restaurant and microbrewery is open for lunch and dinner daily from 11:00 a.m. to 10:00 p.m.

Next throw a corkscrew into the picnic basket and head west on Highway 8 from Hillsboro to **Forest Grove**. This charming town is home to Pacific University, founded in 1849. Stop at the Forest Grove Visitor Information Center, 2417 Pacific Avenue (503-357-3006; visitforestgrove.com) to orient yourself, and ask about a helpful map for self-guided trips to more Washington and Yamhill Counties vineyards and tasting rooms. You could also contact the Willamette Valley Wineries Association at (503) 297-2962 or willamettewines.com or oregonwinecountry.org.

Also located in Forest Grove is **SakeOne Brewery**, 820 Elm Street (503-357-7056; sakeone.com), America's first successful craft sake producer, founded in 1997. The tasting room, which has extraordinary flavors of sake, is open daily from 11:00 a.m. to 5:00 p.m. For good eats outdoors with friendly pub ambience, try **Ironwork Grill** at the ca. 1922 McMenamins Grand Lodge, located at 3505 Pacific Avenue (503-992-3425; mcmenamins.com) at the east edge of Forest Grove. You could also pop into **Bites Restaurant**, 2014 Main Avenue (503-746-6812; bitesrestaurant.com), which serves fusion cuisine in a charming downtown storefront, with innovative dishes like kimchi fries, kai dow, Thai chicken noodle soup, and Korean short rib tacos.

From Forest Grove, take Highway 47 south to Highway 99W and detour west to **McMinnville**, the largest community in the Tualatin Valley. Lovers of antiques can easily find the nearby community of Lafayette and poke through eight classrooms filled with treasures and memorabilia of all kinds, sizes, and shapes at the **Lafayette Schoolhouse Antiques Mall** (503-864-2720), housed in the ca. 1910 school building at 748 3rd Street (Highway 99W). The mall is open daily from 10:00 a.m. to 5:00 p.m.

The monks at the nearby *Trappist Abbey* offer for sale their delicious ginger-date-nut cake, dark fruitcake, and three kinds of creamed honey, including natural, cinnamon, and ginger. From Lafayette turn north on Bridge Street and go 3 miles to the abbey located at 9200 NE Abbey Road, Carlton. The gift shop (800-294-0105; trappistbakery.com) is open daily from 9:00 a.m. to 5:00 p.m. In nearby Amity, at the *Brigittine Monastery*, 23300 Walker Lane (503-835-8080; brigittine.org), the monks turn out legendary truffles and gourmet chocolate fudge. Once you're in Amity, located south of McMinnville via Highway 99W, turn right onto 5th Street and follow the signs about 4 miles to the monastery. It's open Monday through Saturday from 9:00 a.m. to 5:00 p.m.; Sunday 1:00 p.m. to 5:00 p.m.

If you'd like to stay overnight near the antiques and wine country, there are several fine bed-and-breakfast inns to choose from in the McMinnville-Newberg area, among them *A'Tuscan Estate Bed & Breakfast*, a ca. 1928 colonial-style home with elegant European flair at 809 Evans Street (503-434-9016; a-tuscanestate.com), or *Wine Country Farm*, 6855 NE Breyman Orchards Road, Dayton, with five varieties of growing grapes and Arabian horses (503-864-3446; winecountryfarm.com). One of the nicest hotels in Oregon can be found in Newberg. *The Allison Inn & Spa* (2525 Allison Lane; 503-554-2525; theallison.com) is pure luxury in wine country, with views of a vineyard, a full-service spa and fitness center, and delicious food and beverages at their signature restaurant, Jory, named for the rich soil type of the Willamette Valley. New in McMinnville as of 2017 is the *Atticus Hotel* (374 NE Ford Street; 503-472-1975; atticushotel.com). Local art, thirty-six unique and luxurious rooms, and appreciation for local food and wine define this terrific hotel. To splurge, book the Atticus's Penthouse or the Bunkhouse—both of which are divine.

Avid wine lovers will find dozens of options for tasting wines and discovering beautiful destinations. Pause in nearby Newberg to visit *Rex Hill Winery*, 30835 N. Highway 99W (503-538-0666; rexhill.com), and taste fine locally produced wines. While in the tasting room you can also see the winery's inner sanctum, where the wine is carefully created and aged. *Owen Roe Winery* at 2761 E 9th in Newberg (503-538-7778; owenroe.com) has a small tasting room for their delicious wines. In McMinnville, try *R. Stuart & Co. Tasting Room and Wine Bar* (528 NE 3rd; 503-472-4477; rstuartandco.com), located downtown just a few blocks from the winery itself.

TOP ANNUAL EVENTS IN THE WILLAMETTE VALLEY

MAY
Mount Pisgah Arboretum Wildflower Festival
Eugene-Springfield
(541) 747-3817
mountpisgaharboretum.org

JULY
Bohemia Mining Days
Cottage Grove
(541) 942-5064
bohemiaminingdays.org

Da Vinci Days
Corvallis
(541) 757-6363
davincidays.org

St. Paul Rodeo
St. Paul
(800) 237-5920
stpaulrodeo.com

AUGUST
Northwest Art and Air Festival
Albany
(800) 526-2256
nwartandair.org

Scandinavian Festival
Junction City
(541) 998-9372
junctioncityscandia.com

For dining in Dundee, don't miss **Red Hills Market** (155 SW 7th Street; 971-832-8414; redhillsmarket.com) for eclectic fare and deli specialties in a warm and charming space. In McMinnville, the much-loved **Nick's Italian Café** (521 NE 3rd Street; 503-434-4471; nicksitaliancafe.com) serves northern Italian entrees. Other options for informal eats in McMinnville include **Crescent Café**, 526 NE 3rd Street (503-435-2655; crescentcafeonthird.com); **Valley Commissary**, for tasty breakfasts and lunches from an open kitchen (920 NE 8th Street; 503-883-9177; valleycommissary.com); and **Bistro Maison**, 729 E. 3rd Street (503-474-1888; bistromaison.com) for fine dining French food. In nearby Newberg, be sure to stop at **Bar Deux** at 602 E. First Street (503-487-6853; bardeuxnewberg.com), for seasonal shared plates from local produce and purveyors. In nearby Sherwood, detour from Highway 99W at Sherwood Boulevard for popular Stumptown coffee and fresh deli items at **Symposium Coffee Café** in old town Sherwood, 2246 SW Pine Street (503-625-2137; symposiumcoffee.com).

For further information about Yamhill County's fabulous wine country, contact Taste Newberg, 210 N. Blaine Street (503-530-0780; tastenewberg.com) and the McMinnville Visitor Information Center, 328 NE Davis Street #1 (503-857-0182; visitmcminnville.com).

The Heart of the Valley

Head toward the state capital by backtracking about 4 miles from McMinnville via Highway 18 to Highway 221, turning south through Dayton into the heart of the Willamette Valley, and crossing the Willamette River on the *Wheatland Ferry* (wheatlandferry/ccvc.com), one of the last three ferries operating on this historic river. These old-fashioned contrivances are really just cable-operated barges. The ride is short, but you're treated to views upriver and downriver while lumbering across, and the kids will love it. Moreover, the price is right— about $2 to $6 for an auto. The two others in operation are the *Canby Ferry, M.J. Lee II* (clackamas.us/roads/ferry.html), located just north and east of Canby, off Highway 99E, and the *Buena Vista Ferry*, located about halfway between Salem and Albany, near the confluence of the Willamette and Santiam Rivers. Passengers on bicycles or those who travel on foot can usually ride for less than $3. Call or check the websites to determine if the ferries are running; high river waters or mechanical issues may close operations.

In the early days of the territory, when competition for trade along the Willamette River was keen, various boat landings and trading-post sites sprang up on the banks of the river. Just Albany and Corvallis have survived as good-size river towns. Before heading in that direction, though, detour to view a well-preserved collection of vintage tractors, automobiles, trolleys, and various types of farm equipment at *Powerland* Heritage Park, 3995 Brooklake Road Northeast, in Brooks, just north of Salem (503-393-2424; antiquepowerland. com). In late July and early August, you can take in the lively *Great Oregon Steamup* here, with the fun of seeing these enormous mechanical wonders in action. There's even a small 1938 Oregon microbrew truck and a little steam-driven sawmill that usually get fired up and running during the annual event. There are food and beverage booths, too, of course. Visit the museum grounds daily April to September from 9:00 a.m. to 4:00 p.m.

To feast your eyes on acres of stately bearded irises, from stylish yellows and classic blues to exotic purples and seductive pinks, visit the display gardens at a world-renowned central Willamette Valley iris grower. At *Schreiner's Iris Gardens*, 3625 Quinaby Road Northeast, just north of Salem (503-393-3232; schreinersgardens.com), two generations of Schreiners have run the business started in the 1920s by Francis Schreiner. He compiled his first Iris Lover's Catalogue in 1928. The field irises are rotated yearly on about 200 acres; you can see some of these level fields blooming alongside I-5 as you motor north or south between Portland and Salem. Stop at the farm during early spring to enjoy the kaleidoscope of colors in the iris display garden and in the flower display barn. Bulbs can be ordered for later shipment.

If mystical tulips and luscious daffodils are your love, however, beat a path to the spring blooming fields from late March through May at **Wooden Shoe Tulip Farm**, at 33814 S. Meridian Road near Woodburn (503-634-2243; wood enshoe.com). You and the kids can wander through acres of gorgeous blooms, order bulbs, purchase cut flowers, browse the gift shop, and attend the spring festival in March through the second week in May. On festival weekends you'll find specialty foods, Northwest wines, microbrews, live music, seminars, and wooden-shoe crafters. **Note**: On rainy spring days, be sure to pack a thermos of hot chocolate, umbrellas, windbreakers, and sturdy shoes, including extra shoes and warm socks for the kids to change into after field forays.

Salem

In **Salem**, pause for a walk through **Willson Park/Capitol Park Mall**, the lovely grounds of the state capitol at 900 Court Street (503-986-1388). In early spring, dogwoods, azaleas, and rhododendrons bloom about the well-manicured lawns that surround a large fountain. The setting also offers, from atop the capitol dome, a panoramic view of the city and the broad valley where the Calapooya Indians once lived. Inside the rotunda notice the large, colorful murals depicting historical scenes of the territory and Oregon's beginnings.

Nearby, at 1313 Mill Street Southeast, stroll through **Willamette Heritage Center** (503-585-7012; willametteheritage.org), which houses meeting rooms, small shops, boutiques, and eateries, as well as the historic **Thomas Kay Woolen Mill**, in operation from 1889 to 1962. The restored mill now contains the Marion County Historical Society collections, and its displays show the process of changing fleece into fabric. The mill is open Monday through Saturday from 10:00 a.m. to 5:00 p.m. Don't miss the Mission Mill Heritage Gift Shop on the ground level for an awesome selection of books, gifts, and historical memorabilia. You can also tour the woolen mill and walk among the array of historic houses at the village. Be sure to visit the ca. 1841 **Jason Lee House**, the oldest remaining frame house in the Northwest and the structure that served as the territory's earliest Methodist mission. See, too, the **Pioneer Herb and Dye Garden**'s accumulation of old-fashioned herbs and rare dye plants. The garden is located behind the Methodist parsonage.

Vintage Roses and Perennials at ca. 1878 Bush House

Don't miss the *Tartar Old Rose Collection* at ca. 1878 *Bush House* (bushhouse museum.org) where you can see beds of some 300 old garden roses representing varieties and species that came across the Oregon Trail during the mid-1800s. This outstanding collection includes such varieties as Rosa Mundi, a striped ancient gallica that is one of the oldest roses mentioned in literature; the Mission Rose, a wedding gift to early pioneer missionary Jason Lee and his bride, Annamarie Pittman; and the lovely damask rose, Bella Donna.

Large perennial beds, located near the greenhouse, have been redesigned and replanted with huge peonies and gatherings of delphinium, astilbe, yarrow, and coreopsis, among other longtime favorites. You can also see the espaliered apple trees and a fine collection of flowering trees and shrubs. Many of these varieties were planted in the early 1900s by Northwest landscape designers Elizabeth Lord and Edith Schryver. For more information about historic gardens in the area, contact Travel Salem (503-581-4325; travelsalem.com).

Quintessential Salem Experiences

The *Oregon State Hospital Museum of Mental Health*, 2600 Center Street NE (971-599-1674; oshmuseum.org), one of only a handful of museums of its kind in the world, is an amazing place dedicated to telling the stories of the many people who lived and worked at Oregon's State Hospital from the late 1800s on.

Martha Springer Botanical Garden & Rose Garden, Willamette University, 900 State Street (503-370-6300; willamette.edu), is open dawn till dusk.

Salem Riverfront Park, 101 Front Street, featuring the Eco Globe, a beautiful spherical piece of art that includes 86,000 tiles depicting the entire planet Earth.

Salem Art Fair & Festival, Bush's Pasture Park, 600 Mission Street Southeast (503-581-2228; salemart.org), is held mid-July each summer. Go early, and take lawn chairs and a picnic.

Salem Saturday Market, 1320 Waller Street SE (503-585-8264; salemsaturdaymar ket.com). On Saturday May through October starting at 9:00 a.m., find some of the best Willamette Valley plants, flowers, and fresh seasonal produce along with growers, artisans, and crafters.

The woolen mill drew its power from **Mill Creek**, where there are shady places to feed the ducks and reflect upon the not-so-distant past. The large parking area here is a good place to leave your car or recreational vehicle while exploring the nearby historic areas by foot.

Just 4 blocks south, from 12th to 6th along Mission Street, are the marvelous gardens at **Bush Pasture Park, Bush Barn Art Center**, and ca. 1878 **Bush House**, 600 Mission Street SE (503-581-2228; bushhousemuseum.org), an Italianate-style house built by Asahel Bush, a prominent Salem politician and newspaperman. The sunny rose garden, just west of the house, was planted in the mid-1950s and contains more than a hundred beds. You can see and sniff more than 2,000 roses tended by Salem Parks Department garden staff and volunteers.

The extensive grounds offer grassy areas for picnicking and for playing with the kids; there's also a small playground area near the well-stocked gift shop and art center. Notice, too, the large wisteria vine that climbs on the front porch of Bush House; the old vine is draped with a profusion of pale lavender blossoms in mid- to late May. It's a real showstopper. Historic Bush House is open for tours Thursday through Sunday in summer; Friday through Sunday in winter, from 1:00 p.m. to 5:00 p.m.

Just a few blocks east of Bush House and Bush Pasture Park you'll not want to miss visiting **Historic Deepwood Estate**, at 1116 Mission Street Southeast (deepwoodmuseum.org). This estate has fine examples of period English garden rooms, which were designed in 1929 by landscape designers Elizabeth Lord and Edith Schryver. Alice Brown, third owner of the 1894 Queen Anne Victorian house, worked with Lord and Schryver to transform sections of her 6-acre estate into elegant garden rooms.

From the large parking area at the rear, walk onto the main grounds to find the old-fashioned fence and gate that enclose the **Tea House Garden**. Next, walk down stone steps to the formal **Boxwood Garden**; its ornamental fencing forms a background for the precisely clipped boxwood hedges growing here. Then, walk back up the steps, detour through the intimate ivy archway onto the main lawn area, and stop to inspect the ca. 1905 white wrought-iron gazebo. Don't miss the 250-foot-long bed of elegant perennials along the eastern perimeter of the grounds, these flowering plants march in colorful profusion from early spring to late fall. You'll also see dedicated garden volunteers working at Deepwood nearly every Monday morning throughout the year.

You can also browse through the adjacent greenhouse, filled with lush tropical palms, ferns, orchids, and begonias. Deepwood Estate grounds and gardens are open daily dawn to dusk. Call (503) 363-1825 or browse deep woodmuseum.org for current information on house tours, historic preservation underway at the garden, and special events.

Seeking Fresh Air, Produce, and Cider

While in the Salem area plan a trek to **E.Z. Orchards Farm Market** at 5504 Hazel Green Road NE (503-393-1506; ezorchards.com) to purchase fresh produce and orchard fruits, gourmet foods, and artisan goods. And at **Wandering Aengus Ciderworks**, 4070 Fairview Industrial Drive SE (wanderingaengus.com), you can visit the Tasting Room and sample the splendid hard ciders and dessert wines made from uncommon apple varieties. For pleasant overnight lodgings away from town, and especially if you like horses and the out of doors, you could check with the friendly folks at **Airlie Farm Bed & Breakfast**, 14810 Airlie Road in nearby Monmouth (503-838-1500; airliefarminn.com). In the morning you'll enjoy a gourmet farm breakfast. For dozens of wineries and tasting rooms to visit in the Salem area, browse travelsalem.com. and click on Attractions.

Salem's *Riverfront Indoor Carousel*, located in Salem Riverfront Park at 101 Front Street NE (503-540-0374; salemcarousel.org), features forty-two gaily painted carousel horses for you and the kids to ride. The price is right, too, at $1.50 per ride for this Old World-style musical carousel. Also, at the park are an on-site artists' studio, two Oregon Trail wagons, and the carousel gift gallery.

For eateries in the area, plan a pleasant breakfast, brunch or lunch at *Busick Court*, 250 Court Street (503-370-8107), for cozy food downtown; *Amadeus Cafe* at 135 Liberty Street (503-362-8830; amadeussalem.com), which offers lunch and dinner, along with generous happy hour; and *Gilgamesh Brewing Company, The Campus Restaurant and Brewpub* at 2065 Madrona Avenue (503-584-1789; gilgameshbrewing.com), a brewery and restaurant in a former grass seed warehouse. For more information about lodgings, maps, and eateries in the area, visit the well-stocked Salem Visitor Center, 388 State Ste. 100 (503-581-4325; travelsalem.com).

Silverton and Mount Angel

From Salem consider making another detour, this one from I-5 east to Silverton and to *Silver Creek Falls State Park* (oregonstateparks.org). Located in the foothills of the Cascade Mountains, the park contains fourteen waterfalls interlaced with a maze of inviting trails in the cool forest—an especially good option on those occasional 90-degree days in late summer. In autumn a colorful Oktoberfest is held in the nearby community of Mount Angel. Situated on a scenic hill close by, *Mount Angel Abbey* (503-845-3066; mountangelabbey .org) is a classic beauty of a building in red brick; the grounds are lush with many old hardwood trees, flowers, and huge stretches of lawn. The library, designed by Alvar Aalto, is world famous and stores a priceless collection of illuminated manuscripts, as well as a display of rare, hand-printed books. A seminary school of philosophy and theology operates on the grounds, as does a guest and retreat house. At the bottom of the hill, don't miss a stop at the *Benedictine Brewery*, a taproom and restaurant offshoot of the monk community's work.

In nearby *Silverton*, book a guest room at the *Oregon Garden Resort*, 895 Main Street (503-874-2500; oregongardenresort.com), which offers a pool and spa and overlooks the splendid *Oregon Garden*, at 879 W. Main Street (503-874-2500; oregongarden.org), which features a botanical display garden, conifer garden, children's garden, Northwest species garden, and outdoor amphitheater.

For good eats in Silverton, try *The Silver Grille Café*, 206 E. Main Street (503-873-8000; silvergrille.com), for good eats; *Gather Café*, 200 E. Main Street (503-874-4677; gather.cafe), set inside an old downtown building with high tiled ceilings, brick walls and excellent food; *Creekside Grill* (503-873-9700) with good food and creek-side view on the patio; and *Silver Creek Coffee House*, 111 N. Water Street (503-874-9600). For more information about the Silverton area, see silvertonchamber.org.

You can also head east into the high Cascade Mountains on nearby Highway 22, going across 4,817-foot *Santiam Pass* and reaching central Oregon at the Western-style town of Sisters, and near the headwaters of the Metolius River. Santiam Pass, flanked by snowcapped Mount Washington and Mount Jefferson, emerged as the main wagon route into the Willamette Valley from the high desert and rangeland areas; it was scouted up the South Santiam River by Andrew Wiley in 1859. US 20 from Albany roughly follows the old wagon route, connecting with Highway 22 near Hoodoo Ski Area at the top of the pass. If you travel in this direction from the Salem area, be sure to stop in Mill City and pop into *Rosie's Mountain Coffee House*, 647 Santiam Boulevard/ Highway 22 (503-897-2378), to load up with awesome scones, quiches, sandwiches and steaming espresso drinks. For overnight lodging along the way, you could also check out cozy guest rooms at *The Lodge at Detroit Lake*, 175 Detroit Avenue off Highway 22 in the small community of Detroit (503-854-3344; lodgeatdetroitlake.com). Consider a peaceful, restorative stay at *Breitenbush Hot Springs Retreat and Conference Center* (53000 Breitenbush

Rd SE; breitenbush.com), located in the woods north of Highway 22 on the Breitenbush River. The natural hot springs are captured in a variety of pools, and the center offers workshops, classes, retreats and communal meals in a beautiful setting.

River Walking

Visit a renovated covered bridge, *Irish Bend Bridge*, in Corvallis near the campus of Oregon State University. The bridge spans Oak Creek on the Midge Cramer Path west of campus. The bridge, dismantled in 1988, originally spanned the Long Tom River at Irish Bend, a tiny community near Monroe, just south of Corvallis. Local bridge buffs and an army of volunteers worked several weekends to reposition the old covered bridge and give it a new roof and fresh coats of white paint. Another great walking and cycling option in the area is the paved Riverfront Trail Corvallis-Philomath, which stretches 5.8 miles between the two cities. On a bright spring day, there's nothing better than a stroll along these paths, under a canopy of flowering trees. For additional information about the area, contact Visit Corvallis, 420 NW 2nd Avenue (541-757-1544; visitcorvallis.com).

Albany and Corvallis

From Highway 22 wind west and south of Salem via US 20, or south on I-5, to *Albany*. Back in 1845, two enterprising Scots, Walter and Thomas Monteith, bought the Albany townsite along the Willamette River, just 15 miles south of the community of Independence, for $400 and a horse. Each of the three *Albany Historic Districts* offers fine examples of early nineteenth-century architecture. If possible, do the walking tour—you can park your car near the Albany Visitors Association at 110 3rd Avenue (albanyvisitors.com), and find a map there. Some 350 homes—from Georgian revival, colonial revival, and federal to classical, stick, Gothic, and Italianate—have been restored and given status on the National Register of Historic Places. Next to Astoria on the north coast, Albany has one of the most impressive collections of such vintage structures in the state.

Folks can also contact the *State Historic Preservation Office* (503-986-0690; oregon.gov/oprd/OH) for more information about all kinds of vintage structures open to the public at various times throughout the year—from restored homes and historic churches to vintage department stores, carriage and stable companies, and early theaters. These structures are located throughout the state.

Before beginning the walking tour, linger at the visitor center to see old photos of Albany's beginnings and to find helpful maps and information about the historic districts and the July and December ***Victorian House & Garden Tours***. Also plan at least an hour to visit the ***Albany Historic Carousel and Museum***, located at 503 1st Avenue West (541-497-2934; albanycarousel.com). This labor of love developed over a couple of decades, with hand-carved animals created by an all-volunteer effort, and a huge fundraising campaign completed to purchase an antique mechanism and build a charming home for the carousel, a gift shop and a carving studio. Buy a token to take a ride on the animal of your choice, and then visit the carving studio in the basement to see a glimpse of animals-in-progress. Don't miss it!

Good eateries to check out in Albany include ***Sybaris Bistro*** at 442 1st Avenue W (541-928-8157; sybarisbistro.com) for delectable locally sourced fine dining; ***Brick & Mortar Café*** at 222 SW 1st Avenue (541-791-7845; brickand mortarcafe.com) for amazing brunches including a Bloody Mary bar on Saturdays and Sundays; and ***Sweet Red Bistro***, 208 1st Avenue West (541-704-0510), for wine, espresso, and cheese plates.

Before you leave Albany, prepare for a drive into the countryside by grabbing a self-guided map to ten covered bridges in the surrounding area (albanyvisitors.com). At the ca. 1939 ***Larwood Bridge***, crossing Crabtree Creek off Fish Hatchery Road just east of Albany, enjoy a shady park near the swimming hole, along with the nostalgia of an old waterwheel just downstream that has been restored.

Upon arrival in ***Corvallis***, stop at Visit Corvallis, 420 NW 2nd Avenue (541-757-1544; visitcorvallis.com) and get directions to ***Avery Park and Rose Gardens***, located at 16th Street and Allen Lane. Here you can sit amid a fine stand of towering redwoods near the extensive rose gardens while the kids somersault and play Frisbee on the enormous lawn. The roses bloom all summer and into fall.

For a meal in Corvallis, try ***Nearly Normals*** at 109 NW 15th Street (541-753-0791; nearlynormals.com.) for a wide array of vegan and vegetarian options, with protein happily added, or ***New Morning Bakery***, at 219 SW 2nd Street (541-754-0181; newmorningbakery.com), with fresh baked pastries and more.

To stay overnight in style in Corvallis, call the innkeepers at the ca. 1928 ***Hanson Country Inn***, 795 SW Hanson Street (541-752-2919; hcinn.com), a 5-acre estate with a gorgeous sunroom and library. For comfy country digs that come with friendly chickens, lambs, and other farm animals, call the innkeepers at ***Alder Creek Guest Cottage***, 7920 NW Skillings Drive (541-719-8525; aldercreekcottage.com); the kitchenette is stocked with fresh eggs, coffee, bagels, juice, and other treats for preparing your own breakfast.

For a pleasant side trek from Corvallis, collect lunch or picnic goodies and take Highway 34, which locals call Alsea Highway, heading west toward Philomath, Alsea, and then Waldport at the coast. In the community of Alsea, garden lovers can find *The Thyme Garden Herb Company* at 20546 Alsea Highway (541-487-8671; thymegarden.com). Visit the half-acre English-style display gardens and browse in the nursery, which offers a large selection of herbs and flowers. It's open daily from April 15 to June 15. Stop at *Alsea Falls* to enjoy your picnic lunch or for a romantic twilight supper.

For avid fisherfolk, the *Alsea River* offers excellent fly fishing for cutthroat, steelhead, and rainbow trout. In the small town of Alsea, you can find deli items, coffee and espresso drinks, and fishing supplies and gear at *John Boy's Mercantile*, 186 E. Main Street (541-487-4462). You can also find a covered bridge nearby, the ca. 1918 *Hayden Covered Bridge*, off Highway 34, which is still in use; it's located about 2 miles west of Alsea. Or you could take your picnic to a higher vantage point, 4,097-foot *Mary's Peak*, also off Highway 34, where you can enjoy panoramic views from the summit and see one of the rare alpine meadows in the Coast Range. Both Alsea Falls and Mary's Peak offer day-use picnic areas and easy walking trails.

Resuming the trail of the Calapooya Indians, you could continue south on old Highway 99W from Corvallis, past weathered barns, broad fields, and knolls dotted with oaks, to the *William L. Finley National Wildlife Refuge* complex. A large population of Canada geese winters in the Willamette Valley and along the lower Columbia River, feeding on such winter grasses as ryegrass and fescue, as well as on the cereal grains and corn that are planted in fields near the refuge just for their use. Two additional refuges are located about 30 miles north of Corvallis and west of I-5—*Ankeny National Wildlife Refuge* and *Baskett Slough National Wildlife Refuge*. Ask about *Snagboat Bend* and about the *Ankeny Refuge Boardwalk Trail* and the gazebo overlook that offers panoramic views at Baskett Slough Refuge.

The 5,325-acre Finley Refuge was named for the early naturalist who persuaded President Theodore Roosevelt to create the first national wildlife refuges. Along the self-guided *Woodpecker Loop Trail*, open year-round, visitors can also see wood ducks, hooded mergansers (summer nesters), and ruffed grouse, as well as ring-necked pheasants, California and mountain quail, mourning doves, and black-tailed deer. Further information is available at the office of the refuge complex, 26208 Finley Refuge Road, Corvallis (541-757-7236; fws.gov/refuge/william_l_finley). You can also find a pleasant hilltop retreat on this route, Highway 99W, between Corvallis, Monroe, and Eugene, *Bluebird Hill Farm Bed & Breakfast*, 25059 Larson Road, Monroe (541-424-2478; bluebirdhill.biz). You'll find a large guest cottage with comfortable amenities and an outside deck with wide views of the rural setting and the large vineyard. Call ahead for reservations at this lovely spot.

Historic Farms, Modern Purposes

Given the Willamette Valley's historic farming roots, it's no surprise that many charming historic farm properties are to be found around here. Located on a Century Farm just south of downtown Corvallis, *Tyee Century Farm and Wine Cellars* (26335 Greenberry Road; 541-753-8754; tyeewine.com) is a family-owned and -operated vineyard and winery. The vintage milking barn still stands today on this former dairy farm. Visit the on-site art gallery adjoining the tasting room, which offers pinot noirs, chardonnays, pinot gris, and more. In Philomath, *Gathering Together Farm* (25159 Grange Hall Road; 541-929-4270; gatheringtogetherfarm.com) is both a restaurant and a farm that specializes in certified organic vegetable and fruit production. Shop their farm stand for the best seasonal organic vegetables in the valley or visit the restaurant for a truly unbelievable meal. Hours vary seasonally and you should definitely check ahead of time and make a reservation. The menu might include leg of lamb with fingerling potatoes, carrot ginger soup, and cherry crème brûlée to finish.

Tour of Trees

The Oregon State University campus is an excellent place to view the variety of trees and flowering shrubs that can be found in Oregon, without journeying all over the state and hiking on a variety of trails (although that is rewarding too). The college offers a self-guided tour of the historic campus and its trees with the help of a brochure available at Visit Corvallis, 420 NW 2nd Avenue (541-757-1544; visitcorvallis.com). On campus, sign up for a guided tour through the Department of Horticulture (oregon state.edu).

Eugene-Springfield

From the wildlife refuge continue south on Highway 99W through Monroe and Junction City into the southernmost portion of the Willamette Valley, which includes Oregon's second-largest metropolitan area, *Eugene-Springfield*. This region also contains portions of three national forests—Siuslaw, Willamette, and Umpqua—as well as four high Cascades wilderness areas—French Pete, Three Sisters, Diamond Peak, and Mount Washington.

Eugene, home of the University of Oregon, offers not only miles of jogging and bike paths but, especially for chocoholics, the *Euphoria Chocolate Company*, located at 946 Willamette Street (458-201-8750; euphoriachocolate.com). Hiding inside dark and light chocolate truffles the size of golf balls are tempting morsels of ganache or crème Parisienne, a rich creamy center that may be laced with amaretto, peppermint schnapps, pecan, toasted almond, or Grand Marnier; or try solid chocolate, milk chocolate, or coffee royal chocolate. You could also pop into *Voodoo Doughnut*, 20 E. Broadway at Willamette Street (541-868-8666; voodoodoughnut.com), open 24 hours a day, for awesome and quirky doughnuts. *Note*: You can also pop into two Voodoo Doughnut locations in Portland.

Other fun places to eat include *Steelhead Brewing Co.*, 199 E. 5th Avenue, downtown at the corner of 5th and Pearl Streets (541-686-2739; steel headbrewery.com), for a great pub menu and award-winning microbrews made on the premises, and the nearby *Fifth Street Public Market* restaurants and shops, at 296 E. 5th Avenue (5stmarket.com), which include one of Eugene's most popular bakeries on the lower level, coffee shops, and a number of friendly cafes as well. For lunch weekdays and fine dining daily, a choice spot in Eugene's vintage train station is the *Oregon Electric Station*, at 5th and Willamette Streets (541-485-4444; oesrestaurant.com), not far from the Fifth Street Public Market. Ask about reserving one of the elegantly restored and decorated parlor or dining cars, complete with vintage electric side lamps. Another pleasant eatery has two locations: *The Glenwood* (1340 Alder Street; 541-687-0355, and 2588 Willamette Street; 541-687-8201; glenwoodrestaurants .com) offers a large menu with delicious breakfast, lunch and dinner. For an early twentieth-century, European-style city inn and restaurant, check out the ca. 1912 *Excelsior Inn & Ristorante Italiano*, 754 E. 13th Avenue (541-342-6963; excelsiorinn.com); it once was a three-story fraternity house.

Millrace Creek History

Long a part of Eugene's natural and cultural history, the Millrace holds memories for many former University of Oregon students, Eugene's school children, and visitors. Constructed in 1851 by Hilyard Shaw to generate power for the flour mills, woolen mills, and sawmills lining its banks, this narrow stream bubbles up from a pipe that diverts water from the nearby Willamette River. The Millrace then flows through the blackberry vines and ambles behind a number of motels and eateries just across Franklin Boulevard from the University of Oregon campus. For many decades it was the site of college pranks and canoe fetes—often occurring under a full moon. When the water iced over during winter, everyone skated on it, and by the end of the 1920s—when the mills switched to electricity—the Millrace had become the recreational hub of the city.

But in recent decades, the mill race was neglected, becoming overrun with brambles and trash. In 2019, plans to improve and restore the historic Millrace launched, led by the Phil and Penny Knight Campus for Accelerating Scientific Impact. Stay tuned for continued improvements to this Eugene treasure.

Spring Wildflowers Galore

Visit these Willamette Valley sites from April through June and July to see waves of native wildflowers such as bleeding hearts, fawn lilies, shooting stars, and skunk cabbages as well as species of migratory songbirds, geese, ducks, and other wildlife:

William L. Finley National Wildlife Refuge (541-757-7236; fws.gov/refuge/william _l_finley). Located 10 miles south of Corvallis on Highway 99W; go 1.3 miles west at Finley Road to the parking area. It's an open field, about 400 acres with rough terrain and no trail, so it's best to enjoy the spectacular wildflower displays from the road. Ask, too, about **Ankeny** and **Baskett Slough National Wildlife Refuges**, about 30 miles north of Corvallis, west of I-5, which offers a trail up to a viewing gazebo.

Mary's Peak. Drive up to an elevation of about 1,200 feet in the Coast Range, about 10 miles west of Corvallis via Highway 34, where you'll find a variety of native blooms and picnic areas.

Mount Pisgah Arboretum (541-747-3817; mountpisgaharboretum.org). Located just east of Lane Community College in Eugene; follow signs to the Howard Buford Recreation Area. Enjoy picnic areas and walk a network of trails from wetlands and stream banks to the upper, drier sections with hosts of wildflowers everywhere. Stay on the trails, as there are healthy stands of poison oak here.

One of the best places to go for a stroll among masses of elegant rhododendrons is a shady, 15-acre garden glen, **Hendricks Park Rhododendron Garden** (friendsofhendrickspark.org), open daily. The main paths are wheelchair accessible. Situated at Summit Avenue and Skyline Drive, the garden had its beginnings in the early 1950s, when members of the Eugene Men's Camellia and Rhododendron Society donated plantings of azaleas and rhododendrons from their own gardens and their individual propagations. Because of this a number of rare species and hybrids are represented in the more than 5,000 varieties at the garden. From late April to June, enjoy fine magnolias, dogwoods, viburnums, witch hazels, and hundreds of other ornamentals planted among the hardy azaleas and "rhodies." Growing around the edges of the knoll and towering overall are the familiar Douglas fir and stands of white oak. A small playground and places to picnic are located nearby. Pick up a guide to the garden at the upper parking area. Don't miss this splendid garden!

By all means, take the kids to visit the **Cascades Raptor Center**, at 32275 Fox Hollow Road (541-485-1320; cascadesraptorcenter.org), just south of Eugene's city center. You'll see many types and sizes of injured feathered friends, including, for example, golden and bald eagles, ospreys, great horned owls, and peregrine falcons, as well as prairie falcons, spotted owls, and red-tailed hawks. Some injured raptors aren't able to return to the wild, so these feathered friends are housed at the center and often participate in birds of prey educational programs for school youngsters. The center is open Tuesday through Sunday from 10:00 a.m. to 6:00 p.m.; a nominal admission fee helps fund the rehabilitation hospital. The center offers shorter hours during winter months.

If you'd like to explore another delightful outdoor area, especially for springtime wildflowers, head a couple of miles east of Eugene to **Mount Pisgah Arboretum**, a 220-acre natural area nestled within the **Howard Buford Recreation Area**. A place of solitude far from the intrepid joggers and bicyclers, the arboretum offers shady trails and sunny paths along the flank and up the sides of 1,520-foot Mount Pisgah. In early spring you'll see fawn lilies, baby blue eyes, purple camas, and a host of other wildflowers along with more than twenty-five native tree species on the hillside and riverbank areas—this is the east bank of the Willamette River's Coast Fork. This fork, along with the McKenzie River, empties into the main Willamette River channel just north of Eugene. Autumn is a colorful time to visit the arboretum as well. The kids can spot western gray squirrels busily collecting acorns fallen from white oaks. Pocket gophers inhabit a marsh on the upper slopes, and animated frogs chorus beneath a bridge that spans the lily pond near the river. Also keep your eyes peeled for ospreys, pileated woodpeckers, and red-tailed hawks. There are picnic tables and restrooms on the grounds near the headquarters cottage.

Information about the arboretum, workshops and guided hikes, the annual Spring Wildflower Show & Plant Sale, the Fall Festival & Mushroom Show, and a map can be obtained from Friends of Mount Pisgah Arboretum (541-747-3817; mountpisgaharboretum.org). **Note**: Be sure to stay on the established trails, as there are healthy stands of poison oak in the areas away from these paths. Almost everyone is allergic to every part of the low-lying poison oak plant.

For classy overnight accommodations in Eugene, consider **The Campbell House Inn**, located on the east side of Skinner's Butte at 252 Pearl Street (800-264-2519; campbellhouse.com). Originally constructed in 1892, the structure has been fully restored as an elegant thirteen-room boutique hotel inn. We're talking deluxe here—four-poster beds, fireplaces, whirlpool tubs, telephones, Wi-Fi, private baths, and sumptuous breakfasts.

Perhaps Eugene's finest lodging is **Inn at the 5th**, 205 E 6th Avenue (541-743-4099; innat5th.com). Located adjacent to the 5th Street Market, this place is super-classy, with unique art on the walls in every room, room service provided by Marché Restaurant, an on-site spa, and plenty of charm. The lobby is very elegant without being stuffy and is home to an amazing table made from a maple tree that used to stand on the site.

If you pass through the Eugene-Springfield area during September or October, consider taking a walking tour of the **University of Oregon** campus. The outing provides a pleasant visual overdose of autumn hues clustered on a wide variety of well-established native and non-native tree species, and you'll find plenty of places to park in and around the campus just off Franklin Boulevard.

Favorite Places in October and November for Fall Leaf Lovers

College campuses: University of Oregon (Eugene); Oregon State University (Corvallis); Lewis and Clark College (southwest Portland); Marylhurst University (Lake Oswego–southwest Portland); Reed College (southeast Portland)

Columbia River Gorge, western section, between Portland and Hood River

Highway 242, the old McKenzie River Highway from McKenzie Bridge to the top of McKenzie Pass

Hoyt Arboretum (southwest Portland)

Japanese Garden (southwest Portland)

Junction City

A leisurely and pleasant drive from nearby **Junction City**, especially with a well-filled picnic basket, loops west along pastoral Highway 36, across Bear Creek, along the Long Tom River, around Triangle Lake, through Deadwood and Swisshome to Mapleton and the tidewaters at the mouth of the Siuslaw River at Florence. Return to Eugene on Highway 126, through Walton, Elmira, and Veneta. Linger at **Triangle Lake** for your picnic or stop along the way and pick out a river-worn rock to sit on. While listening to the singing of the streams and rivers, relax into nature's setting and feel the warmth of the afternoon sun—maybe even take a snooze. Along the way are several waysides and picnic areas, some with boat landings, but there are no campgrounds on this particular route.

If you travel through the area around the third weekend in March, go north about 2 miles on Highway 99W from Junction City and turn west on Ferguson Road to enjoy some 6 miles of daffodils that bloom in profusion early spring along the roadsides and fences during the annual **Daffodil Festival**. Go early in the day and stop at the **Long Tom Grange** (541-998-6154; junctioncity.com) also on Ferguson Road, for enormous gooey cinnamon rolls and delicious sticky buns along with displays of flowers, quilts, local arts and crafts, antique cars, and farm animals. In early August, you could take in Junction City's colorful *Scandinavian Festival* (541-998-9372; junctioncityscandia.org), which includes not only bright costumes and music galore, but also folk dancing, crafts, and tasty Scandinavian foods as well as a microbrew and wine terrace, beer gardens, and Scandia runs. For more information about the Lane County area, including lodging, browse eugenecascadescoast.org.

Central Cascade Mountains

East from Eugene-Springfield via Highway 126, travel 60 miles to access Highway 242, the *McKenzie Pass Scenic Byway*. After driving through the tiny communities of Vida, Blue River, and McKenzie Bridge—each hugs the banks of the McKenzie River like a dedicated trout angler—turn onto Highway 242, just east of the McKenzie District Ranger Station (541-822-3381; fs.usda.gov /willamette), for one of the best displays of fall colors in the region. *Note*: This Highway 242 route is closed with the first heavy snowfall (usually late November) and does not reopen until at least Memorial Day. Check with the McKenzie District Ranger Station for current information and road conditions (541-822-3381).

That characteristic nip in the air signals the return of another season in the Northwest woods, and autumn declares its arrival with leaves turned bright crimson, vibrant orange, and vivid yellow. On the quiet winding Highway 242 that loops and twists about 20 miles to the top of *McKenzie Pass*, soft breezes whisper through tall Douglas fir branches and stir the colored leaves of big-leaf maple, vine maple, alder, and mountain ash.

You're in the *Willamette National Forest* now—the largest of eighteen national forests within Oregon and Washington and one of the largest in the United States. The original incentive for finding a route across the Cascades in this area was the discovery of gold in Idaho nearly 150 years ago. In 1862, Capt. Felix Scott and a couple of colleagues, John Cogswell and John Templeman Craig, formed a party at Eugene to deliver supplies to the Idaho mining area. Under the auspices of his firm, the McKenzie Salt Springs and Deschutes Wagon Road Company, John Craig collected tolls at McKenzie Bridge until 1891. He lived nearby for many years and is buried at the McKenzie Pass summit.

Rugged Outdoorsman Dee Wright and Scenic Highway 242

In the early 1930s, Dee Wright supervised a crew of Civilian Conservation Corps (CCC) workers who constructed the rock observatory that sits amid the lava fields at the top of **McKenzie Pass**. It is said that Wright was a skilled woodsman and trailmaker, and colorful storyteller. He first lived near Oregon City among the Molalla Indians and learned their culture, folklore, and survival skills. He became a government packer and learned intimately the natural terrain of the Cascade Mountains between Mount Hood and Crater Lake. One of his most stubborn mules was named Dynamite.

Dee Wright was a rugged outdoorsman who thrived on adventures. This colorful character, well known in the early West, died in 1934 at the age of 62, just before the CCC project at the top of McKenzie Pass was completed. The USDA Forest Service named the structure **Dee Wright Observatory** in his memory.

Don't miss stopping at this incredibly scenic spot, with its wide-angle views of not only massive solidified lava flows in every direction, but also of the series of gorgeous snowcapped mountains in the Cascade Mountains' volcanic chain. You can also hike along a paved walkway through the lava fields. The drive up winding Highway 242 to the top of 5,325-foot McKenzie Pass is especially scenic in mid to late October, when the autumn colors are brightest. For current information and road conditions, stop first at the McKenzie District Ranger Station on Highway 126 (541-822-3381; fs.usda.gov/willamette), just east of McKenzie Bridge.

Sometime around 1910, an automobile chugged over the summit, probably with extra fuel, water, and a supply of axes and saws to remove limbs and trees that always seemed to plague early travelers on the rutted, bumpy gravel, and dirt roads. Weather permitting, you will reach the top of 5,325-foot -McKenzie Pass via the scenic and very winding road, Highway 242, with relative ease, however, and you may decide to detour into the parking area to walk stone steps up to the **Dee Wright Observatory**. From this tower-like stone structure, constructed in the early 1930s by the Civilian Conservation Corps, you can peer through eleven narrow windows, each focused on a particular mountain peak; the peak's name and distance from the viewpoint are carved into the stone.

To the southeast you'll see Belknap Crater, Mount Washington, the North and Middle Sisters, and Mount Scott; Mount Jefferson and Mount Hood hover over lesser peaks to the north. If time allows, walk the 2-mile trail—it's part of the **Pacific Crest National Scenic Trail**—up **Little Belknap Crater** to see fissures, lava tunnels, and spatter cones. Like Lava Cast Forest near Bend, it's an intriguing, close-up encounter with those massive lava fields of the high central Cascade Mountains, which cover thousands of acres with at least three layers of the rough black stuff.

Geologists believe the fires deep inside Oregon's Cascade Mountains crest are just napping and may someday erupt again, as did Mount Saint Helens to the north, in Washington, in May 1980.

Blue River and McKenzie Bridge

The McKenzie District Ranger Station (541-822-3381; fs.usda.gov/willamette), just east of McKenzie Bridge, will have current weather and road information for the mountain area and directions to nearby Forest Service campgrounds. Located on Highway 126, the ranger station is open from 8:00 a.m. to 4:30 p.m. on weekdays. Maps of the nearby *McKenzie River National Recreation Trail* are also available. The scenic trail traverses 26 miles of varied terrain. Some stretches are suited for beginning hikers and families with young children; others are rough and steep, favored by the many hardcore mountain cyclists who tackle the trail each year. *Note*: Scenic McKenzie Pass and Highway 242 are closed by snow during winter months; Highway 126, however, remains open year-round across Santiam Pass to Sisters, Redmond, Bend, and central Oregon.

You can also linger awhile and call the staff at *Belknap Hot Springs* (541-822-3512; belknaphotsprings.com) to reserve a comfortable guest room in the historic lodge on the banks of the McKenzie River, a couple of miles beyond the ranger station. There also are several cabins—bring your own bedding—and forty-two camping/recreational vehicle spaces available, all within walking distance of two hot mineral spring swimming pools. You can also walk to a scenic section of the McKenzie River Recreation Trail from the upper campground. Then, take the footbridge across the river, near the lodge pool, and enjoy a short walk to the splendid woodland garden areas.

By continuing east on Highway 126 a few miles from Belknap Hot Springs, you can stop and see a pair of lovely waterfalls that drop over basalt ledges across the bubbling McKenzie River. Named *Koosah Falls* and *Sahalie Falls*, they are within a short walk of each other from the parking area. Sahalie Falls pathway is wheelchair accessible. The trail connects to the greater McKenzie Trail, which you can travel in either direction from here.

Playing hide-and-seek with Highway 126, the snow-fed *McKenzie River* has long been known by lovers of fishing. According to lively accounts from old newspapers of the early 1900s, "wet flies were disdained by the swiftly traveling denizens of the rapids and many misses suffered before anglers acquired the knack of handling the rod properly . . . whether trout bite or not, there are times when a fisherman must stop fishing and tell fish stories." For current regulations and angler's licenses, stop at a grocery store or sporting goods store before heading upriver. You can also contact the Oregon Department of Fish and Wildlife for helpful maps, brochures, and current regulations (503-947-6000; dfw.state.or.us/). On the website you can see the comprehensive list of protected birds and mammals as well as hunting information and regulations for big game, upland game birds, waterfowl, and trapping fur-bearing animals.

Recipe for a Hot Spring

The many mineral springs in the area were long known to Native peoples, who believed they held restorative and healing powers. Most hot springs contain about twenty-four different minerals, from potash, arsenic, silica, and potassium to chlorine, calcium, sodium, sulfuric acid, and bicarbonic acid. *Belknap Hot Springs*, discovered by R. S. Belknap around 1869, was a longtime favorite of families living in the Willamette Valley. The lodge was built across the river from the location of the mineral springs, and by 1910 a daily motor stage from Eugene had been established—the trip on the original dirt and gravel road took a whole day. During the season of 1890, some 700 lodge guests were registered, at a cost of $15 per week; one could tent camp at a weekly rate of $1.50.

On your visit you'll notice billows of steam rising from the hot springs on the far side of the McKenzie River; the 130-degree mineral water is piped across the river to the *Belknap Hot Springs* and outdoor pool (belknaphotsprings.com). The mineral water is cooled to a temperature of about 102 degrees Fahrenheit in the swimming pool and is perfect for soaking one's weary bones at the end of a day of hiking and exploring the area. *Terwilliger Hot Springs* is also nearby on the McKenzie River corridor, although it is undeveloped and requires a short hike in. There is still a day-use fee to pay at the parking lot, to cover maintenance of the area.

For information about guided river fishing in the well-known McKenzie drift boats (541-726-5039 or 800-32-TROUT; mckenzierafting.com), as well as about other guided rafting trips, contact the Visitors' Association of Travel Lane County in Eugene, 745 Olive Street (541-484-5307; eugenecascadescoast.org and mckenziechamber.com). For comfy overnight stays along the McKenzie River, contact the innkeepers at ***Eagle Rock Lodge Bed & Breakfast***, 49198 McKenzie Highway 126, Vida (541-822-3630; eaglerocklodge.com), which offers several cozy guest rooms in the main house and carriage house and come with names such as Kingfisher, Owl, Osprey, Dragonfly, and Caddisfly. The comfortable rooms come with fireplaces, overstuffed chairs, and sofas. River sounds and the rustle of Douglas fir tree tops help you drift gently to sleep, and mornings bring hot coffee and hearty breakfasts. Or, you can contact the owners at *Inn at the Bridge Cabins*, 56393 McKenzie Highway 126, McKenzie Bridge (541-822-6006; mckenzie-river-cabins.com/), farther off the beaten path where you can hole up in a splendid cabin that features two bedrooms and two baths along with a river rock fireplace living room and fully equipped kitchen for preparing your own eats. Each cabin also comes with French doors to a screened-in porch that opens to the pleasant grounds that slope gently down to the McKenzie River. Another great option is *Loloma Lodge*, 56687 McKenzie Highway 126, McKenzie Bridge (541-813-6018; lolomalodge.com), a restored historic destination with cabins in close proximity to the river.

Oakridge and Willamette Pass

A final detour into this section of the central Cascade Mountains is accessed via Highway 58, just south of Eugene and winding about 30 miles east up to the community of *Oakridge*. Along the way notice the Southern Pacific Railroad tracks, a historic transportation link to the upper Willamette area that has operated since 1912. In the early 1930s, as many as five-passenger trains passed through Oakridge each day, with stops at Fields, McCredie Springs, Cascade Summit, and Crescent Lake on the east side of the pass. Rotary snowplows, mounted on the trains, kept the Cascade line open during the winter, and the train crews stopped at a cook house at the summit for hot meals.

In good weather a popular excursion in those early days was to get off the train at Diamond Creek, hike down a trail to *Salt Creek Falls*, enjoy a picnic beneath tall firs, and then take the next train back home. Travelers can do the same using an automobile. The falls are located about 20 miles east of Oakridge via Highway 58, and there you can hike a short trail to this spectacular frothy ribbon, which cascades some 286 feet down into a small canyon. These are the second-highest falls in the state.

Next continue east on Highway 58 to the 5,128-foot summit, *Willamette Pass*, to see one of the state's oldest ski areas. Of course, the original rope tow built by Roy Temple and fellow ski enthusiasts from Oakridge in the 1940s is now gone, but in its place rises a chairlift that carries a new crop of skiers nearly a mile to the top of 6,666-foot *Eagle Peak*. Roy and his wife, Edna, ran the original ski area for a number of years and lived at Cascade Summit, at the west end of nearby Odell Lake. Edna remembers making and serving chili, hot dogs, cupcakes, and coffee at the ski shack, with a roaring bonfire out in front. You can see historic artifacts and memorabilia about Oakridge, the ski area, and the upper Willamette River region at *Oakridge Pioneer Museum*, 76433 Pine Street (541-782-2402). The museum is open Saturday from 1:00 to 4:00 p.m. and other times by appointment.

For an overnight stay just west of Oakridge, consider **Westfir Lodge and Mountain Market** (541-246-9007; westfirlodge.com), located in the former office of a company logging town. The Office Bridge still stands across the street, and the lodge is a terrific base camp for adventures onto many mountain biking trails and the Aufderheide Scenic Drive, which connects north from here to Highway 126. East of the Willamette Pass summit, at a brisk elevation of 4,800 feet, check with the friendly staff at the ca. 1923 **Odell Lake Lodge & Resort** (541-433-2540; odelllakeresort.com), located at the sunny southeast corner of the lake. There is moorage space at the marina, and motorboats, canoes, rowboats, and small sailboats are available to rent by the hour or day. In the summer and fall, anglers fish for kokanee salmon, mackinaw lake trout, and native rainbow trout on the 5-mile-long, 300-foot-deep lake; during winter, cross-country skiers and snow bunnies flock to the area from the valley. The small restaurant in the lodge is open seasonally.

Covered Bridge Country

Cottage Grove

Continuing south on I-5 from the Eugene-Springfield area, take exit 174 at **Cottage Grove** and, bearing to the east about a mile past the Village Green Inn, stop at the Cottage Grove Ranger District station located at 34963 Shoreview Drive (541-767-5000; fs.usda.gov/umpqua) to pick up maps and information about covered bridges and historic mining areas. From nearby Row River Road, take the two-lane back roads past vintage covered bridges into the **Bohemia Mine** area, enjoying the rural countryside along the way.

With good brakes and a radiator full of water, adventurous travelers can negotiate the narrow and steep, winding gravel road to **Fairview Peak** and **Musick Mine**, at the top of 5,933-foot **Bohemia Mountain**. On a clear day you can see snowcapped Mount Shasta to the south, the gossipy snowcapped Three Sisters mountains to the north, and the lower Coast Range to the west. Along the 70-mile loop drive are other places to stop as well.

Although some 400 miners once called the **Calapooya Mountains** in this area home, now gentle breezes rattle broken, rusted hinges and scuttle through a fallen-down cookhouse, blacksmith shop, or remnants of an old hotel or store. The mines flourished from 1890 until 1910, with some activity after World War I, but most of the mines have given way to wind, rain, snow, and time. In the old days it took 6 to 8 horses from 8 to 10 hours to pull a load of supplies and mining equipment up **Hardscrabble Grade**, the steep, 6-mile trail.

Today smooth country roads reach into the Bohemia mining country, wrapping around green hills and pastures where woolly sheep and multicolored cows graze peacefully in the sun. Check at the Cottage Grove Ranger District Station (541-767-5000; fs.usda.gov/umpqua) if you're interested in public gold-panning areas—there are several in the immediate area. **Note**: Even though a shack may look long forgotten and deserted, it may actually be someone's headquarters for mining exploration or assessment work; the mines are on private land and are not to be disturbed by travelers. Inquire at the Ranger Station.

A wagon road was the first main route into the Row River area; it wound along the river through Culp Creek to **Currin Bridge**, a covered bridge built in 1925 over the Row River. In the surrounding Cottage Grove–Eugene–Springfield area, it's possible to explore nearly twenty of the fifty-three covered bridges still standing in the state. Calling forth a bit of horse-and-buggy nostalgia or images of kids with fishing poles and cans of worms, most covered bridges are under the protection of local historical societies. Although most are no longer for public use, a few do remain open to automobile traffic and, of course, to artists, photography buffs, and folks with fishing poles. In Cottage Grove, the **Covered Bridge Festival** is celebrated in early October (cgchamber.com and eugenecascadescoast.org).

From exposed trusses and rounded portals; to Gothic-, portal-, or louvered-style windows; to tin or shingled roofs, the covered bridges in this area are more numerous than in any other section of the state. Five are in the immediate Cottage Grove area, and four are still in active use for automobiles, bicyclers, and hikers. The longest covered bridge in the state is **Office Bridge**, spanning 180 feet across the north fork of Middle Fork of the Willamette River at Westfir, near Oakridge. The shortest, at just 39 feet, is **Lost Creek Bridge**, located in southern Oregon.

Visiting Covered Bridges

ALBANY-CORVALLIS AREA
For helpful maps and current information, contact the Albany Visitors' Association (541-928-0911; albanyvisitors.com) or Visit Corvallis (541-757-1544; visitcorvallis.com).

Hoffman Bridge (1936); spans Crabtree Creek
Irish Bend Bridge (1954); spans 100 feet over Oak Creek on the Oregon State University campus
Larwood Bridge (1939); spans 103 feet over Crabtree Creek
Ritner Bridge (1926); spans Ritner Creek
Shimanek Bridge (1966); spans 130 feet over Thomas Creek

COTTAGE GROVE AREA
Contact Travel Lane County (541-484-5307; eugenecascadescoast.org).

Centennial Pedestrian Bridge (1987)
Chambers Bridge (1936)
Currin Bridge (1925)
Dorena Bridge (1949)
Mosby Creek Bridge (1920)

EUGENE-SPRINGFIELD-WESTFIR AREA
Contact Travel Lane County (541-484-5307; eugenecascadescoast.org)

Goodpasture Bridge (1938); spans the McKenzie River
Lowell Bridge (1945)
Office Bridge (1944); spans the north fork of Middle Fork of the Willamette River
Parvin Bridge (1921)
Pengra Bridge (1928); spans 120 feet over Fall Creek
Unity Bridge (1936)

OTHER HELPFUL RESOURCES
Cottage Grove Museum
(541) 942-4269
cottagegrovemuseum.com

Cottage Grove Ranger District Station
34963 Shoreview Drive
(541) 767-5000
fs.usda.gov/umpqua

Covered Bridge Society of Oregon
covered-bridges.org

Oregon Covered Bridge Festival
(541) 942-2411
cgchamber.com

In the 1930s, there were more than 300 covered bridges in the state, but by the 1950s their numbers had dwindled to fewer than 140. The ***Covered Bridge Society of Oregon*** is dedicated to preserving and restoring the remaining bridges and also promotes the study of the bridges' history and unique construction. A helpful map and brochure showing all 53 bridge locations in twelve different areas of the state can be obtained at the Cottage Grove Visitor Center, 700 E. Gibbs Avenue (541-942-2411; cgchamber.com and covered-bridge.com).

For easy hiking into meadows carpeted with alpine wildflowers in July and August, near Cottage Grove, try the ***June Mountain Trail***, the ***Adams Mountain Trail***, or the ***Hardesty Trail***—maps and information are available at the ranger station on Row River Road. Keep alert, too, for some of the forty kinds of edible wild berries that grow in the region. Tiny wild blackberries ripen in August, salal berries are abundant in forested areas, and Oregon grape berries are plentiful in late summer and fall. All make delicious jams and jellies, and all were used by the Native tribes as well.

In early spring you can see waves of blooming purple camas that carpet the swales along I-5 between Creswell and Cottage Grove. Long ago the Native peoples gathered the tiny bulbs of the purple camas for winter food and steamed them in large pits lined with heated rocks and wet grass, covered over with hides to hold in the heat.

In mid-July, Cottage Grove celebrates **Bohemia Mining Days** with a tour of historic homes, a lunch barbecue at Historic Snapp House, and fiddlers' contests. The Prospector's Breakfast on Sunday at the top of Bohemia Mountain ends the three-day celebration (541-942-2411; cgchamber.com). You can also see Bohemia mining memorabilia at the **Cottage Grove Museum**, housed in the ca. 1897, octagonal, former church building located at Birch and H Streets (541-942-4269 for current hours; cottagegrovemuseum.com). For cozy accommodations, you can check with **Lily of the Field Bed & Breakfast**, 35722 BLM Rd 20-2-28, Cottage Grove (541-942-2049).

For tasty local eateries in the Cottage Grove area, pop into **Stacy's Covered Bridge Restaurant**, 401 Main Street (541-767-0320; stacyscoveredbridgerestaurant.com), for tasty entrees; **Buster's Main Street Café**, located on 811 Main Street in the historic Cottage Grove Hotel (541-942-8363; bustersmsc.com), for eggs Benedict, steak and eggs, Philly cheesesteaks, Reubens, and more; and **Jack Sprat's Restaurant** at 510 E. Main Street (541-942-8408; jackspratsbrats.com) for comfort food. For coffee and espresso drinks that get rave reviews from local coffee lovers, you can stop at **Rally Coffee Café**, 1220 Main Street, or at the drive-thru, **Hot Shots Espresso**, 375 E. Oregon Avenue, on your way into or out of Cottage Grove back to I-5.

From there you can head north on I-5 to Eugene and Portland or head south on I-5 to Roseburg, Grants Pass, historic Jacksonville, Medford, and Ashland-Shakespeare town, in the southern Oregon region. From there you can continue to the northern California border over the scenic 4,300-feet Siskiyou Pass Summit passing in the shadow of snowcapped 14,162 ft. Mount Shasta! Or, you could detour from Grants Pass onto Highway 199 and head west toward the **Oregon Caves National Monument** (nps.gov/orca and oregoncaveschateau.com) and the southern Oregon coast. You could also continue from there on Highway 101 to northern California and the splendid **Redwood National Forest** region (redwoods.info). Happy Travels!

OTHER ATTRACTIONS WORTH SEEING IN THE WILLAMETTE VALLEY

Historic Carousel & Museum
Albany
albanycarousel.com

Oregon Country Fair
Veneta
oregoncountryfair.org

Enchanted Forest
Turner
enchantedforest.com

Salem Peace Plaza
Salem
peaceplazasalem.org

Evergreen Aviation & Space Museum
McMinnville
evergreenmuseum.org

Tokatee Golf Club
Eugene-McKenzie Bridge-Blue River
tokatee.com

Places to Stay in the Willamette Valley

CORVALLIS AREA

Alder Creek Guest Cottage
7920 NW Skillings Drive
Corvallis
(541) 719-8525
aldercreekcottage.com

Alsea Valley Bed & Breakfast
19237 Alsea Highway 34
Alsea
(541) 487-4526

Best Western Corvallis
925 Garfield Street
Corvallis
(541) 758-8571
bestwesternoregon.com

Bluebird Hill Farm Bed & Breakfast
25059 Larson Road
Monroe
(541) 424-2478
bluebirdhill.biz

Leaping Lamb Farm
20368 Honey Grove Road
Alsea
(541) 487-4966
leapinglambfarm.com

COTTAGE GROVE

Lily of the Field Bed & Breakfast
35722 BLM Rd 20-2-28
541-942-2049

Village Green Resort
725 Row River Road
(541) 942-2491
villagegreenresortand
gardens.com

EUGENE—VIDA— MCKENZIE BRIDGE

Belknap Hot Springs
McKenzie Bridge
(541) 822-3512
belknaphotsprings.com

Best Western Greentree Inn
1759 Franklin Boulevard
Eugene

(541) 485-2727
bestwesternoregon.com

The Campbell House Inn
252 Pearl Street
Eugene
(541) 343-1119
campbellhouse.com

Eagle Rock Lodge Bed & Breakfast
49198 Highway 126
Vida
(541) 822-3630
eaglerocklodge.com

Inn at the Bridge Cabins
56393 Highway 126
McKenzie Bridge
(541) 822-6006
mckenzie-river-cabins.com

Inn at the 5th
205 E 6th Avenue
Eugene
(541) 743-4099
innat5th.com

MCMINNVILLE—FOREST GROVE

Atticus Hotel
375 NE Ford Street

McMinnville
(503) 472-1975
atticushotel.com

**A'Tuscan Estate Bed &
Breakfast**
809 NE Evans Street
McMinnville
(503) 434-9016
a-tuscanestate.com

**McMenamins Grand
Lodge Hotel**
3505 Pacific Avenue
Forest Grove
(503) 992-9533
mcmenamins.com

**Twisted Willow (ca. 1892)
Dutch Colonial Bed &
Breakfast**
509 NE 9th Street
McMinnville
(503) 472-5787
twistedwillowinn.com

HELPFUL WINE COUNTRY WEBSITES

**Oregon Wine Advisory
Board**
oregonwine.org

Oregon Wine Press,
McMinnville
oregonwinepress.com

Visit Lane County
eugenecascadescoast.
org

**Willamette Valley
Wineries Assoc.**
willamettewines.com

Wine Press Northwest
winepressnw.com

HELPFUL TELEPHONE NUMBERS AND WEBSITES FOR THE WILLAMETTE VALLEY

**Albany Visitors'
Association**
(541) 928-0911
albanyvisitors.com

**Corvallis Visitor Infor-
mation Center**
(541) 757-1544
visitcorvallis.com

**Cottage Grove Visitor
Information Center**
(541) 942-2411
cgchamber.com

**Covered Bridge Soci-
ety of Oregon**
covered-bridges.org

**Eugene Convention &
Visitors' Association of
Lane County**
(541) 484-5307
eugenecascadescoast.
org

**Forest Grove Visitor
Information Center**
(503) 357-3006
forestgrove-or.gov

**McKenzie Ranger
District Station**
(541) 822-3381
fs.usda.gov/willamette

**McMinnville Visitor
Information Center**
(503) 472-6196
visitmcminnville.com

**Middle Fork/Oakridge
Ranger Station**
(541) 782-2283
fs.usda.gov/willamette

Taste Newberg
(503) 530-0780
tastenewberg.com

Oakridge Chamber
(541) 313-6758
oakridgechamber.com

Travel Salem Visitor Center
(503) 581-4325
travelsalem.com

Silverton Visitor Information Center
(503) 873-5615
silvertonchamber.org

State Historic Preservation Office
oregonheritage.org

USDA Forest Service

Cottage Grove Ranger District
fs.usda.gov

Washington County Visitors' Bureau
(503) 644-5555
tualatinvalley.org

MONMOUTH

Airlie Farm Bed & Breakfast
1410 Airlie Road
(503) 838-1500
airliefarm.com

SALEM–DETROIT–SANTIAM PASS

Best Western Plus Mill Creek Inn
3125 Ryan Drive SE
(503) 585-3332
bestwesternoregon.com

The Grand Hotel
Salem
201 Liberty Street SE
(503) 540-7800
grandhotelsalem.com

The Lodge at Detroit Lake
175 Detroit Avenue, Highway 22
Detroit
(503) 854-3344
lodgeatdetroitlake.com

SILVERTON

The Edward Adams House Bed & Breakfast
729 S. Water Street
(503) 873-8868
edwardadamshousebandb.com

Silverton European Style Inn
310 N. Water Street
(503) 873-1000
silvertoninnandsuites.com

ST. PAUL–AURORA

Feller House Bed & Breakfast
21625 Butteville Road Northeast
Aurora
(503) 678-0268
thefellerhouse.com

Places to Eat in the Willamette Valley

ALBANY

Brick & Mortar Café
222 First Avenue W.
(541) 791-7845
brickandmortar.cafe

Novak's Hungarian Restaurant & Bakery
208 SW 2nd Avenue
(541) 967-9488
novakshungarian.com

Sweet Red Bistro
208 1st Avenue W.
(541) 704-0510

Vault 244 Bistro
244 First Avenue W.
(541) 791-9411

CORVALLIS

The Beanery Coffee House
500 SW 2nd Street
(541) 753-7442
allannbroscoffee.com

New Morning Bakery
219 SW Second Street
(541) 754-0181
newmorningbakery.com

Sam's Station Café
1210 NW 29th Street
(541) 752-6170
samsstation.com

COTTAGE GROVE

Backstage Bakery & Café
25 S. 7th Street
(541) 767-0233

Rally Coffee Café
1220 Main Street
(541) 214-5461

Stacy's Covered Bridge Restaurant
401 E. Main Street
(541) 767-0320

EUGENE

Ambrosia Fine Dining Restaurant
174 E. Broadway Street
(541) 342-4141
ambrosiarestaurant.com

Full City Coffee & Palace Bakery
842 Pearl Street
(541) 344-0475
full-city.com

Oregon Electric Station
27 E. 5th Avenue
(541) 485-4444
oesrestaurant.com

Steelhead Brewery
199 E. 5th Avenue
(541) 686-2739
steelheadbrewery.com

Voodoo Doughnut
20 E. Broadway
(541) 868-8666

FOREST GROVE

Ironwork Grill
McMenamins Grand Lodge
3505 Pacific Avenue
(877) 992-9533
mcmenamins.com

HILLSBORO—BEAVERTON

Cornelius Pass Roadhouse
4045 NW Cornelius
Pass Road
(503) 640-6174
mcmenamins.com

Helvetia Tavern
Helvetia Road, off US 26
(Sunset Highway)
(503) 647-5286

MCMINNVILLE

Cornerstone Coffee Café
216 NE 3rd Street
(503) 472-6622

Golden Valley Brewery & Pub
980 NE 4th Street
(503) 472-2739

Nick's Italian Café
521 NE 3rd Street
(503) 434-4471

Valley Commissary
920 NE 8th Street
(503) 883-9177
valleycommissary.com

NEWBERG

Coffee Cottage Cafe
808 E. Hancock Street
(503) 538-5126

SALEM

Flight Deck Restaurant
2680 Aerial Way SE
(503) 581-5721
flightdeckrestaurant.com

Gerry Frank's Konditorei Café
310 Kearny Street SE
(503) 585-7070
gerryfranksconditorei.com

Rosie's Mountain Coffee House
647 Santiam Boulevard/
Highway 22
Mill City
(503) 897-2378
rosiesscones.com

Sassy Onion Cafe
1244 State Street
(503) 378-9180
sassyonion.com

SILVERTON

Chocolate Box
115 N. Water Street
(503) 873-3225
silvertonchocolateboxshop.
com

Creekside Grill
242 S. Water Street
(503) 873-9700

O'Briens Cafe
105 N. Water Street
(503) 873-7554

Silver Creek Coffee House
111 N. Water Street
(503) 874-9600

VENETA

Our Daily Bread Cafe & Bakery
88170 Territorial Road
(541) 935-4921
ourdailybreadrestaurant.
com

Appendix: Travel Planning Resources

Oregon Department of Aviation
(flight maps, sight-seeing)
(503) 378-4880
aviation.state.or.us

Oregon Department of Fish and Wildlife
(Oregon fishing information)
(800) 720-6339
dfw.state.or.us

Oregon Historic Cemeteries Association
(503) 378-4168
oregoncemeteries.org

Oregon Marine Board
(503) 378-8587
boatoregon.com

Oregon road and mountain pass conditions
(800) 977-6368
tripcheck.com

Oregon State Historic Preservation Office
oregon.gov/oprd/HCD/SHPO

Oregon State Parks campground information
(800) 551-6949
oregonstateparks.org

Oregon State Parks campground reservations
(800) 452-5687
oregonstateparks.org

Oregon Tourism Division
775 Summer Street Northeast, Salem
(800) 547-7842
traveloregon.com

Oregon Wildlife Refuges
dfw.state.or.us/

US Bureau of Land Management (BLM)
(503) 808-6002
blm.gov/or/district

USDA Forest Service campground reservations
(877) 444-6777; TDD reservations, (877) 833-6777

Index